BALANCING T

BALANCING THE LOAD

WOMEN, GENDER AND TRANSPORT

Edited by Priyanthi Fernando and Gina Porter

ZED BOOKS
London & New York

in association with
International Forum for Rural Transport and Development

Balancing the Load: Women, Gender and Transport
was first published in 2002 by
Zed Books Ltd, 7 Cynthia Street, London N1 9JF, UK,
and Room 400, 175 Fifth Avenue, New York, NY 10010, USA

in association with
The International Forum for Rural Transport and Development (IFRTD),
113 Spitfire Studios, 63–71 Collier Street, London N1 9BE
Tel: +44 (0) 207 713 6699   Website: www.ifrtd.org

The International Forum for Rural Transport and Development provides a
framework for collaboration between individuals and organizations interested in
the access and mobility needs of rural people in developing countries. Through
advocacy, information-sharing, knowledge-generation and networking, this global
network facilitates and promotes the successful application of improved policies
and practice.

Distributed in the USA exclusively by Palgrave, a division of
St Martin's Press, LLC, 175 Fifth Avenue, New York, NY 10010, USA

Designed and typeset in Monotype Garamond by Illuminati, Grosmont
Cover designed by Andrew Corbett
Printed and bound in Great Britain by Bookcraft Ltd, Midsomer Norton

A catalogue record for this book is available from the British Library

Library of Congress Cataloging-in-Publication Data applied for

ISBN 1 85649 981 2 Hb
ISBN 1 85649 982 0 Pb

CONTENTS

ACKNOWLEDGEMENTS

The editors would like to thank the Gender and Transport Thematic Group of the World Bank, particularly Michael Bamberger and Jerry Lebo, for funding the publication of this book. Their support for the wider dissemination of the methods and outcomes of the Balancing the Load, gender and transport research programme brings new audiences to the challenges of improving rural accessibility and mobility in the developing world. It also recognizes the value in hearing the voices of researchers from the South who may not have had opportunities to share their views and experience.

This book is prepared as a component of the Balancing the Load programme and special thanks are due to the main sponsors of this programme, the Infrastructure and Urban Development Division of the UK Department for International Development. Their support and advice has been gratefully received since the very beginning of the initiative. Indirect yet equally vital support has been received from the Swiss Agency for Development Cooperation through their core funding of the International Forum for Rural Transport and Development Secretariat.

Grateful thanks are extended to colleagues at the IFRTD Secretariat for their continued support, and to the team at Zed Books for their enthusiasm and commitment to this publication.

Finally we would like to acknowledge the vital contribution of all the researchers involved in the Balancing the Load programme. This includes those whose written words may not appear in this book, but whose ideas, experiences and inputs into discussions are fully reflected in the final work.

ACRONYMS AND ABBREVIATIONS

ADB	Asian Development Bank
AMTS	Ahmedebad Municipal Transport Service
CIDA	Canadian International Development Agency
DDC	Dairy Development Corporation
DWCRA	Development of Women and Children in Rural Areas programme
GSRTC	Gujarat State Road Transportation Corporation
GTZ	Deutsche Gesellschaft für Technische Zusammenerbeit
IFAD	International Fund for Agricultural Development
IFRTD	International Forum for Rural Transport and Development
ILO	International Labour Organization
IMT	intermediate means of transport
ITDG	Intermediate Technology Development Group
ITSL	Intermediate Technology Development Group, Sri Lanka
Ksh	Kenya shillings
KTDA	Kenya Tea Development Authority
NGO	non-governmental organization
PHC	primary health centre
PRA	participatory rural appraisal
RHD	Roads and Highways Department
RIDO	Rural Infrastructure Development Organization
Rs	rupees
SDC	Swiss Agency for Development Cooperation

SEWA	Self-Employed Women's Association
SLGA	Soba Local Government Area
SNV	The Netherlands Development Organization
Tk	Taka
Tsh	Tanzanian shillings
UNDP	United Nations Development Programme
USh	Ugandan shillings
VDC	Village Development Committee
VTTP	Village Travel and Transport Programme
WFP	World Food Programme
Z$	Zimbabwe dollars

INTRODUCTION

BRIDGING THE GAP BETWEEN
GENDER AND TRANSPORT

Priyanthi Fernando and Gina Porter

This book is about women, gender and transport. When the case studies that form the main part of this book were commissioned, there were only a few pioneering studies on the subject (notably Doran, 1990; Bryceson and Howe, 1993; Malmberg Calvo, 1994a). Transport professionals were mainly concerned about how transport infrastructure, mainly road networks and feeder roads, could be efficiently and cost-effectively constructed and maintained. The emphasis for poverty eradication was on reducing isolation and improving people's 'access' to goods and services. There was a general assumption that if infrastructure was provided, transport services would follow, people's mobility would improve and they would be able to travel and access goods and services easily.

The discussion has since moved on. It is now recognized that 'mobility' is crucial for accessing goods and services and that roads are simply not enough (Dawson and Barwell, 1993). The transport sector is paying greater attention to the need to stimulate transport services, particularly in rural areas of the lower-income countries, and is more conscious of the need to enable rural people to have and use transport technologies, particularly the more affordable 'intermediate means of transport' (IMTs)[1] (Malmberg Calvo, 1994b; Barwell, 1996; Starkey, 2000)

Gender, however, has not been fully integrated into the mainstream of either the infrastructure debate or the debate on rural transport services and IMTs. Agencies promoting labour-based road construction and maintenance as a means of creating employment and incomes have made an effort to increase women's participation in labour-based activities. There are a number of 'pilot projects' and several guidelines, toolkits and the like that encourage transport sector professionals to develop more gender-sensitive transport interventions (Booth et al., 2000). But, despite evidence (mostly from sub-Saharan Africa) that women and men in rural house-holds have responsibility for different transport tasks, that women often carry a heavier burden in terms of time and effort spent on transport, and that, with less access and control over resources, they have fewer oppor-tunities than men to use transport technologies that could alleviate their 'burden', gender issues are still peripheral to much of rural transport policy and practice (Sibanda, 2001).

While transport professionals have taken little account of gender, issues of access and mobility have also been marginalized in much of the discourse on gender and development. Gender analysts, focusing on gen-der roles, resources and relations, have rarely considered in detail the role that improved transport plays in providing women with the resources to meet their practical needs (e.g. enabling them to fulfil their responsibilities for water and firewood collection). Few have looked at how improving access and increasing mobility can address more strategic gender issues. Women's transport burden contributes to women's time poverty. Lack of time is a key constraint to women building up their assets and reducing their vulnerability. By reducing women's transport burden, development interventions can increase their productivity and incomes and enhance their assets; they can also have more time to rest, to enjoy social life, to participate in community activities. Increasing women's mobility can em-power women to take greater control of their lives by increasing their access to markets and their exposure to education, training and informa-tion, and by providing more opportunities for their political participation.

The case studies in this book aim to support the dialogue between transport and gender professionals. Written by individuals on both sides of the divide, they use a gender perspective to look at a range of transport issues in a variety of locations. Mainly they are about poor women in rural and urban communities, and how transport and transport interventions affect their lives. Through their diverse experiences we are able to develop some insights into how gender relations and the gender division of labour influence women and men's transport needs and patterns and their access to and use of transport infrastructure and technologies. Their stories also illustrate how transport provision (or lack of it) impacts on their lives. We hope that this will add to the growing body of knowledge used by both transport professionals and gender specialists in their work.

The rest of this chapter gives a background to the methodology of the research programme that generated the case studies and highlights some of the key issues arising from the selection of case studies in this book.

THE RESEARCH PROGRAMME

The research programme used a small amount of funds from the UK Department for International Development and initiated an innovative research/training/capacity-building approach that provided a somewhat unusual means of gathering a wide spread of data over a short period and in diverse settings.

Potential participants were identified through a variety of means, but in particular through the international and national networks of the International Forum for Rural Transport and Development. They were invited to submit broad ideas for a small piece of original in-country research on gender and transport which could be completed in six months within a modest budget of US$1,000. Those who submitted proposals were invited to a one-week workshop early in 1998 (Kampala for Africa, Calcutta for Asia).

This preliminary workshop was crucial to the development of the individual case studies. Participants at the workshops worked with each other and with facilitators to help shape the research design for their study. Through a series of preliminary briefings by facilitators, followed by small group sessions (where groups were mixed by country, academic background and gender) and then by group and individual presentations, each researcher identified and refined his or her research questions and developed specific activities needed to obtain answers to those questions. Participants decided on the methods they would employ, the timetable for the research and the format for their final presentation.

Following completion of the research, the participants prepared their results for presentation and discussion at a regional seminar (held in Sri Lanka in June 1999 for Asian participants and in South Africa in July 1999 for African participants). In particular, they were asked to consider the implications of their results for the preparation of guidelines for people involved in rural transport – communities, practitioners and policy makers. The regional seminars, to which 150 policy makers and practitioners were also invited, gave project participants an opportunity to reflect on the results of their own research in its broader regional context, drawing comparisons with work elsewhere and, hopefully, contributing to locally targeted policy interventions.

This approach proved to be a cost-effective exploratory research tool and an effective methodology for harnessing local knowledge, expertise and latent research skills. Almost all the case study contributors were African or Asian NGO workers, activists or researchers working closely with the communities that they researched. Two-thirds were women. The programme created opportunities for raising awareness of issues, getting a wide range of stakeholders committed to their resolution and disseminating the results effectively.

THE CASE STUDIES

This book includes 19 case studies from those prepared for and discussed at the final regional seminars:[2] 10 from Africa and 9 from Asia, representing 9 African countries and 4 Asian countries. They encompass semi-arid, savannah and rainforest environments; plainlands and mountain topography; Muslim, Hindu, Buddhist and Christian populations; economies ranging from semi-subsistence to the highly commercialized; rural and peri-urban localities; and areas with high and low population densities.

The authors of the case studies have approached gender and transport from a variety of angles, and have employed a range of research methods. Most use a mix of participatory rural appraisal techniques involving key informant interviews with checklists and observation, sometimes coupled with larger semi-structured questionnaire surveys and/or focus groups.

THE THEMES

There are major regional differences between Asia and Africa, particularly in the provision of transport services and the prevalence of a variety of modes of transport. In the Asian countries, the public sector plays a much more active role in the provision of transport services (buses and railways). Construction of roads and development of transport infrastructure in Asia seem to stimulate use of IMTs such as bicycles, rickshaws and motorcycles, as well as motorized transport. In Africa this is not necessarily the case.

The similarities in the gendered impact of transport provision between the regions are, however, more striking than the differences. In the following sections we pick out some of the major themes that cut across the regions. The themes are not exhaustive. The case studies include insights into many more issues that will be of interest to transport and gender professionals but that, for considerations of space, we have not included here.

The significance of culture

Perhaps one of the most significant overall observations in these, as in so many other, gender and development studies is that cultural rules are rarely unfavourable to men! They merely reinforce unequal gendered power relationships within households. Men can usually travel where they wish, by whatever means are available, so long as they have the funds (though Rao's study in Bihar India [Chapter 13] indicates that low-caste men have travel problems because of harassment by officials). By contrast, women may be constrained by restrictions on where, how and with whom they travel. And there are other constraints on women's mobility imposed by work burdens inside and outside the home and by lack of access to resources which could generate funds to purchase transport. Despite these constraints, women in much of sub-Saharan Africa and in Asian countries like Nepal travel vast distances each day in their traditional capacity as (unpaid) porters.

Culture is a strong determinant of women's ability to use transport technologies, though there are important local variations in what transport is permissible for women to use and what is not. In eastern and northern Uganda women ride bicycles while in the central region 'bicycles are the property and domain of men' (Iga, Chapter 5). Among some ethnic groups in Burkina Faso women are forbidden to ride bicycles, in some regions they are given a donkey as part of their dowry, while in Yatenga province bicycles and donkeys are almost exclusively used by men, and tradition strictly forbids women to ride donkeys and horses, which will 'incur the risk of young girls losing their virginity' (Ouedraogo, Chapter 11). Women in Africa and Asia seem to have internalized these cultural conventions. In Yatenga province, Burkina Faso, as in Ahmedebad, India, they rarely question the tradition or complain and are often more willing to contribute to purchase a means of transport for their husbands or grown-up sons than to purchase their own (Ouedraogo, Chapter 11; Shresthova et al., Chapter 16)! In Tanzania, Mwankusye finds that both men and women subscribe to the socially constructed attitude that IMTs are for men.

Some religious practices, notably the practice of female seclusion in some (but by no means all) Muslim areas such as parts of Bangladesh and northern Nigeria (Yunusa et al., Chapter 10; Matin et al., Chapter 12), influence gender roles and shape women's ability to benefit from transport improvements. Yunusa et al. suggest that road improvement in their study village has had a substantial impact on men, who now make more use of improved transport services for taking the sick to hospital, produce to markets and refuse to their farms. There is less impact on women because secluded women do not generally travel out of the village, and as the majority of women do not own farmland, they have not benefited from improved road access to agricultural inputs and markets. The availability of improved transport services may not aid women much if they are unable to take advantage of the improved access, and as Robson (2000) suggests in another study, the availability of bicycles and motorbikes can actually reinforce seclusion if women are no longer needed as 'beasts of burden'.

These studies strongly suggest that we should not consider the influence of culture or religious traditions as immutable. Conventions like female seclusion rarely apply where extreme poverty prevails (Callaway, 1987, pp. 56–68; Porter, 1989; Robson, 2000). In Bangladesh, despite the practice of female seclusion, women from poorer, destitute families face fewer restrictions on their mobility than do more well-to-do women, whose families are more concerned with maintaining the family's *izzat* (respectability and honour). Matin et al. (Chapter 12) provide several examples of poor women who have been driven by economic circumstances to challenge social and religious conventions and become more mobile. Changing perceptions of bicycles as a 'modern' means of transport have meant that women riding bicycles in the town of Narayanghat in Nepal are considered desirable wives (Seddon and Shrestha, Chapter 18), and in the cashew-processing area of Sri Lanka the introduction of processing technologies has significantly changed women's status and mobility patterns (Wettasinghe and Pannila, Chapter 20). One of the most encouraging case studies is Nitya Rao's review of a cycle-riding scheme linked to a literacy programme in Pudukkottai, Tamil Nadu, India (Chapter 13). Women in Pudukkottai still do not own bicycles, and their use of bicycles has in many cases led to increased workloads, but Rao argues strongly that women have gained self-confidence and self-esteem from learning to cycle. Rao's study also shows how a 'critical mass' of women challenging conventions can effect changes in social and cultural attitudes.

Household structures and women's roles

Household structures, family composition and size, and women's role in the household affect the gender allocation of tasks and responsibilities and women's mobility and transport burden. These link to cultural factors, like the prevalence of female seclusion, as discussed above, or the practice of polygamy. Musa (Chapter 8) shows how women in polygamous house-holds in Jebel Si in Darfur, Sudan, have sole responsibility for their children because men are too poor to maintain more than one wife. In Dumka, Bihar, India, men helped women in tasks relating to the collection and sale of forest products, but in larger households, where a number of adult women in a household were able to share these tasks, men concentrated on farming and wage labour (Rao, Chapter 15). In the Zimbabwe study, Chingozho (Chapter 3) emphasizes that bigger and older families own more IMTs, a reflection of both needs and assets.

Many of the case studies show that women's productive and repro-ductive burdens can be particularly heavy in female-headed households, and that they differ from male-headed households in the way they access and use transport technologies. In many of the case study villages they comprise a significant proportion of poor households. Chingozho makes a distinction between female-headed and female-managed households and points out that in areas of Zimbabwe the latter benefit from the remit-tances of migrant men, and thus are able to afford IMTs.

Some studies identify the specific transport needs and responsibilities of children. Mashiri and Mahapa (Chapter 2) show that there is a significant travel demand in Tshitwe, Northern Province, South Africa, created by children going to school. Two of the Indian studies refer to the particular difficulties young girls face when travelling on public transport to school (Shresthova et al., Chapter 16; Mukherjee, Chapter 17). Kaumbutho (Chapter 7) illustrates how the demand for children to transport goods in Kenya can affect their educational opportunities. And Chingozho (Chapter 3) points out that the introduction of IMTs may not necessarily assist children's access to education since they may then be put in charge of the equipment.

Transport interventions can impinge on gender roles. Many of the studies observe that the introduction of IMTs or motorized transport has shifted some women's tasks to men, especially where ownership and use of such equipment confers status and becomes a male prerogative, as discussed by Bryceson and Howe (1993). While this may reduce women's workload, it can also reduce their income if, as in Bihar (Rao, Chapter 15), men start to take over marketing activities. While in some instances im-proved access can make the receipt of remittances easier (Musa, Chapter 8), in others it can aid migration and thus affect household size and composition. Seddon and Shrestha (Chapter 18) suggest that in their Nepalese case road construction has caused a shift from extended to nuclear families, which has increased women's workloads.

Seasonality

The seasonality of transport demand is often conceptualized in terms relating to evacuation of harvests, reaching markets and transporting agricultural inputs. At the household level, the different seasons play a much more significant role. The case studies show that women and men in poor households engage in a mix of livelihood strategies that vary with the seasons. Often women and men (most often men) migrate in search of wage labour when there is no farm work, or they engage in poorly remunerated activities such as gold washing (Tuya, Burkina Faso) or salt farming (Banaskantha, Gujarat, India). Among the Santhal villages in Dumka district, Bihar, India (Rao, Chapter 15) households are dependent on the collection and sale of forest produce for half the year and on wage labour and cultivation for the other half.

These different activities result in seasonal changes to transport patterns and tasks. In the agricultural season in Tuya, women walk around 16 to 44 kilometres daily to collect water, to go to the farm and to market, but they walk even greater distances when gold washing replaces farm work. For most of the year, villagers in Dumka district, Bihar, travel locally on foot or on bicycle, but when travelling to West Bengal as wage labourers they need to use motorized transport. Women and men working in the salt pans in Banaskantha move with their families to the vicinity of the pans so that they can walk to and from work.

Seasons also bring changes to transport infrastructure and affect women's and men's ability to use different types of transport technologies and to access services. In many South Asian countries, the monsoon season makes rural roads and other infrastructure impassable, isolating villages and creating considerable hardship for women's and men's travel. Banaskantha, an arid area, is flooded every two years, causing considerable damage to the rural roads. During the monsoon, 40 per cent of the Gujarat State Road Transportation Corporation's buses do not operate. In some of the Bangladesh villages where the country boat and the *donga* (a canoe made from the hollow trunk of a palm tree) are the only modes of transport during the five to six months of the rainy season, women rarely travel, children do not go to school, government extension workers do not come to the villages, and immunization and other health services are interrupted.

In coastal Ghana, the ability of women traders to use transport services varies with the seasons. Post-harvest time, women have sufficient funds to use the *tro-tros* (minibuses) and taxis that go to the markets; at other times they consider these too expensive and walk (Porter, Chapter 9).

Kaumbutho's study (Chapter 7) highlights the bottlenecks caused by damage to local infrastructure, such as bridges, and illustrates how rivers can pose formidable barriers to mobility and access, especially during the rainy season. For the Nkone community, the Nkone Bridge is the only route through which motorized vehicles or IMTs can reach the villages from the main towns – so when the rains wash away the bridge, there is a major impact on the gender allocation of transport tasks. Men, who do not head-load but use intermediate or motorized means of transport, no longer take responsibility for transporting inputs into the village or produce out of the village and the transport tasks shift to women and children. Women, who also have the responsibility for children's safety, have had to 'throw' children across the river so they can get to school (Kaumbutho).

Location and patterns of urban–rural interaction

Location can have a crucial impact on mobility patterns and transport burdens. Women and men who live in areas remote from good roads and frequent transport usually face particular difficulties. In coastal Ghana, where women are mainly responsible for produce marketing, poor and unreliable transport services may mean that women living in off-road villages arrive too late at urban markets to sell their produce, or their produce may have deteriorated by the time it reaches market (Porter, Chapter 9). Gender relationships and responsibilities also restrict women's ability to stay away from home for long periods, so infrequent transport services prevent their reaching markets further away (Porter, Chapter 9; Rao, Chapter 15). This has an impact on their potential to maintain and expand their commercial activities. In their Bangladesh study, Matin et al. (Chapter 12) made a basic distinction between villages close to and those remote from the paved road, but their findings suggest that patterns of mobility are complex, and depend on the interplay of cultural and access factors.

Proximity to urban centres and higher density of transport in urban and peri-urban areas does not always make access any easier. Women in the rural areas on the outskirts of Calcutta who travel to the city, primarily to earn an income as domestic servants, vendors, industrial workers or labourers in government institutions, spend almost twelve hours outside their homes, and have to cope with overcrowded and irregular public transport, long waits, lack of facilities and harassment by pickpockets and from transport officials. The stress of both commuting and carrying out their domestic responsibilities often takes a toll on their health and on the health and wellbeing of their families (Mukherjee, Chapter 17).

The studies indicate also that there are issues relating to transport service routes and fares. The *boda boda* services in Uganda had little impact on meeting women's transport needs because a majority of women's transport tasks did not require travel along those routes (Iga, Chapter 5). And many of the low-income women in Ahmedebad and Calcutta either walked or evaded paying fares because the transport costs were prohibitive (Shresthova et al., Chapter 16; Mukherjee, Chapter 17).

Safety

Safety is becoming a major issue in the transport sector as the huge cost of traffic accidents to national economies and individual households becomes increasingly apparent. The Global Road Safety Partnership website shows that of the 700,000 people killed and over 10 million injured in road accidents annually, 70 per cent are in the South,[3] and that this costs a country a minimum of 1–3 per cent of its GNP annually.

The transport sector has focused its attention on the vulnerability of pedestrians, cyclists and people using other slow-moving IMTs to the high speeds and lack of concern of motorized vehicle drivers. Kwamusi Paul (Chapter 6) argues that from a gender and rural transport perspective, the concept of safety takes on wider meaning. Women walking on village paths and tracks are not likely to be at risk from being knocked down by motor vehicles. But they are often injured from falling, from sharp objects and thorns, or from animal bites and attacks. Women with head-loads are particularly vulnerable, especially when distances are long and they are tired and when paths are slippery or overgrown. Such accidents often happen while women are engaged in domestic tasks such as collecting water or firewood. They are considered 'personal injuries' and are rarely, if ever, considered as part of the safety problem.

Sexual harassment on crowded public transport, and at night-time when bus stops or railway station platforms are badly lit, when the lack of transport services forces women travellers to 'hitch' rides, is another aspect of transport 'safety' for women. Sometimes, too, poor women (and even poor men) are also faced with harassment from the authorities. The fear of harassment and concerns about safety restrict women's mobility. It is common for girls to be kept away from school if there is no 'safe' transport, and some women prefer to walk than to use an unsafe transport service (Bid et al., Chapter 14; Latif, 1999).

Women also suffer indirectly from road accidents. Their role as caregivers means that they have the responsibility of nursing accident victims and caring for the disabled in their households. Often this puts added pressure on their time and compromises other tasks, reducing their productivity and ability to maintain their families.

Diverse stakeholders and the exercise of power

To address their transport needs, or to acquire and use transport technologies and services, communities usually have to negotiate with more powerful stakeholders – policy makers, transport providers, district engineers, financial institutions, and so on. For communities physically distant from centres of decision making, the repeated lobbying required to obtain assistance is usually quite difficult and the travelling alone is a heavy burden. Poor rural women are particularly disadvantaged because of their poverty, their lack of education, their limited access to information and, most important, their lack of political power. Women's transport needs, for both reproductive and productive purposes, are generally ignored in transport policy statements or planning procedures in the South as in the North (Mashiri and Mahapa, Chapter 2; Seddon and Shrestha, Chapter 18; Ghimire, Chapter 19).

The case studies provide several instances of communities making representations to the authorities to upgrade their infrastructure or to provide improved services, with no result (Kaumbutho, Chapter 7; Porter, Chapter 9; Bid et al., Chapter 14). Unscrupulous contractors, lack of support from technical personnel, insufficient financial resources or lack of knowledge of the processes of making representation have frustrated their efforts.

Women's limited savings and lack of access to land and other collateral, coupled with poverty and low levels of literacy, often make it difficult for them to obtain credit from formal institutions. Typically, women's income-generating activities operate with very small sums of capital, generated by them or through NGO or government assistance (Mashiri and Mahapa, Chapter 2; Mwankusye, Chapter 4). This heavily compromises their ability to invest in time-saving transport. And, as Mwankusye points out (Chapter 4), because women are less mobile and have less time than men, they have fewer opportunities to access outside information, and their knowledge of formal credit and IMT options is limited.

Integrated approaches

Conventional transport solutions such as road investments do not automatically bring equal benefits to men and women. In Nepal, road construction has led to positive changes in agricultural production, resulting mainly from greater access to markets (Seddon and Shrestha, Chapter 18; Ghimire, Chapter 19) and has stimulated transport services (buses) and the greater use of IMTs (motorcycles, bicycles and rickshaws) (Ghimire, Chapter 19). However, the 'total stock' of household transport tasks has largely remained the same (with new tasks replacing tasks that now have become easier because of improved transport), and, with no changes in gender relations or the gender division of household labour, the workload for women has increased.

Integrated approaches that combine transport with other interventions can have a more positive impact for women, particularly if they take into account women's and men's transport-related roles, resources, constraints and priorities. The construction of feeder roads in the Jebel Si area of North Darfur, Sudan, by the international NGO Oxfam improved food security and women's livelihoods, mainly because Oxfam played a pro-active role in integrating transport provision with service provision (Musa, Chapter 8). Improved access enabled Oxfam staff, women's organizations and local authorities to reach the villages. They provided immunization and other health services, set up a revolving fund for drugs, provided wells and hand pumps, rehabilitated schools, started literacy classes for women, initiated training in food processing, upgraded women's skills for engaging in small enterprises, effected timely distribution of food aid during droughts and, most importantly, encouraged women's participation in the village committees and the rural council. The roads enabled women to travel to meetings and return to their homes the same day. They now have more access to information and are able to identify their own needs and to explore ways to address them.

In Pudukottai, the District Collector, the top bureaucrat in the district, a woman, led the planning of the mobility component of the literacy campaign. She recognized that if the campaign was to be successful it needed to address itself specifically to the needs and problems of the women in the district. As a result, the campaign explicitly aimed not only to enable women to address their practical transport needs, but also to improve their strategic position by boosting their self-confidence (Rao, Chapter 13).

IMPLICATIONS AND FUTURE DIRECTIONS

This volume does not claim to fill all the gaps in our knowledge on women, gender and transport. There is still a great deal more to be learned about the impact of various transport interventions (such as roads, IMTs and subsidized transport services) on gender relations and gendered work burdens, and particularly how they affect specific categories of women, such as porters. We know very little about what transport interventions can offer elderly and disabled women. The case study on gender and safety (Paul, Chapter 6) raises a number of issues that need to be further investigated. There is also a need to expand the geographical coverage of our research. We have little information about gender issues in rural transport in Latin America, in China or in the transitional economies of Eastern Europe, while in Asia and Africa data on urban women and transport are remarkably scarce (Booth et al., 2000).

This book illustrates clearly that mobility and access are key elements in determining women's ability to carry out their productive, as well as reproductive, roles. The case studies show that women make a significant economic and social contribution to their families and their communities, which is often invisible and unrecognized. A gender analytical approach to transport planning and analysis can uncover this contribution and help initiate interventions that meet women's practical needs and reduce their time poverty. It also cautions that transport interventions do not necessarily reduce the total stock of transport tasks and can introduce new tasks and responsibilities that may increase women's time burden. Another important point, strongly argued by Matin et al. (Chapter 12), is that a focus on reducing women's *transport burden* is not enough. The cultural conditions that restrict women's *mobility* limit their physical orbit and their command over the political and social processes that determine their lives, and it is just as important to address gendered power relations and enable women to have greater mobility and more control over transport decision making in the household as well as in the wider political context.

The case studies also demonstrate how gender-blind conventional approaches to transport issues can be, and how important it is to look at needs and impacts from a gender-disaggregated perspective. It is important, too, to recognize that women (and men) are not homogeneous and that gender characteristics will be complicated by other factors such as age, occupation, disability, and so on. The studies point to the complexity of factors that influence both transport demand and supply at the household and community levels, the significance of gender roles and the influence of gender inequality on transport provision. They highlight the importance of integrating gender analysis into all levels of transport planning, management and implementation if transport interventions are to be more effective in stimulating poverty reduction and social justice. They make a strong case for imaginative, integrated and targeted approaches that will work through multidisciplinary teams of social scientists, gender specialists, transport planners and technical specialists working closely with women and men in local communities.

NOTES

1. Intermediate means of transport, or IMTs as they are often called, are those transport technologies that fall between walking and four-wheeled motorized transport such as cars and trucks. They include pack animals, animal carts, bicycles, rickshaws, motorcycles, three-wheeled scooters, etc.
2. A full set of papers is available in summary form in the IFRTD publication of the proceedings of the Balancing the Load seminars.
3. Read 'developing countries', 'Third World'.

2

SOCIAL EXCLUSION AND RURAL TRANSPORT: A ROAD IMPROVEMENT PROJECT

TSHITWE, SOUTH AFRICA

Mac Mashiri and Sabina Mahapa

Developing communities in rural South Africa face a daily transportation burden that limits their participation in the mainstream economy, entrenching their isolation. The problem is not transitory. Socio-economic and political relations in South Africa are characterized by dualism between urban and rural areas, between developed and developing rural areas and between women and men. This dualism is endemic and does not merely reflect a necessary gradualism that will allow one sector to catch up with the other. Unless there is radical intervention it is likely that rural South Africa will continue to reproduce individuals who are socio-economically deprived.

Research indicates that the socio-economic and cultural aspects of being female or male significantly influence activities, resources and opportunities in rural South Africa. The transport burden is largely shouldered by women (Marais, 1987; Mashiri, 1997). The reduction of this burden is an indicator of the success of interventions aimed at improving the quality of rural life. It can only be accomplished by unravelling the nature of this burden and by understanding how responsibilities for transport are distributed between men and women, who has the greater burden, and how this creates special gender-specific needs.

Rural communities perceive transport not as a problem in itself, but always as part of a far more general socio-political and economic problem (Tarrius, 1984). Decision makers have grossly underrated the significance of understanding the needs of rural communities as a basis for generating innovative solutions to rural transport and development. The analysis of transport systems has largely excluded the study of rural household transport characteristics, even though the household is the locus of the transport demand (Bryceson and Howe, 1993). This has been exacerbated by the fact that innovative integrated planning has largely been sacrificed for sectoral planning despite the many shortcomings associated with the latter.

The poor, who are largely women, experience the greatest access problems. Conventional transport policies, however, tend to treat communities as homogeneous without recognizing that women and men have widely varying mobility and accessibility needs. They also tend to equate their current travel patterns with their needs. Where there are gross inequities in income distribution, such as in South Africa, effective demand alone is nowhere near describing the *real* needs of communities (Mashiri et al., 1998). Very often those who might be expected to have the greatest need for transport, given their rural socio-economic conditions, are also those who ask for nothing, or whose voices are not heard. This is a critical problem for techniques such as origin-destination surveys and activity logs. The techniques must enable non-demand from this disadvantaged social stratum to be interpreted. There is therefore a need to revisit the traditional definition of transport to mean

> the movement of people and goods for any conceivable purpose, including the collection of water or firewood, by any conceivable means, including walking and head-loading. (see Bryceson and Howe, 1993; Ali-Nejadfard, 1997)

Three strands of thought support this definition: (a) the mode of travel used need not necessarily be motorized or conventional; (b) the choice of mode needs to be catered for in planning, no matter how unimportant it may seem to planners; and (c) trip purposes should not be disregarded at the discretion of planners (Bryceson and Howe, 1993).

This chapter uses this overarching definition of transport as it relates to gender issues against the backdrop of the Tshitwe road upgrading project. It aims to make a case for reorienting the way rural transport needs are perceived, planned and provided for, with a view to targeting interventions better, particularly those addressing the mobility and accessibility needs of rural women and children. It also sets out to appraise critically the sustainability of poverty alleviation attributes of labour-based road-works, and their impact on women. It also briefly explores the role that non-motorized modes of transport might play in reducing the transport burden of the Tshitwe community.

In aiming to improve the material conditions of rural women through improved access, the first step is to understand women's travel needs, and the extent to which lack of access constrains the fulfilment of those needs. It is also critical to investigate how gender and gender relations affect transport deprivation, and how more appropriate and more gender-sensitive interventions can help reduce this deprivation.

Although the conventional definition of transport as referring to roads and vehicles has been found to be inappropriate for rural areas, where most travel and transport is on foot and away from roads (Dawson and Barwell, 1993), it is still used in the transport sectors of many provinces in South Africa, and was employed in the planning and implementation of the Tshitwe project. Consequently, although women in Tshitwe are responsible for most of the transport demand, they were not recognized by policy makers as transport stakeholders. In assessing the level of transport demand and resources, women's, and indeed the community's, needs were ignored. The Tshitwe community's current travel patterns were confused with their travel needs. Where data have been collected on the travel and transport burden experienced in the rural areas of the Northern Province, they have tended to be highly generalized and aggregated.

THE TSHITWE COMMUNITY

The village of Tshitwe, situated in the far north of the Northern Province of South Africa, is typical of the settlements in the province. The Northern Province is one of South Africa's least urbanized. More than 83 per cent of the total population of 4.8 million live in rural areas. This province has the highest poverty levels in South Africa (Baber, 1996) and it incorporates three former 'homelands', which were characterized by graft, corruption and abject poverty.

Tshitwe is situated in the former homeland of Venda and is relatively remote, characterized by relatively high population density, an underdeveloped and inadequate agricultural base, and high levels of out-migration. The nearest higher order settlement[1] is 40 kilometres away at Makhado. Tshitwe is bounded by the perennial Njelele River 8 kilometres on its western side. This river is a formidable barrier to access to other villages and schools in the rainy season. To access vans driving up to Makhado and beyond, Tshitwe residents have to walk about 10 kilometres and cross the river. With heavy rains, the river becomes a monster and the path that crosses the river is impassable.

The study involved structured interviewer-administered questionnaire surveys, unstructured interviews, observations and discussions. Base data were collected from adult household members of 140 households, yielding a total sample of about 1,000 persons. A target group approach to data collection (Zils, 1987) was used to include rural women in the sample effectively. Unstructured interviews were targeted at women and general discussions involved both women and men. The study also used an activity-based approach, different to conventional demand-based analysis of travel behaviour. This approach treats travel explicitly as a derived demand, and was designed to be indicative of the community's travel patterns and its transportation needs as they relate to access to socio-economic opportunities.

THE TSHITWE ROAD-UPGRADING PROJECT

The Tshitwe road-upgrading project commenced in March 1997 with a budget of approximately US$300,000 to upgrade 15 kilometres of road. The project recruited 47 women and 67 men on a rolling basis, largely from within walking distance of the road. It aimed to engender a sense of community participation and ownership, reduce costs and institute equity in the distribution of employment opportunities. Women's tasks on this project were non-technical and largely menial, such as carrying stones. Men undertook all tasks remotely resembling elementary technology. Men were also paid much more than women. These men and women upgraded the road from a not so well-engineered gravel road to a bitumen surface of mostly four-metre paved width.

The Tshitwe road upgrading, especially its projected year-round oper-ability and substantially lower costs of operating freight and passenger vehicles, was expected to benefit the agricultural economy in the area through higher farm-gate prices, lower costs of delivering productive inputs (fertilizer, seeds, etc.), cheaper and more reliable availability of trucking services and better accessibility to agricultural extension services. How-ever, overall levels of agriculture activity and land productivity have not improved. Off-farm employment, except for food vendoring that ended with the project's closure, has not been sufficiently stimulated. The supply of road passenger services has not improved at all as there are no buses or combi-taxis, only occasional vans passing by. The access time to mar-kets and other socio-economic activities has not changed because no significant additional transport services have been attracted to the road. Given its location on the slopes of the mountains which form natural boundaries of Tshitwe, the road has doubtful long-term prospects. In addition, road maintenance is likely to be a problem given that, other than carrying stones, women, who would be expected to help in this regard, did not learn any appropriate skills.

DEMOGRAPHIC CHARACTERISTICS OF THE TSHITWE COMMUNITY

The greater majority of the study respondents were female heads of households. Women are either *de facto* household heads because their husbands are migrant workers, or employed and resident in urban areas, or *de jure* household heads because of separation or divorce. A significant number of women-headed households were banished from other populous Venda villages and deported to Tshitwe after being suspected of witch-craft (a phenomenon largely associated with women). Female-headed households had fewer financial assets than male-headed households and, particularly the *de jure* female-headed ones, were more often than not on the extreme end of the poverty spectrum.

The greater majority of the households had between five and eight members, which suggests a relatively high dependency ratio. The age–sex distribution shows a preponderance of school-going youths. The relatively limited agricultural pursuits (dry land cropping and animal husbandry), pension income and the relatively meagre remittances have combined to influence positively the relatively high school attendance ratio. However, the drop-out rate, especially of girls, is high, for a variety of reasons, including distance to schools and affordability. The schools are unable to attract quality teachers and the quality of education is poor. The presence of students in a household implies regular travel demand as well as greater demands on the household's disposable income. The greater majority of the trips generated in Tshitwe are school-related. While a considerable number of pupils walk upwards of five kilometres to a primary school, secondary school students travel much longer distances.

The study indicated that some households had at least one member who earned a regular income, largely as a migrant worker. The presence of income-earning members in a household implies regular travel demand. Many villagers thus depend on an external economy, as it is extremely difficult to produce consistently for their subsistence needs. A significant number of Tshitwe households, however, depend entirely on subsistence agriculture for survival. Women sometimes barter their crops or livestock for daily necessities at the local corner shop. Villagers, especially women, also supplement their incomes through the sale of beer, crops, livestock and livestock products; remittances from migrants; local employment; non-farm activities; and pensions and transfers from household members. Inevitably, most households find it extremely hard to make ends meet. Their travel and transport are largely limited to procuring subsistence living.

The study established that many villagers owned wheelbarrows and animal-drawn vehicles as well as bicycles and donkeys. These non-motorized vehicles are used largely for carrying goods. Although women own and use these modes, especially the wheelbarrow and the donkey, the majority of owners, especially of the more expensive bicycles and carts, were men.

Walking is by far the dominant mode of travel. Tshitwe residents have to walk upwards of eight kilometres just to access motorized transport and then pay US$2 for the round trip to Makhado, which is expensive for most households. Some pupils walk relatively long distances, especially to high schools. Save for serious illnesses, regular visitations to health centres, the nearest one of which is ten kilometres away, are rare. Rural health centres have become conduits for the dissemination of vital development information since the advent of the new political dispensation. The Tshitwe community is missing out on this information.

GENDER ISSUES IN ACCESSIBILITY AND MOBILITY

Tshitwe women's gender roles have a powerful influence on their travel and transport patterns. The women engage in a range of activities that require transport:

- *Domestic*: fetching water and firewood (in larger households, women have to repeat these trips several times); cooking; caring for children and the elderly; trips to the grinding mill.
- *Economic*: marketing goods and services at pension pay points and other places; tilling, sowing and weeding the fields and gardens; harvesting and carrying harvests from the field to the homestead or market; sewing; brewing beer; and so on.
- *Social*: taking children to schools, taking sick people to health centres and babies to the clinic for weighing and vaccination; attending funerals, religious meetings, societies and community projects.

Fuel for both cooking and lighting is a major concern. While women and children walk upwards of five kilometres to collect firewood for domestic use, men usually use animal-drawn carts to collect wood for sale.

While women have both domestic and economic roles, much of their time is spent in the transport component of those roles, leaving little or no time for other productive socio-economic activities. A woman's day in Tshitwe consists of more than eighteen hours of activities which sustain the household, but which are less central to the market, such as collection of water and firewood, subsistence farming and informal sector activities.

A steady decline of readily accessible firewood supplies through massive deforestation and a decline of reliable and potable water resources through recurring droughts have exacerbated the magnitude of these tasks. Commercialization of firewood has also placed increasing demands on women's labour time for fuelwood collection.

The survey also indicated a clear differentiation by gender in terms of access to the means of production, such as land, agricultural implements, livestock and extension services, as well as finance, information, training and markets, which impacted negatively on women's socio-economic pursuits.

Villagers perceived that poor accessibility levels and the lack of transport services have negatively affected them in many ways. Although the majority of respondents indicated that they would have liked to travel further to improve their livelihoods by marketing their products, services and labour to a wider and diverse market, and undergo further education and training, it was not always possible because of accessibility problems. This is particularly the case with women. This latent demand for transport that is invisible to market forces remains unfulfilled. In view of the inadequate access to socio-economic opportunities, most respondents showed a willingness to emigrate permanently to other areas where these opportunities are perceived to exist.

Small, medium and micro-enterprises constitute a link between traditional and modern, between rural and urban, and between those who 'have' and those who 'have not'. The lack of adequate roads and transport services makes it too cumbersome and time-consuming for women to engage profitably in enterprises involving travel. Consequently they often lack access to markets and are unable to participate in wage labour or trade. Enterprising Tshitwe women were able to sell various goods and services to local and foreign personnel working on the project because not much start-up capital was required. But they are unable to access credit to undertake small enterprises beyond petty food vendoring or for agricultural inputs, for a variety of reasons: Tshitwe women are functionally illiterate; lack financial education; are unable to present projects in a way acceptable to financial institutions; are not used to banking language and requirements; and are bound by restrictive family regulations. These factors have conspired to elevate informal sources of credit, such as family borrowing, savings, savings clubs, friends, unscrupulous money lenders, to favoured status.

Tshitwe women generally have limited savings because they often spend most of their meagre resources on the daily necessities of the household. This heavily compromises the affordability of labour-saving devices and limits their ability to afford and access transport. In many such households, children, particularly girls, become, of necessity, labour resources from an early age. Women's potential to participate in socio-economic activities is influenced and ultimately limited by the inadequate opportunities resulting from their isolation.

Women's ability to utilise family savings (even savings they might have accumulated themselves) and to access credit for financial investment is limited because their creditworthiness, in the eyes of formal institutions, is either weak or non-existent. The traditional land tenure system discriminates against women by allocating land in communal areas to male members of the household. Divorced women have no right to the land they had been cultivating whilst married. Without the financial inputs necessary to leverage meagre cash holdings and to purchase inputs, women continue to work at inefficient levels. It is thus critical to encourage and strengthen financial clubs dominated by women, which could be used as a substitute for collateral; finance long-term investment in agriculture and the informal sector; provide a cushion for economic downturns and income gaps; and serve a function similar to a line of credit to provide for liquidity.

CONCLUSIONS AND RECOMMENDATIONS

A functioning infrastructure is a precondition to the access of inputs and information and for the sale of market produce in areas that are characterized by small-scale agriculture, such as Tshitwe. Developing a minimum infrastructure is a precondition for the implementation of a poverty-oriented development strategy because it frequently presents the only opportunity in the short run for additional jobs with consequent multiplier effects. However, the choice of response measures is critical to the success of intended rural projects.

This study shows that the provision of infrastructure in remote, sparsely populated and economically disadvantaged areas can be cost-inefficient, and can result in only marginal improvement to the economies of these settlements, without maximizing value for money. Road investments are only likely to induce a response in production when the costs of moving produce to the market are reduced and higher farm-gate prices obtained. They are unlikely to have much effect if they merely improve the quality of the road surfaces and all-weather capabilities as peak transport demand occurs in the drier periods of the year (Hine, 1984). The upgraded Tshitwe road has not improved the schoolgoer's transport problem, nor is it likely to, because what school goers need is not a high-quality road surface but the introduction of an efficient transport service.

Priority should be given to ensuring continuous and hardened tracks and paths to enable efficient cart and bicycle transport to the nearest major road. Investments in building minor, low-level footbridges, minor drainage works and other small-scale remedial spot improvements which extend vehicle access and keep routes open to motor vehicle traffic are likely to be more cost-effective (Hine, 1993; Howe, 1997b). Increasing the use of non-motorized transport, such as bicycles, and the provision of credit facilities to purchase non-motorized transport modes could provide an efficient transport service.

The labour-based road-upgrading project alleviated, temporarily, the financial problems of Tshitwe women and men. To this extent, one of the objectives of the project has been fulfilled. But the financial windfall was short-lived. In most cases, men spent their wages on consumer goods from the urban areas, with no redistribution of those resources back to the rural sector. Women used their savings to purchase local goods and services. And, because more men were employed on the road upgrading and their remuneration was much higher than that of women, there was no positive impact on the balance of payments of the village. Not much money from the project was circulated in the community and therefore the expected multiplier effect was insignificant.

However, what is of interest in terms of spatial reorganization is that a significant proportion of the Tshitwe population is willing to give up its current life to settle in areas with better opportunities. Without reading too much into such an opinion, it may well be that spatial reorganization of the rural communities with a view to matching the resource base of the province with population distribution could be implemented with the support of the communities.

Tshitwe women share specific problems related to their unequal access to resources and services and to their relatively limited participation in public life. Their responsibilities as custodians of basic household liveli-hood predominate. The extent to which women's tasks would be eased by the road depended on the flow of services following the upgrading work. However, it is clear from this study that services do not follow automati-cally unless they are specifically planned for. In addition, there was no effort made to integrate the project with other existing sectoral develop-ment strategies. The poor, largely women and children, still walk great distances. Although agricultural practice is characterized by small volumes of modern inputs, such as extension services and fertilizer, access to these inputs is still limited. The transport burden has not been reduced at all. In fact, where higher agricultural yields are achieved, it has increased as the majority of head-loading chores that women and children perform remain.

And, because these (women's) activities are invisible, particularly to the policy makers, women, many of whom are the sole household breadwinners, invariably suffer. In rural South Africa, more than 63 per cent of women live in poverty and so it is critical to classify women as an explicit target group for purposes of instituting specific measures (Larcher and Dikito, 1991) and to develop strategies tailored to their specific needs and circumstances. It is therefore necessary to develop policy guidelines and strategies for the various levels of government to include women in the assessment of their own transport needs and to improve gender-sensitive planning, dissemination and implementation of transport solutions.

Conventional transport planning, with its unambiguous emphasis on roads as the panacea for all transport problems, is thus, at best, an incomplete response. The necessity to pay greater attention to the examination of the *real* access needs of rural dwellers differentiated by gender cannot be over-emphasized. Road investment must be complemented with other measures which address, in a more holistic manner, the totality of communities' accessibility needs. Not only have non-motorized transport modes been found to have synergistic linkages with other transport modes, but they could also ameliorate the transport burden of Tshitwe women and men in the short term and ultimately act as a catalyst for sustainable long-term socio-economic development (Mashiri, 1997).

The Tshitwe road-upgrading project reflects a preoccupation of policy makers with high-technology fixes and efficiency rather than the thorough examination of the needs of the beneficiary communities, which could have resulted in a different, less expensive, but more sustainable gender-sensitive solution to the same problem. It is thus critically important to realize that ignoring, underplaying or misunderstanding gender differences in the economy of the household, and by extension of the village, could lead to expensive and irrelevant development projects. It is also necessary to target interventions not only with regard to improvement of the physical infrastructure (where the roles of all types of infrastructure are recognized), but also on the means of transport (including non-motorized transport modes), and the quality of services. This should be done within the ambit of an integrated rural development framework by way of a multi-sectoral and gender-sensitive approach which starts with the condition of the poor, their resources, aspirations and problems.

NOTE

1. A high-order settlement is a settlement which has a number of shops (including restaurants) of various types selling urban goods such as furniture, sometimes a post office, a church or churches, reticulated sewerage and water, electricity, a clinic, a pension pay-out point, a high school, etc.

3

INTERMEDIATE MEANS OF TRANSPORT AND GENDER RELATIONS

ZIMBABWE

Dorris Chingozho

The population of Zimbabwe is estimated to be around 12 million people. With an average annual population growth rate of 3.1 per cent, down from 3.3 per cent due to the HIV/AIDS pandemic and other social and economic factors, 51.2 per cent are female (Central Statistical Office, 1998). About 75 per cent of the population live in rural areas deriving a substantial portion of their livelihood directly from agriculture. The daily sustenance of the rural people demands a lot of time in terms of travel and transport. Men and women have different roles, and although men are assuming some women's roles and vice versa the difference is still marked, and women have a greater workload than men. Many gender specialists and groups have emphasized health, education and economic empowerment without looking at the critical issue of transport.

The Intermediate Technology Development Group (ITDG)[1] carried out a transport project from 1992 to 1995, in partnership with the Institute of Agricultural Engineering in Zimbabwe and support from IT Transport UK.[2] The project implemented a broad-based national programme for disseminating low-cost vehicles (also called intermediate means of transport or IMTs) and introducing split-rim, wheel- and axle-making technology (developed by ITDG) to small workshops. It aimed at mitigating transport problems and related time constraints faced by households in communal areas by increasing and broadening the product range and the availability of good-quality, low-cost transport devices.

Five main types of IMTs are used in rural areas: Scotch carts (ox carts), wheelbarrows, water carts and water carriers (barrows), pushcarts and bicycles. They can be used both for personal travel and for movement of goods. The ownership of motor vehicles in the rural areas is very low, largely restricted to prosperous local businessmen.

This chapter assesses the impact of improved transport on women in areas where ITDG's transport project programme and other initiatives have been implemented. Its aim is to document how interventions promoting the use of IMTs have changed the gender allocation of the transport burden and have impacted on gender relations. The study hopes to contribute to a more gender-sensitive planning of transport in rural and peri-urban areas, and to assist transport planners in Zimbabwe to integrate rural transport policy into broader developmental policies and objectives.

Many of the conclusions in this chapter are drawn from an analysis of ITDG project evaluation reports and of reports of other organizations such as the World Bank and the ILO, complemented by fieldwork in areas where the ITDG technology was disseminated, including Chivi, Nyanga, Murombedzi and Chivhu. Zhombe, Binga and Chiredzi were not visited during this survey as they were covered by an earlier evaluation (Orr and Njenga, 1995). Surveys were also carried out in two villages in Chiota communal lands as well as in Gokwe. Chiota was selected for its high prevalent usage of IMTs. In Gokwe there is a high level of IMT usage in cotton and maize farming, which operates on a commercial basis.[3]

The study used structured discussions with village leaders and other key informants to obtain data about the communities and an overview of their travel patterns, transport constraints and problems.

WOMEN'S TRANSPORT NEEDS

Agricultural activities

Agriculture is a major activity and the main means of survival in the households interviewed and generally in most areas of Zimbabwe. A lot of time is spent on travel and transport relating to agriculture. In the rainy season cultivation takes place in the rain-fed fields, and in the dry season in irrigated plots and gardens. Both periods require transporting inputs such as fertilizers and manure to the fields and transporting produce to the homesteads for storage. Transport is also needed for marketing purposes. Most of the produce is marketed at central marketing points, for example the Grain Marketing Board or the Cotton Company, as well as at business centres, especially for garden produce.

In the two villages surveyed in Chiota people travel about 4 kilometres to their nearest business centres: Landos and Arda Centre at Mandodya. Women farmers in these two villages rely on individual initiatives and efforts in marketing maize, sunflower and cotton crops to these commercial centres. Some use buses and at times individually or cooperatively hire trucks to ferry goods, particularly vegetables, to Harare's main horticultural market. Harare is only 65 kilometres from Chiota, and in households where the vegetable crop is substantial and of good quality there is the expectation of receiving a higher price for the crop. Some women expressed confidence that during good economic times the investment in hiring a truck was justified by the successful sale of the crop.

Firewood collection

All the households interviewed use firewood as their source of energy. Women who head-load collect firewood on average twice every week. In Chiota firewood is collected over distances of more than 3 or 4 kilometres, involving two hours of walking and another hour of collecting. This translates to sixteen hours per month for head-loaders. Village Development Committees are adopting stern policing measures to reduce deforestation. Women head-loaders not only have to travel longer distances, incurring more trips and an increased transport burden, but also sometimes have to do so at night. The increasing time allocated to collection of firewood has affected women's other duties, such as preparing meals. Often women leave girls to cook or allocate boys to collect firewood.

Grain milling

An average family consumes four 20-kilogram tins of mealie meal per month. Every week, women on average head-load one tin of maize and small girls head-load half a tin (10 kilograms). This translates to four trips per month involving two hours of walking and one hour of waiting, making three hours per trip and twelve hours per month. The waiting time at the mill is determined by the seasonal changes in the availability of maize. It is high soon after harvesting and goes down as maize stocks subside, peaking again the following season. The number of grinding mills available at the commercial centre also affects waiting time.

Longer journeys

Besides going to the grinding mill and procuring basic food items, travel to the commercial centres is infrequent because for high-value goods and for administrative functions people need to go to the towns. Of those surveyed, 44 per cent go to the commercial centre to board buses to the major cities, 33.3 per cent to sell produce and buy agricultural implements and about 29.6 per cent for social gathering and beer drinking. Income levels and consumption patterns determine the frequency of travel to the centres. High-income, female-managed households access the centres more than female-headed households, who have relatively lower incomes.

OWNERSHIP AND USE OF IMTs

The ownership of IMTs in all the areas studied is largely determined by incomes, entrepreneurial skills and social status. IMT owners tend to have more income than have non-owners. Ownership is also determined in some cases by the potential for income-generating activities. For example, animal-drawn carts or bicycles, especially those that have a front-load carrier (used to deliver products by most rural traders), are mostly found in households that engage in off-farm income-generating activities. IMT ownership is also influenced by terrain conditions, with greater ownership in areas of fairly flat topography. Ownership is also influenced by family size and age. Young and small families have lower IMT ownership patterns than do bigger and older families. This may have to do with different task demands associated with family size and age.

There are two categories of households that need special mention: female-headed and female-managed households. They generally comprise up to 40 per cent of the total households. Female-headed households are composed of widows, divorcees and unmarried women with children. Some of these households are poorer than the average household in the community. Female-managed households are commonly a product of out-migration by the male household head (Mannock Management Consultants and ILO, 1997). In the two villages of Chiota, from a sample size of 27 households 33.3 per cent were female-headed and 37 per cent were female-managed, compared to 29.7 per cent that were male-headed.

IMT ownership, particularly bicycles and carts, is lower among female-headed households than among female-managed households. The former usually depend on borrowing or hiring devices. In Chiota this difference is determined by the differences in income between the two types of households. Female-headed households have lower income levels and low-value assets. They own a smaller range of IMTs, which are usually old or worn out and often not functional. For the majority of the households, new transport devices are necessary but well beyond their reach. The female-managed households have higher income levels, depending mainly on remittances from their husbands. In some instances the women in these households are not engaged in serious income-generating activities. Female-headed households, mainly widows, source their incomes from working sons or daughters but mostly from agricultural activities and peanut butter production.

Local availability of IMT manufacturers also influences the ownership of IMTs. For instance, IMT technology is prevalent in the areas where workshop owners were trained in the technology and where ITDG in collaboration with other NGOs – the Organization of Rural Associations for Progress, Christian Care, Life Sowing Ministries and the Agricultural and Rural Development Authority – disseminated the technology. Most of these agencies allocated the low-cost vehicles to particularly needy individuals or to cooperatives engaged in group activities.

In many areas, IMT ownership is concentrated among the more commercially minded farmers, where Scotch carts and wheelbarrows have an important role in carrying inputs to the field and harvested crops from the fields. A study by the Ministry of Transport with support from the ILO (Mannock Management Consultants and ILO, 1997) revealed that cart owners in Chipinge had an average 45 per cent higher overall income than the sample and that the greatest share of this higher income comes from agriculture. Bicycle owners are few and there seems to be a link to status particularly among male-headed households. The studies in Chiota showed that out of a random sample of 27 households, only 44 per cent owned a bicycle.

USES OF IMTs IN THE HOMESTEAD

Bicycles

Bicycles are used predominantly by men and boys, sometimes with accompanying loads, both within and outside the villages even in quite difficult terrain conditions. Their use by women is limited. Female-headed households have bicycles only because their late husbands or their children used them, not usually as a result of their direct efforts and needs. These bicycles are largely old and in disuse. Though women indicated that they were allowed to use them, they seem to be still embedded in the culture that women do not ride bicycles.

Bicycles are used to access distant areas such as commercial centres and clinics and to visit friends and relatives outside the villages. In areas where there are employment opportunities in the surrounding farms, men use bicycles to travel to and from work.

Although bicycles are technically suited for carrying loads to the grinding mills as they are fast and can traverse small and difficult paths, they are not used for this purpose save when carrying light loads. This is largely due to the fact that a large number of households with bicycles also have carts. The carts are more efficient at carrying large quantities and can be used to carry grain on a cooperative basis that eliminates the need to transport small quantities of grain individually. In Chiota, there was no indication of the commercial use of bicycles such as hiring, except that they are lent free of charge in the community. This suggests that bicycles have only a limited economic role. Their main function is as a status good which aids household travel in general, rather than any specific income sector.

In Murombedzi the situation is somewhat different. Here bicycles are the most common means of accessing the commercial centres and they are also used for commercial activities such as carrying milk cans on carriers to the Dairy Processing Centre at Murombedzi Business Centre. Here too they are predominantly used by men and boys.

Scotch carts

Whilst not every household owns a Scotch cart, a two-wheeled animal drawn cart, it is the most widely owned and predominant form of load-carrying IMT in the areas surveyed. There are three main ways in which carts are used by the community: for day-to-day household requirements; for lending to other members of the community in exchange for labour, for example for weeding, brick moulding and firewood collection; and for hiring (this is a recent phenomenon due to the hard economic times).

Carts are used to move relatively large amounts of goods quickly over a given distance. Whilst their use varies from area to area, their primary purpose is to meet agricultural transport needs. These include ferrying agricultural inputs (like artificial fertilizers, manure and top-soil) to fields and produce from fields such as crops and maize stalks for cattle pens or carrying building materials such as bricks, stones and water. They are also used for carrying produce to market. In Chiota, firewood is collected through the use of Scotch carts. In Murombedzi, they are used in small business enterprises to carry goods for sale, such as beer containers. In Nyanga, women have been liberated from the drudgery of head-loading water through the use of water carts for agriculture and brick-moulding.

Leasing carts for a fee varies from place to place. There is a mix of hiring and sharing largely dominated by sharing. In Chiota, Chivhu and Chivi, a large majority of the farmers do not offer hiring services. It is considered socially unacceptable to hire out carts, which are primarily viewed as a household tool for the reciprocal benefit of the community at large. In Chiota 82 per cent of the respondents said they share their carts in exchange for labour and only 55 per cent hire their carts out. Income generation was not given as the primary reason for purchasing Scotch carts. However, owing to the hard economic times the situation is quickly changing. Cart owners generate some infrequent but vital income by hiring out to non-cart owners.

Hiring fees range from as little as Z$40 per load in Chivi to as high as Z$80–100 in Chiota depending on the duration and purpose of the task and the amount and nature of the material being carried. Building materials such as gravel and bricks attract the highest fees and firewood and crops the lowest. Hiring carts to ferry grain to the grinding mill is rare, except among large-scale poultry farmers. Dairy and poultry farmers in Murombedzi Business Centre carry heavy and sometimes bulky loads to and from the grinding mill at the growth centre for grinding stockfeed and buying oil cake from an oil-making cooperative there. If the grinding mill is too far to head-load or to use wheelbarrows or converted water barrows, women and men collaborate and carry grain for a number of households in a single cart.

The use of carts for commercial purposes, especially crop marketing, is determined by distance, household income and consumption patterns as well as the nature and range of services provided by the centre. In areas of critical transport shortages involving long distances, farmers (both men and women) cooperatively use Scotch carts and/or hire trucks to move their crops to the nearest Grain Marketing Board or Cotton Company of Zimbabwe points of purchase. However, the movement of small quantities is done with wheelbarrows.

Usage of Scotch carts in the surveyed areas extends beyond the owners due to significant levels of sharing, borrowing and hiring, particularly during periods of peak agricultural transport demand.

Wheelbarrows

The Ministry of Transport/ILO study (Mannock Management Consultants and ILO, 1997) suggests that wealthier families purchase wheelbarrows for their utility function. This, they argue, begins when households begin to construct brick houses roofed with corrugated sheets to replace their mud and thatch dwellings. The wheelbarrow continues to be useful as a load-carrying aid for both male and female members for fuel, water and maize-milling needs. This is confirmed by results from Chiota in particular, where a large majority of the respondents argued that a wheelbarrow is the most convenient way of carrying out lighter tasks and there-fore essential in the rural areas.

The wheelbarrow has a 'neutral' gender image; that is, it is not per-ceived as an exclusively 'male' or 'female' vehicle, unlike the bicycle, which tends to be seen as transport for men.

Water carts

Water carts are available in areas of critical water shortage such as Chivi, where transporting water involves long distances. In Nyanga, the farmers who had two water carts donated for testing purposes have found them helpful in alleviating the transport burden to water gardens and to ferry building materials, including grass for thatching. Households in Chiota have accesss to reliable boreholes near to or at home (on average not exceeding 500 metres). They therefore do not need water carts as water can easily be carried using wheelbarrows or by head-loading.

Without the drums a water cart can be used as a cart for transporting firewood. It has become the most effective IMT for firewood collection as more forests are progressively depleted and distances for collection increase. Cart owners have another advantage in that physical access by cart to firewood sources is not a major problem. Moreover, women indi-cated that there are no difficulties associated with storage of firewood; thus carts can be fully loaded so as to avoid frequent trips.

Water barrows

In Chivhu, the water barrow has many uses. It carries two 20-litre or even two 60-litre plastic drums of water per trip. Modified as a wheelbarrow, it can also be used to carry maize to the mill or to carry firewood.

The water barrow can also be converted to serve as a ripper (which can plough a furrow for planting seeds) and a planter. This multipurpose application makes it user-friendly, particularly for women and children, significantly reducing the time and effort for planting. One artisan in Chivhi is working with farmers to develop a viable and appropriate design of water barrow for agricultural use.

Donkeys

Ownership of donkeys is associated with poorer households. Donkeys are also prevalent in drought-prone areas. With proper harnessing techniques they are resilient animals and form a convenient means of local transportation.

BENEFITS ACCRUING TO WOMEN

Time saved and activities

The use of IMTs has created both direct and indirect benefits for women. The gains vary depending on the wealth status of the family and the household size, which determine the type and number of IMTs owned. First, the use of IMTs has shortened the travel times involved in the various transport journeys. Second, they have substantially increased the efficiency with which loads are carried: for example, women are finding that transporting maize, firewood and manure by cart is more efficient and quicker than by head-loading.

Transportation of agricultural inputs and produce has been made efficient by the use of Scotch carts. Using a cart has also reduced the time and frequency of firewood collection from twice a week to once every month depending on family size and consumption patterns. Women spend only two hours per month using the cart, but a large proportion of the households (70–80 per cent) still head-load because they have no access to IMTs.

The use of carts and wheelbarrows has reduced the time devoted to going to the grinding mill to about nine hours a month. The number of women going to the grinding mill has also dropped. Out of the households surveyed, 74 per cent send boys using the carts or the wheelbarrows. Girls and mothers go to the grinding mills when they are travelling to the centre for other reasons, such as buying basic commodities, including cooking oil, paraffin and soap.

Role changes

Traditionally men have dominated all the tasks that involve the use of livestock, such as oxen and donkeys. Activities that involve harnessing oxen to Scotch carts and driving them have been men's tasks. The increased use of IMTs has led to the involvement of men in household duties that would normally be done by women. Men have increasingly assumed responsibility for some transport tasks, such as fetching firewood, going to the grinding mill, taking the sick to clinics and so on, as long as they can use IMTs, especially Scotch carts. Men are involved in firewood and water collection particularly when it involves long distances and when larger quantities are required such as for big functions and gatherings (e.g. weddings and funerals). Only 7.4 per cent of the women indicated that their husbands participate in water collection for domestic purposes. This is partly due to the fact that a high number of males are always absent from the rural areas. However, even in the households where men are present it is mainly boys who are involved in water collection, indicating a general male attitude to water collection as women and children's work.

These shifts in the allocation of roles are largely a result of the use of IMTs. Owing to the Economic Structural Adjustment Programme men are migrating back to the rural areas and are working alongside women in income-generating activities. It is also argued that men get involved in activities such as firewood collection when they find women's workload to be interfering with their interests and expectations, such as when women are delayed from preparing food.

Utilization of time saved

All the evidence from the surveys and other earlier work and case studies suggests that the use of IMTs significantly reduces women's transport burden. However, as Ian Barwell (1996) acknowledges in case studies from sub-Saharan Africa, we also found that the question of time saved and its utilization is more complex than imagined. The release of time seems to usher in new demands and tasks: for example, more water may encourage better/more cleaning, calling for more trips to the water source; time that was used going to the grinding mill is used to increase the number of vegetable beds or to feed more chickens. Whilst leisure time is beneficial because a consistently huge workload has unsatisfactory economic, social and health implications, rural women felt pushed by the need to meet the food self-sufficiency of the family and to get surplus produce for sale. They stressed that, unlike urban women, they cannot 'rest' because they have to ensure the survival of the family. 'While an urban woman can rest, a rural woman hardly gets the time; she can only rest when she goes to sleep', said one woman.

The women across the various areas use time saved to participate in women's clubs and cooperatives. In Chiota, as in Nyanga and Chivi, they use the time saved to do gardening projects. They are also involved in buying and selling goods on credit. Some have started or expanded income-generating activities such as peanut butter production, poultry and pig-rearing. Some are increasingly engaged in casual labour. The study shows that for many rural women income-generating activities tend to take place on a relatively small scale within the local area. Women indicated that the ability to start activities is constrained more by lack of start-up capital than by limited time availability.

DESIGN ISSUES

The ITDG's Manufacture and Design of Low Cost Transport Devices Project improved the supply of Scotch carts and made significant strides in developing other low-cost devices. Its impact on alleviating the transport burden of women and low-income households was broadly positive (Dawson, 1995). Women in areas where IMTs are widely used are positive about the impact of the transport devices brought into the household, although access and degree of benefits are not always equal.

The ITDG project developed two low-cost transport technologies directed mainly at tasks normally carried out by women. These are the water barrow and a donkey cart that is light enough to push by hand or be pulled by a single donkey. This is important, for two reasons. First, much of the country is still recovering from the recent droughts that decimated large numbers of cattle, and there are still few households that own cattle. Second, it is more culturally acceptable for a woman to go to the field and catch a donkey and hitch it to a cart than to do so with an ox. The small cart is also useful for day-to-day activities like taking maize to the mill or collecting water close to a borehole, where ox carts are not allowed since the heavy cart damages the surrounding areas. More fundamentally, women reported using the carts themselves as men are usually away.

The ITDG-designed vehicles are suitable for women because they are easy to use, easy to harness the donkey to and light to lift. The design of the water carriers is also suitable and even small children can use them with great ease. The water barrow has an advantage over the wheelbarrow because it has compartments for carrying water tins, unlike wheelbarrows, from which tins drop off.

Communal area small-scale farmers in Nyanga pointed out that the cart can be used both as a water cart and as a Scotch cart, making it more ideal and indispensable to many farmers, particularly those where water sources are far from their homesteads. The water barrow can also be converted and used as a wheelbarrow to carry firewood. It can be re-inforced to act as a ripper to make furrows for planting seed, as well making it much more convenient for women's varied and demanding tasks.

The ITDG-designed split-rim Scotch carts are simpler to manage and women reported that they can easily change the tyres in the event of a puncture instead of waiting for assistance from men. While all of the interviewed users were very enthusiastic about the split-rim technology, the relief that comes with the use of any IMT was of greater importance to them than a particular technology. The main issue was the ability to purchase the products. While IMTs reduce the transport burden, the question of affordability must be addressed. The manufacturers cannot just make products and sell below their cost to meet the needs of farmers. In meeting the IMT needs of communities it is essential for development workers and planners to take into account the objectives of the manufacturers as well.

CONCLUSION

Several insights emerge from this survey. The development, dissemination and use of low-cost and appropriate IMT technology have substantially increased the availability of IMTs in rural areas and helped alleviate women's transport and travelling burden. This has been complemented by the increasing involvement of men in household duties. Some tasks (e.g. water collection) are more rigidly allocated to women. Women in households where such changes have taken place have managed to find time to engage in other social, economic and even political activities. They do not, however, find time to rest because they need to meet other pressing household obligations, and the time saved ushers in new demands and tasks.

The ownership and use of IMTs depends on income level and family size. IMTs are primarily purchased for household use, though, owing to economic hardships, some IMT owners are beginning to hire them out. Most female-headed and female-managed households do not own or use IMTs. In some areas 70–80 per cent of the women continue to head-load firewood. Women from the female-headed and female-managed households lack constant ready money to pay for the hire of transport services, especially if cash instead of kind or labour services is demanded. Hiring would eat up the little they get in the way of remittances, instead of using the money to satisfy pressing household needs. They depend on borrowing or sharing IMTs with those who have them.

NOTES

1. ITDG is an international NGO with offices in Bangladesh, Kenya, Nepal, Peru, Sri Lanka, Sudan and Zimbabwe.
2. IT Transport is a private consultancy firm.
3. Chiota and Chivhu are in Mashonaland East province, Nyanga in Manicaland province, Murombedzi in Mashonaland West province, and Chivi in Masvingo province.

4

DO INTERMEDIATE MEANS OF TRANSPORT REACH RURAL WOMEN?

TANZANIA

Josephine A. Mwankusye

In Tanzania, where over 75 per cent of the population is rural, and small-holder agriculture is the backbone of the country's economy, women are the main actors in agricultural production. Women are also responsible for about 90 per cent of food-processing activity, and water and firewood collection. Because women have limited access to improved means of transport, they carry out most of these activities by walking and carrying. Most of their travel and transport takes place along footpaths and tracks, and head-loading accounts for 73 per cent of all transport requirements.

Since the 1980s several efforts have been made by government and donors to develop the activities of both men and women in the rural sector but their impact has been very marginal due to inefficient transport. Considerable efforts are now being made to improve the rural travel and transport situation. The Village Travel and Transport Programme was formulated in 1994 by the Tanzanian government, and with support from several donors is being implemented in ten selected districts (Iramba, Muheza, Morogoro, Masasi, Mbozi, Kasulu, Sumbawanga, Mbulu, Meatu and Mbinga). Proposed project interventions included improvement of paths, roads and drainage structures: improvement of access to selected services, mainly water, milling machines and fuelwood; and promotion of the use of intermediate means of transport (IMTs). The programme emphasizes empowering women to own and get access to IMTs.

The key question is are the benefits from these interventions reaching rural women? Are the existing socio-cultural relations and the gender division of labour in rural transport being considered?

BACKGROUND: THE CONTEXT OF RURAL TRAVEL AND TRANSPORT IN TANZANIA

Transport demand in rural areas

In Tanzania the rural travel and transport demand is characterized by travel for domestic activities such as collection of water and firewood, and the processing of food crops at grinding mills; for agricultural production; for marketing agricultural produce and livestock products; for accessing services; and for social purposes. Much of this travel and transport takes place within a district, along paths and tracks, on foot and using IMTs. A rural household makes an average of between 35 and 52 trips a year within a district and about four trips outside, mainly by bus. During the rainy season a large proportion of the paths and tracks become impassable because of lack of drainage structures such as culverts and wooden bridges at stream and river crossings, making many villages inaccessible.

The rural transport network in Tanzania comprises a hierarchy of paths and tracks, and feeder, district and trunk roads (Kaira et al., 1993). Feeder roads (usually earth roads) connect village centres to district regional roads. The village *godowns* (stores) and crop collection/buying centres are usually located along these roads. The major transport modes on feeder roads are walking/porterage, bicycles, pack-animals, animal carts, handcarts, wooden bicycles and wooden trucks. Some villages get access to motorized transport on market days when trucks and some four-wheel-drive vehicles visit the villages to buy produce from the markets.

District roads (mostly gravel) connect division centres to district headquarters and in some cases are served with a scheduled bus service. Ward *godowns* for produce are usually located along these roads for easy access by the lorries. Trunk roads (usually all-weather) serve long-distance traffic, and in most cases have no significance for the local population.

Women and rural travel

In Tanzania, as in many sub-Saharan Africa countries, men and women are assigned distinct roles based on a gender division of labour. Apart from transportation of agricultural produce and household needs, rural women are mostly responsible for taking the sick to health centres or hospitals, especially children and expectant mothers. Reliable health services are often located at district headquarters. To obtain such facilities women must travel an average distance of about 8 kilometres, sometimes by bus but usually on foot.

Female-headed households, which form 27 per cent of the population (Bureau of Statistics, 1995), are the most marginalized within Tanzanian rural society. These households are smaller, have fewer adults, and have lower total incomes and incomes from agriculture. The absence of a male partner and lack of access to IMTs contribute to the scale of the transport burden faced by the women in these households.

Measures to alleviate rural transport problems

In 1987, the Tanzanian government through the Ministry of Transport, Communications and Works drafted a National Transport Policy, the main objective of which was to ensure that the transport services of the country are reliable, fast, safe, responsive, up-to-date and economic. The Policy acknowledges that over 75 per cent of the country's population live in rural areas and are engaged in subsistence agricultural production, and recognizes that in order to improve and attain efficiency in the performance of the agricultural sector, the rural transport system must be improved.

Government and donor-funded programmes

There have been a number of rural transport programmes initiated in Tanzania by the government in collaboration with donors. One such initiative, the Makete Integrated Rural Transport Project (MIRTP), substantially improved the rural mobility in Makete district from 1985 to 1996. The project improved rural infrastructure (feeder roads, footpaths/tracks) and social services (water sources and grinding mills) and promoted the use of IMTs (mainly donkeys and wheelbarrows). During an impact assessment in 1992, 58 per cent of households interviewed said the bicycle was the most useful IMT for their transport tasks, 30 per cent said a donkey was the most useful, and 3 per cent preferred an animal-drawn cart (Chiwanga et al., 1992). If time is valued in terms of opportunity costs, the annual monetary benefits of the use of IMTs amounted to US$9.74 per household. Women benefited with 54 per cent of the total time savings.

The Tanga Integrated Rural Development Project, supported by the Deutsche Gesellschaft für Technische Zusammenarbeit (GTZ), initiated an animal draft power component from 1981 to 1993. The project introduced animal power into an area with few cattle and no tradition of using animals for work. Although, in numerical terms, the project results were not spectacular, animal power has become firmly established within the area. The project's activities included the introduction of donkey carts, ox carts and the development of prototype heavy rollers for clearing fields.

In 1987, the Mbeya Oxenization Project was established with support from the Canadian International Development Agency. The project worked in close cooperation with farmers, government institutions and local entrepreneurs. A number of women were also sensitized to the use of animal power for agriculture and rural travel.

The Centre for Agriculture Machinery and Rural Technology was established in 1981, and is engaged in designing, developing, testing and producing agricultural implements. Since its establishment much time and effort have been expended in developing prototype equipment and ox carts.

IMTs (mainly bicycles) have been provided through project assistance in a number of rural areas under programmes initiated under the Structural Adjustment Programme and the Economic Recovery Programme between 1982 and 1985. In 1984 the Dutch government under a commodity support programme donated a grant of NFL1 million, which purchased about 50,000 bicycles for cotton farmers in Shinyanga and Mwanza regions. These two regions were selected because the Dutch government had been providing support for the cotton industry there, and because – although farmers (both women and men) had a strong tradition of bicycle ownership – there was a shortage of bicycles.

Interviews with farmers showed that 92 per cent were using bicycles primarily for work purposes, with family care and domestic activities as secondary purposes (Cooksey et al., 1987). Unfortunately, these statistics only relate to male farmers; no women bicycle owners were interviewed.

THE STUDY

My study is based on a literature review of past and present rural development programmes, particularly in Tanzania; information obtained from principal informants/villagers and district/village government officials; interviews and focus group discussions during field visits in villages; and participatory observation.

Four key questions were examined:

- Is there any relationship between women's economic/household activities and the use of IMTs in the study area?
- Do women have access to IMTs?
- What are the specific uses of IMTs?
- What are people's perceptions of women's use and ownership of IMTs?

The study focused on three villages, two from Morogoro rural district (Bunduki and Maguruwe) and one in Muheza district (Potwe). Morogoro and Muheza districts are among the seven pilot districts which are currently implementing the Village Travel and Transport Programme (VTTP)

Bunduki and Maguruwe villages

These are among the pilot villages for the VTTP in Morogoro. They are situated along the Uluguru Mountains, about 57 kilometres from Morogoro town. They have high potential for vegetable and fruit production, but are not connected by motorable roads. Villagers use very steep slippery tracks and paths to reach the market and other social amenities about 16 kilometres away. About 70 per cent of the agricultural produce is perishable fruits and vegetables. Poor transportation and the lack of reliable marketing and processing arrangements lead to substantial losses of these perishables. The footpaths and tracks within the area are in a very poor condition, so accessibility to the villages is always difficult, and the situation becomes worse during the rainy season. The two villages have a total of 6,340 inhabitants, 61 per cent of whom are women (Census, 1988). Female-headed households comprise 25 per cent and 27 per cent respectively of all households in Bunduki and Maguruwe.

Potwe village

Potwe village is one of the pilot villages for VTTP in Muheza district. It is located 8 kilometres from the Tanga-Dar es Salaam main road in a region of rolling terrain. The village has high potential for fruit, vegetable, maize and bean production. However, owing to clay soils, during the rainy season accessibility within the village area becomes very difficult. The village has a total of 3,134 inhabitants according to estimates from the 1988 population census, of which 60 per cent are women. In Potwe 26 per cent of the households are female-headed.

Economic conditions

The study areas are all characterized by high population densities. Small-scale agriculture prevails: the major food crops grown are maize, cassava, beans and bananas. Cash crops include coffee, cardamom, tea, sisal and sesame. Potwe village benefits from sisal- and tea-processing industries. Bunduki and Maguruwe villages produce tropical and temperate fruits and vegetables.

Household decision-making and authority are based on nature of production and management of resources. Men make the decisions on land use patterns, the type of crops to be grown and where, decisions which in some cases affect women's ability to provide food crops for household consumption. Owing to increasing land scarcity over the Uluguru Mountains, men in Bunduki and Maguruwe are cultivating cash crops near their homesteads, and food crops are cultivated further away. Women have no alternative but to walk between 7 and 10 kilometres to reach food crop fields.

The gender division of labour has always assigned women the unpaid, productive and reproductive roles, which usually take place at home and are therefore unrecognized. Maguruwe and Bunduki are matrilineal societies and women have some access to land and other means of production; however, women's access to land is so limited that it does not emancipate them from their disadvantageous position.

Men in these societies control the management of household income and other resources such as fertilizers, oxen and IMTs. IMTs are used mainly for household economic activities and less for women's tasks. Societal values reinforce the decision-making powers of men and dictate the nature of the division of labour and the ownership, control and distribution of resources within households (Mwaipopopo, 1994). Women's lack of access to IMTs is the result of their inability to control available household resources to their advantage.

Transport and IMTs in the study area

Despite some efforts to promote the use of IMTs, few people own and use them (see Table 4.1) – about 73 per cent of all transporting is done

TABLE 4.1 Ownership of IMTs in the villages

| | **Potwe** | | | **Maguruwe and Bunduki** | | |
	Total	Women	Men	Total	Women	Men
Bicycles	50	4	46	4	1	3
Handcarts	60	0	60	0	0	0
Donkeys	2	0	2	2	0	2
Wheelbarrows	70	0	70	10	0	10
Motorcycles	0	0	0	4	0	4

Source: Study findings, October 1998.

by head-loading. Women carry up to 30 kilograms on their heads and walk distances of up to 20 kilometres.

A number of families in Potwe village have bicycles; however, ownership and bicycle use are largely restricted to men. One man commented: 'I paid money to marry my wife, how can she own a bicycle?' Two women who own bicycles are Maternal Health Clinic attendants and two others are farmers.

In Bunduki and Muguruwe the Ward Executive Officers and the Agricultural Extension Officers own the motorcycles. In Bunduki village the Ward Executive Officer has both a motorcycle and a bicycle, but his wife walks some 5 kilometres outside the village to obtain milling services. The motorcycle is strictly used for official trips and sometimes personal travel but not to assist with household activities.

There is little experience of animal keeping in the area, though the villages of Maguruwe and Bundkui benefited from an NGO donkey promotion in 1996. Wheelbarrows, common in both areas, are mainly used by men for construction purposes.

Financial constraints

The high acquisition price of IMTs, which is beyond the cash income-earning capacity of most rural households, constrains their ownership and use. The situation is worse for women. A majority of rural women earn very little cash per annum because traditionally men own cash crops (see Table 4.2). Though women remain the main producers of these crops, the

TABLE 4.2 Women's earnings

	Potwe		**Maguruwe and Bunduki**	
	% of total	Av income (Tsh)	% of total	Av. income (Tsh)
Agriculture	70	9,000	75	8,000
Agriculture and petty business	10	15,000	7	24,000
Business	18	30,000	13	30,000
Government employees	2	35,000	2	35,000

Source: Study findings, October 1998.

actual produce is men's property. The main source of income for the majority of rural women is the surplus food crops produced. In female-headed households the situation is even worse. Most of these women struggle to meet basic household needs such as school fees, medical requirements and food. They cannot number the purchase of IMTs among their top priorities.

Women's income-generating activities

Rural women embark on various income-generating activities to supplement their household requirements. This they do through participation in women's groups, the majority of which operate on small sums of capital generated by them or through government and donor or NGO assistance. Though experience has shown that low-income women entrepreneurs repay their loans and use the proceeds to increase their income and assets, many formal credit schemes still favour men.

There are four women's groups in Maguruwe and one in Bunduki. In Maguruwe one group is engaged in crop production and two in poultry. In Bunduki, the women's group is engaged in vegetable production. There are six women's groups in Potwe village, four of which produce maize and vegetables while two keep poultry.

Transport problems hamper the activities of women's groups. The women's groups in Potwe village lose about 10 tons of the vegetables they

TABLE 4.3   Estimated prices of commonly used IMTs in the study area

	Price (Tsh)	Maintenance costs (Tsh)
Bicycle	65,000	18,000
Bicycle with trailer	78,000	–
Hand cart	36,000	18,000
Ox cart	450,000	67,000
Donkey	132,000	67,000
Donkey cart	180,000	75,000
Wheelbarrow	18,000	15,000

Source: Study findings, October 1998.

TABLE 4.4 An example of the economics of rural bicycle ownership (Tsh)

Investment cost	
Purchase of bicycle life	65,000
Depreciation (per annum)	17,188
Annual operating cost	
General and maintenance	30,000
Tyres and tubes	50,400
Total	80,400

produce per season due to unreliable means of transport. Members of the groups felt strongly that IMTs, preferably pushcarts and bicycles with trailers, could assist them in carrying their produce from the field to the marketplace, and would reduce the losses from head-loading. But they have too little income to purchase an IMT.

A study of the economics of ox cart ownership in Rukwe district showed that credit made an ox cart much more affordable to an owner of oxen, and that the capital required could be reduced by 75 per cent if the cart were to be bought on credit (Barwell, 1996). But women's income-generating activities operate with very little capital, so very few women can obtain such credit.

Lack of skills and information on the use of IMTs

Because women are less mobile than men and tend to have less access to outside information, their knowledge about IMTs is limited. In some cases women may know what option they would prefer but may need more information, which they cannot get.

There is also a perception that when collecting water and firewood, as well as taking grains to the milling machines, women will have some time to chat and discuss social affairs, and if such facilities are located further away they will have more time to talk. Discussions with women in Potwe and Bunduki villages challenge the veracity of these perceptions. These women would prefer more time to accomplish their multiple tasks.

Martha Bernard is a 42-year-old woman, who lives in Bunduki village. She is a mother of six who has been earning her livelihood through pottery for thirty years. For thirty years Martha has been carrying clay on her head and walking 14 kilometres twice a week. Sometimes she has to spend a night at Maguruwe village, where clay is obtained. Currently the VTTP in Morogoro district is demonstrating the use of donkeys in Bunduki village. Martha could not believe her eyes when she saw a donkey carrying clay. From that day she promised that she would build up some savings and buy at least one donkey to assist her in carrying clay and other household activities.

The difficult terrain

Widespread use of IMTs is also hampered by the poor condition of rural transport infrastructure (paths, tracks and roads). The hilly terrain in Maguruwe and Bunduki substantially affects the use of IMTs by both men and women. There are only four bicycles in the villages, of which one is owned by a female clinic attendant, but she uses it very rarely.

Socio-cultural constraints and attitudes

There are no strong cultural restrictions on the use of IMTs by women in any of the three villages. However, there is a socially constructed attitude within the community that men should own and use means of transport, including IMTs. Married women are considered as men's property, just like any other assets within the family. Unfortunately this attitude prevails even among women.

Several women do not perceive the long hours and effort spent on water and firewood collection as a problem. They have always performed these tasks and accept them as part of their life. When asked why they carry goods on their heads instead of using bicycles, they responded that this is the way they have been brought up.

The use of IMTs for domestic activities

In theory the use of IMTs can generate a significant reduction in time and effort spent by women in collecting water and firewood. For instance the use of a wheelbarrow with a payload of 50 kilograms compared with head-loading (20 kilogram capacity) can reduce the time spent on water transport by 60 per cent.

In all three villages there is very little use of IMTs for household activities. In Potwe village, where the terrain permits the use of IMTs, about 50 per cent of households own bicycles and wheelbarrows; however, only 1 per cent of bicycles are used for domestic activities (mainly taking grain to milling machines). Women spend a lot of time searching for and ferrying water and firewood, estimated to average 16 to 24 hours per week or about two to three working days (24 hours). Such activity reduces the time and energy spent on productive work in agriculture and other income-generating activities. IMTs are not used for water and firewood collection because of the extremely strong cultural tradition that water and firewood collection is predominantly the responsibility of women and girls (who do not own IMTs). In some areas the terrain and footpaths from the houses to the source of water and firewood are often unsuitable for use of IMTs, so women prefer walking and head-loading

About ten households in Maguruwe and Bunduki villages own wheelbarrows, which are used for carrying sacks of fertilizer but rarely for domestic activities. In most cases the barrows are bought for transportation of bricks and water in house construction.

Two minor reasons for the limited use of IMT for water and firewood collection are the lack of containers for water transport and the fact that firewood is transported in long pieces that cannot be loaded onto a donkey.

Economic viability

Discussion with women vegetable producers in Potwe village revealed that they felt the use of IMTs has direct benefits for economic rather than domestic activities. In Makete, where the use of donkeys was strongly promoted, the main reason for their purchase was the heavy burden stemming from the transportation of heavy crops, especially potatoes from the field. Donkeys were only bought if their use generated an increase in revenues, which could quickly compensate for the high investment costs. The promotion of the use of IMTs in Makate, especially donkeys, reduced women's transport burden by 15 per cent (MIRTP Evaluation Report, 1992). The animals were used for transportation of crops from the field (the task which is usually done by women) (64 per cent), sending grains to milling machines (65 per cent), and the purchase of fertilizer (87 per cent). The purchase of a donkey was rational only in areas with a strong market orientation. However, in a number of cases men use IMTs for water and firewood collection for commercial purposes.

A rural woman's working schedule

Time	Activity
4.35 a.m.	Wakes up
5.00 a.m.	Washes up and prepares food for the young
5.00–5.30 a.m.	Walks to the field
5.30–3.00 p.m.	Field activities
3.00–4.00 p.m.	Collects firewood and comes home
4.00–5.30 p.m.	Pounds and/or sends grains to the milling machine

Lack of time to acquire new technologies

In Potwe a small percentage of (mainly elderly) women indicated that even if they had an opportunity to acquire a bicycle or donkey, they would not have the time to learn how to use it. The traditional division of labour leaves rural women with multiple roles as mothers, wives and farmers. They are governed by daily necessity and strain to provide every family member with food and other necessities. A woman's daily schedule and her multiple roles keep her busy from morning till evening, so when new technologies are introduced it is the men who have the time to learn and benefit.

In Maguruwe village, when the Donkey Promotion Project was introduced in 1995, five male farmers were trained at Sokoine University. Discussion with villagers revealed that women could not participate in the programme since they had to remain at home to take care of their families.

CONCLUSION

It is evident that, though efforts have been made to promote the use of IMTs in rural Tanzania, the impact of such efforts in reducing women's transport burden has been minimal. Head-loading is still the dominant means of transportation for the majority of rural women. There are no strong cultural constraints on the use of IMTs by women, but the prevailing socio-cultural attitudes limit ownership of means of transport to men; these attitudes are not absolute and can be changed. Some communities are learning from their experiences and interventions.

An implicit assumption of many IMT promotion strategies is that everyone in a rural area can participate in and benefit from the use of

IMTs. It is forgotten that there are wide variations in households' capacity to invest labour or financial resources in transport. The gender of the household head is often a determining factor. Female heads of families struggle to provide food, shelter and clothing for their children. The cost of investing in a means of transport is too high for them, especially if they have to devote additional time to work and to pay for the transport facilities.

The low level of income among rural women is another major constraint on their use of IMTs. Other constraints are the lack of familiarity with IMTs and lack of time to learn and acquire new technologies.

Efforts should be made to promote the use of IMTs by women through the mass media, demonstrations and community development initiatives and to challenge the cultural norms that prohibit women from owning IMTs. These could include sharing experiences from successful programmes, encouraging communities to balance the cultural division of labour, and using women's organizations/groups to sensitise women to the use of IMTs for both productive and household activities. Deliberate efforts should also be made to introduce credit schemes for women as individuals as well as women's groups, and to consider the provision of credit for purchase of IMTs.

NGOs should be encouraged to provide IMTs in rural areas. Financial and technical assistance should be given to local artisans to produce IMTs which are more suited to the specific area. It may also be necessary to adapt IMT designs to suit use by women. Women's bicycles should be given priority.

5

BICYCLES, *BODA BODA* AND WOMEN'S TRAVEL NEEDS

MPIGI, UGANDA

Harriet Iga

Rural transport in Uganda is not well developed, with most districts having remote areas not easily accessible from district headquarters. The major mode of transport is by road. The classified road network comprises 8,000 kilometres, while rural feeder roads account for 22,000 kilometres. The most common means of rural transport is by walking and head-loading along road paths, tracks and rails. Culture and tradition tend to limit load-carrying activities to women, making them shoulder most of the transport chores in the household.

The purchase price of bicycles, draught animals and animal carts is expensive for many rural households. Ownership and use of personal means of transport is very low and limited to well-to-do households. There are some crude and inefficient locally made wheelbarrows that are used to transport firewood, water and other household goods, but these are also limited to a few middle-class families. In households where intermediate means of transport are available, men and boys tend to take over the duties that are the preserve of women.

In areas where terrain permits usage, bicycles are common. This is particularly true of Eastern and Northern Uganda, where they are used as bicycle taxis. Women cycle in these areas, unlike in the Central Region, where bicycles are the property and domain of men and women are merely passengers who ride sideways on the rear luggage rack.

The bicycle and motorcycle taxis that have emerged in recent years, and which are locally referred to as *boda boda*, provide a link between rural areas and rural towns in many districts in Uganda. Unlike bicycles, which are used intensively in Eastern and Northern Uganda, motorcycle *boda boda* taxi services have become popular in the urban and peri-urban areas of the Central Region. The fares range from 50 cents to US$3, depending on the distance travelled. Where both modes of transport are in operation, motorcycle taxis charge higher fares.

This study analyses *boda boda* operation and its impact on women's travel needs. It aims to find out the gender composition of *boda boda* taxi users and operators; determine significant transportation activities carried out by *boda boda* taxi services; assess how these services meet the needs of women; determine constraints faced by women and men who use/operate these services; and find out the gender differences in demand for these services.

The study was carried out in rural towns of Mpigi district and covered a total of 195 respondents from both rural and peri-urban areas in Nansana, Nabweru, Kulambiro and Kazo, between 6 and 8 kilometres from Kampala city.

MPIGI DISTRICT PROFILE

Mpigi district lies within the central part of Uganda and is the gateway both to and from Kampala, the capital city. Its population according to the 1991 population census was 913,867 people, with an estimated population of 1,066,400 for 1996.

The district is situated on the northern shores of Lake Victoria. It borders the districts of Mubende, Kiboga and Luwero in the north, Kampala in the east, Masaka in the southeast and Lake Victoria in the extreme south. The district encompasses an area of approximately 6,278 square kilometres, of which 5,531 square kilometres are covered by water. The major economic activities carried out in Mpigi district are agriculture, fishing, forestry/lumbering and trade.

Women play the biggest role in production, especially in the provision of labour. They carry out most of the activities, including land clearing, ploughing, planting, weeding and harvesting, and also perform the supporting role of health care, child-bearing, cooking, fetching water and firewood for the family. Most of these activities require some form of transport.

There are three types of roads in the district: all-weather tarmac, all-weather murram or gravel, and dry-weather (dirt) roads. The latter are the most common. Of the total road network of 851 kilometres in the district, 110 kilometres are tarmac roads, 267 kilometres are all-weather murram or gravel, and 474 kilometres are dirt roads. Rural areas are mainly served by footpaths. Most urban roads are not tarmacked and are poorly maintained. This, coupled with poor drainage, leads to their very fast deterioration.

In Mpigi district, there are three institutions responsible for rehabilitating and maintaining road infrastructure: the Ministry of Works, Transport and Communication, which is responsible for the construction and maintenance of trunk roads; the Ministry of Local Government, which is responsible for construction of feeder roads and, in conjunction with the District Works Department, for their rehabilitation and maintenance; and the Entebbe Municipal Council and Mpigi Town Council, which are responsible for construction, rehabilitation and maintenance of roads in areas under their jurisdiction.

OVERVIEW OF *BODA BODA* OPERATION

Boda boda operators perform a type of taxi service (that is, an intermediary transport service). They operate for hire from road stands (stages) in towns, trading centres and along the main roads, and their activities include personal travel, transportation of passengers, and movement of goods on a commercial basis. Bicycles are used to transport charcoal, water and agricultural produce while motorcycles mainly transport passengers and goods for businesspeople.

Boda boda services are still new in Mpigi district, although they are rapidly spreading all over the country. The services were introduced in this area between 1996 and 1997. Each *boda boda* stage had a minimum of ten registered operators with a minimum of two or three stages in a village. Many village opinion leaders felt that *boda boda* services bridged the transport gap between the rural and peri-urban areas and eased travel within the rural towns. They also created jobs for the youth and veterans (retrenched army personnel) and were a means of income generation.

Operators

Boda boda taxi operation is predominantly a male job. In Central Uganda, tradition does not allow women to ride bicycles, although they can be carried on them. A few young women in the region have started riding motorcycles, but not as a form of taxi. The operation of *boda boda* is monopolized by men.

The typical profile of a *boda boda* operator is that of a young man, usually a school dropout who is engaging in the taxi service as an economic enterprise. Of the twenty-five operators randomly selected and interviewed, 52 per cent were aged between 20 and 29 years and 28 per cent were aged between 30 and 39. Three-quarters had never gone to school, or had dropped out at primary level. The majority were married, and only the few under 20 years old were single.

The owners of the bicycles and/or motorcycles employed 68 per cent of the operators. The rest used bicycles or motorcycles belonging to their relatives or friends. Thirteen motorcycles were Yamaha Mate-C50s, eight were Suzukis and only four were Roadmasters, a type reported to be very strong. Yamahas and Suzukis are commonly used for taxi operation because they are relatively cheap. The carrying capacity for the motorcycle varies between 100 and 200 kilograms while that of the bicycle varies between 70 and 100 kilograms. The operators had been in the transport service for a period of between one and four years. They started work at 7.30 a.m. and went on till 9.00 p.m., although some operators went on until midnight.

All *boda boda* operators had to be licensed and insured and were supposed to belong to an association and receive registration numbers. Of the 25 operators, 19 were insured while 6 were not, and only one bicycle was not licensed. In Uganda, because of the high poverty level, and because it is mainly the low-income earners who own bicycles, it is very rare to find a bicycle that is insured. All the operators pointed out that they were well trained. Many of the operators belonged to membership groups/associations mainly for identification, discipline and management of the stage. Most of those interviewed belonged to the Bwaise Veteran Association.

Boda boda operators face certain constraints which to some extent compromise their effectiveness. These include insecurity at night, non-payment of fares by some passengers and arrests by the police. In addition, they pointed out that the roads are rough and dusty, and slippery during rainy seasons. This limits the extent to which *boda boda*, especially bicycles, can be used effectively.

Users

In rural and peri-urban areas of Mpigi district, *boda boda* taxis are used for personal movement, for going to market, for social visits, for attending burials and the church/mosque, for transportation of goods (agricultural produce and shops/domestic purchases), for going to school and for commuting to work. They are also used for connecting from homes/households to taxi stages, especially in areas that are not easily accessible to taxis. This is done on a daily basis.

People of different social classes use the *boda boda* services, although the majority of the users seem to be those who work outside their villages and the business community. Other users include students going to school, patients going for treatment, and criminals (thieves), especially at night.

The gender composition of the users was hard to determine because operators could not estimate whether the majority were male or female users. Village opinion leaders were of the view that the majority users were men and it was observed that there were between 5 and 20 women a day, which is on the low side. Generally, it can be concluded that the majority of *boda boda* users are men. Women used *boda boda* taxis for social visits and for going to burials and to clinics. They also used them to connect to taxi stages and workplaces.

The travel distances ranged up to 7 kilometres for motorcycles and 5 kilometres for bicycles. Motorcycle operators charged higher fares than did bicycle operators. Many of the users are not comfortable with the motorcycle charges, which range between USh 500 (US$0.5) and USh 3,000 (US$3), depending on the distance travelled. Although bicycles are uncomfortable, they are preferable as they are cheaper, and many women opt for them.

Users, especially women, faced a number of constraints, which included bad sitting positions, leading to falls, and operators' speeding, leading to accidents, and high taxi charges. Women faced cultural taboos, such as body contact with the operators (having to hold them around the waist) and the need to sit with legs apart, showing their thighs. However, these taboos are dying out and are not so serious as to stop women from using *boda boda* services. Women users pointed out that the current motorcycles do not require that women hold the operators' waists or sit astride and that they have a back support to prevent them falling off.

IMPACT OF *BODA BODA* SERVICES ON WOMEN

The study interviewed 150 randomly selected women in the district. A majority of the households to which these women belonged had no transport assets. Only 29 households had bicycles, 2 had motorcycles and 1 a car. All the transport assets belonged to the women's husbands, except for the car, which the woman had inherited from her deceased husband. Husbands use these modes of transport for business activities and for getting to work. The male owners of five bicycles and one motorcycle used them for *boda boda* transport services.

Neither the women nor the men had considered the need to have any assets such as wheelbarrows and bicycles in their homes to ease the household workload. Both sexes neglect women's travel needs since some of these needs are considered as women's roles which they are obliged to fulfil. The way in which women's needs are prioritized varies. In peri-urban and urban communities, they are met to a large extent as women have access to all types of transport to carry them to their places of work and for other needs. This is because many of the urban women are employed or engage in business/marketing activities.

The travel needs of rural women in Mpigi district include going to the garden (field), fetching water, collecting firewood, going to the market and to social occasions; women do not have any transport assistance for these activities except when making personal trips such as visits and burials.

Women were aware of the time and energy which their transport responsibilities occupy and pointed to household chores such as cultivation, fetching water, collecting firewood and cooking as the most time consuming. They walk long distances to the gardens, which are up to 4 kilometres away, and which could take a minimum of one hour's travel to and fro. The distance covered for fetching water is up to 3 kilometres, which also takes a minimum of one hour. Water has to be collected about four times a day.

Agricultural produce is also transported daily, and is particularly time-consuming and difficult during harvesting seasons. Women generally carry loads on their heads because very few of them can afford hiring *boda boda* services. It is mainly their husbands and male relatives who market the produce using bicycles and motorcycles, which they own or hire.

Women carry out most of the domestic work in addition to their productive roles and they rarely have the time to be involved in income-generating activities. They expressed an interest in having adult/functional literacy programmes as a starting point for them to get involved in income-generating activities. They observed that this can help them raise money to buy their own transport assets.

Women use *boda boda* services as needs arise. Rural women sometimes use *boda boda* services for personal journeys but not as a means of easing their domestic workload. Most of them pay their own fares, except for students and a few who ask their husbands.

Boda boda transport service charges were found to vary according to the distance travelled: for instance, findings showed that up to 1 kilometre the charge was USh 500 (US$0.5) on a motorcycle and USh 200 (US$0.2) on a bicycle, and between 2 and 4 kilometres it was USh 1,000 to 1,500 (US$1–1.5) for a motorcycle and USh 500 to 800 (US$0.5–0.8) for the bicycle. However, at night motorcycle charges increased to as much as USh 5,000 (US$5).

The high charges, and sexual harassment in the form of vulgar language, force women to walk. Other constraints on the use of *boda boda* services included insecurity at night, the risk of accidents from speeding, and the rough dusty roads, which are also slippery during the rainy season.

SUGGESTIONS FOR IMPROVING TRANSPORT

Women made several suggestions to improve transport in the area. They suggested that the relevant authorities should repair, grade and tarmac the roads to encourage transport operators to reach remote areas. They appealed to the *boda boda* taxi operators to reach hilly areas which were not easily accessible. Women also suggested that they should be given access to credit facilities to enable them to invest in the transport business, and to acquire transport assets for domestic use.

Women also suggested the introduction of women-friendly bicycles for female riders. They felt that the introduction of bicycles and wheelbarrows would entice male members of the family to participate in domestic chores.

CONTRIBUTION OF *BODA BODA* SERVICES TO COMMUNITY DEVELOPMENT

Boda boda services have a positive and significant impact on the development of their localities. The services have promoted trade and created jobs in the rural areas and have bridged the transport gap between the rural and peri-urban areas, and are therefore a potential which needs to be promoted to boost community/rural development. However, the capacity of these services to benefit women has been limited. *Boda boda* operators are mainly men; because women's travel is centred on their homes and the village, the services do not significantly help to meet their travel needs.

6

GENDER AND SAFETY IN RURAL TRANSPORT

BUSIA, UGANDA

Kwamusi Paul

In recent years, improving rural transport has become a concern of policy makers in Uganda, where 90 per cent of the population is rural and agriculture is the mainstay of the economy. Efficient rural transport services are important for increasing accessibility, for reducing time and effort, and for easing barriers to services and social facilities.

Promoting improved rural transport requires consideration of a number of issues. One is how gender relations affect rural people in terms of access, management and control of transport services and safety. In Uganda there is little systematic examination of rural transport issues in overall transport planning. Despite an increasing accident rate on rural roads, there is relative neglect of the accident problem amongst transport planners. It must also be remembered that although rural travel accidents are common on rural roads, rural travel extends to include paths and tracks. There is little documentation on the relationship between safety, gender and rural transport.

This research uses a multidisciplinary approach to investigate safety and gender issues in communities in Uganda. The study aims to improve understanding of how the access, use and control of intermediate means of transport (IMTs), particularly bicycles, impact on safety in a wider context.

There is a need to establish that safety is a rural travel issue. It is commonly assumed that since rural travel involves walking and cycling, where the travel speeds are quite low, the issue of safety does not arise, and efforts should be directed towards accessibility. Safety, like comfort, is considered an urban transport phenomenon.

BACKGROUND TO THE PROBLEM

The problem of safety has been mainly defined in terms of accidents. Essentially, there has been little attempt to integrate safety with other rural travel issues at policy or local level. While studies have shown that the behaviour of road users towards safety is a problem, there has been little attempt to link this behaviour to gender. It has also been assumed that the problem of accidents can be solved by public awareness initiatives alone, with little recognition given to local knowledge.

First, a series of questions need to be asked regarding safety and accidents in rural transport. Is there a problem of accidents in rural transport? If so, how can they be reduced? How can the management of safety in rural travel be sustained? What is lacking in current assessments?

Second, the relationship between gender, safety and rural transport needs to be defined. How can gender help us understand the management of safety? What are people's transport priorities? What are men's and women's perceptions of safety? What is the potential for community initiatives in accident reduction?

Third, what are the issues relating to policy options and in terms of interventions? What could be the wider policy option? What is the nature of the current transport system? How does it affect safety? What are the position and status of safety issues in overall transport management? How much priority should policy processes give to people's involvement? How can local knowledge and initiatives be integrated into the process?

THE STUDY

The main objectives of the study were threefold: to investigate how gender relates to safety in rural travel; to examine the impact of the accident burden on women; and to provide useful recommendations with regard to safety in rural travel.

Several research questions and issues needed to be answered and investigated at community and policy levels.

Research priorities

At the community level the questions relate to how road safety is perceived and managed by road users, how safety is influenced by gender, how accidents compromise rural accessibility, and how safety is a limitation on the use of IMTs.

At the policy level, research needs to establish what the safety issues in rural travel are at present, how these influence a framework for better management of road safety, how road safety can be managed locally, and how the community, and women in particular, respond to the lack of road safety.

Methodology

The study first examined the literature and conducted discussions with safety managers in Busia and elsewhere in Uganda. This was complemented by surveys in Busia district to identify the various aspects of safety management.

Busia is located in Eastern Uganda. It is bordered by Kenya to the east, by Tororo district to the north and by Iganga district to the southwest. Busia has a total of 65 kilometres of classified roads, 298 kilometres of feeder roads and an undetermined amount of community roads and paths. The district was selected for two reasons. First, because it is known to have the highest number of bicycles per population in the country. Public hire bicycle taxis (*boda boda*) originated in Busia, and bicycles are a crucial means of travel in the rural areas. Second, women are marginalized with regard to bicycle use and have limited access to and use of bicycles.

A cross-section of people were interviewed: community leaders, women leaders, peasants and community extension workers. Much of the information was collected through active interviews using a semi-structured questionnaire. Stratified, proportional and systematic random sampling was used to ensure the representativeness of the different groups.

The study had certain limitations. The research period (six months) was a relatively short one in which to examine and research the issues involved in the study, and the resources limited the scope. Busia is a relatively new district and it was quite difficult to secure background statistics needed for the study. Also inland water transport is an important mode of transport in the district, especially on Lake Victoria, but for reasons of time and resources the study limited its focus to land (road) transport.

TRANSPORT MODES AND SAFETY

Walking

Walking is by far the predominant mode of mobility in Busia district for personal, economic and domestic activities. Generally women carry out more walking journeys than men, largely because of their domestic responsibilities.

Although walking is largely seen as a safe mode of transport, it can be subject to significant risk. Much of this risk is attributed to being knocked down by bicycles or motorcycles. However, the study findings showed that risk was perceived in a number of other ways, including accidental falling, injury from thorns and sharp objects, tripping over potholes, and being bitten by snakes and insects or attacked by other animals.

Falling can result from head-loading, slippery paths, stumbling and falling into holes. Injuries that result from falling are largely minor, though sometimes fractures occur. Knee and toe injuries are common. All the respondents had fallen at some time while walking. One explained it with a local saying: 'A child grows up by falling.' Head-loading contributes to falling because of the instability of walking. Most head-loading is done by women; loads are heavy and the distances covered are long. This causes fatigue and contributes to the risk of falling. Head-loading also reduces peripheral vision and hearing; women may find it more difficult to see or hear approaching cycles or vehicles.

During the wet seasons many people fall due to the slippery surface of the roads and paths. On some overgrown paths morning dew can also cause slipperiness. Stumbling increases when paths are uneven and toes are often injured on stony surfaces. Visibility is poor on rural roads and paths, especially on moonless nights and in the early hours of the morning. Very few people can afford to travel with torches. Injuries can also happen when travelling in a hurry, such as running to avoid the rain.

Snakes and insects pose risks in rural travel. This is especially the case for women collecting firewood and clearing bush for cultivation. There are many dangerous tropical insects, such as scorpions, tsetse flies and Martis. Bulls, baboons, dogs and billy goats are also known to attack travellers. Women seem more vulnerable to these attacks, though it is not clear why.

Cycling

Bicycles are the most commonly used IMTs in Busia district. Accidents from bicycles can occur by falling off the bicycle or through collision with other cycles, vehicles and pedestrians.

Accidents from falling off bicycles are common. Women passengers are particular victims because of the way they sit on the bicycle. Accidents also occur when bicycles collide on village paths and sometimes when cyclists hit domestic animals. Collisions with motorists occur more often on feeder roads and on the classified road network. Many rural paths are narrow and can only serve as single cycle lanes, leading to greater risk of accident. Many of these accidents are serious and often fatal.

There are several causes of cycle accidents. Many cyclists disregard right of way and keep-left regulations. Women cyclists are commonly acknowledged as being more careful than men and some women have cited lack of safety as a reason for their lack of interest in cycling. Most accidents occur when cyclists are riding at a very high speed. Bicycles also tend to be old and poorly maintained and many riders ignore brake defects. The cost of new bicycles and spare parts is often unaffordable for rural people. New bicycles have a 58 per cent excise tax and there is 65 per cent tax on spare parts. This has compromised safety and has led to the use and adaptation of older bicycles. A traffic count in Busia revealed that over 90 per cent of the bicycles have no front lamps even when they are being used at night. Cyclists say they cannot afford the price of a cycle dynamo and that they are also afraid of lamp theft.

Alcohol consumption is common in the rural areas, particularly during the post-harvest and festive periods. Drunken riders affect safety by riding on village paths, knocking down fixed objects and pedestrians. Drunken pedestrians also contribute to accidents by staggering and by not giving way to other road users.

Rural travel commonly involves transporting goods from one place to another. In order to reduce the distance travelled, some riders overload their bicycles beyond the limits of safety, causing balancing and stability problems, leading to accidents.

Safety in bicycle use is not regulated. The police are reluctant to enforce safety among cyclists beyond handling accident cases because there is considerable political outcry when cyclists' interests seem affected. Also there is no mechanism for ensuring safety in rural areas, where the police have little access. The local administration is more concerned with the *boda boda* bicycle taxis, from whose owners they can collect revenue.

A large number of second-hand 50cc motorcycles have been introduced into the rural areas, particularly for *boda boda* services. They have increased safety concerns because of their higher riding speed, the lack of competence of their riders and their greater contribution to accidents.

While women are most commonly the victims of accidents when walking, men are more involved in cycling and motoring accidents. This is because men do most of the cycling, their cycling speeds are high, and they tend to carry bigger loads. They are also greater risk takers.

ACCIDENTS IN RURAL TRANSPORT

There is a significant element of risk and a lack of safety in rural transport in both cycling and walking. The fact that rural transport is characterized by low speed is irrelevant. One reason why safety has been a peripheral concern in rural travel and transport is the lack of data to support the problem. Only 7 per cent of the road accidents in rural travel are brought to the notice of the police and only 20 per cent of the victims seek medical assistance.

There is a strong belief among local people that accidents are a result of bad omens caused by supernatural powers. So most accident victims prefer traditional healers to modern medicine, even for severe accidents involving fractures. What is important, however, is that accidents are kept secret, and people are unwilling to reveal details of the accidents to outsiders, either the police or the medical authorities. This causes problems in the collection of accident data and makes many of the accidents 'invisible' to official institutions.

Many accidents are caused by recklessness on the part of road users. The community has its own mechanism of resolving conflict by compensating the aggrieved party. Elders and clan leaders arbitrate, even in the case of fatal accidents. The guilty party is fined according to what the community deems appropriate. In most cases the aggrieved party is compensated by having his or her bicycle repaired or, in the case of death, by payment of animals to the family. After such a resolution, the aggrieved are reluctant to report the accident to the authorities.

In many cases, the person who is injured is related to or has a friendship with the guilty party. It is therefore seen as inappropriate to report the accident to the police.

THE ACCIDENT BURDEN ON WOMEN

Owing to their disparate transport needs, women and men face different kinds of risk. The study shows that women suffer from lack of safety both directly as travel accident victims and indirectly as post-accident victims. Whereas women are mostly the direct victims of accidents related to walking, men are most likely to suffer cycling and motoring accidents. Despite the fact that men take greater risks than women, and women are more conscious of safety than men, women are nevertheless prone to travel accidents, principally through head-loading.

Most of the accidents that befall women happen while they are engaged in domestic tasks such as collecting fuelwood and water. Accidents from walking are seen more as personal injuries. The narrow perception of safety with regard to cycle/pedestrian or motorist/pedestrian accidents means that many accidents occurring in rural areas are ignored, especially those involving women.

In addition, women suffer indirectly from accident-related factors. They have the responsibility of nursing accident victims, whether male or female, which increases the burden on them. Where victims are hospitalized, it means extra travel to the hospital, usually several kilometres away, on foot. Providing care also compromises productive tasks such as agriculture, especially when the accident happens during crucial farming periods like planting or harvesting. The increased burden posed by providing care to accident victims often means that women pay less attention to their other responsibilities, particularly the care of children.

The research reveals that rural travel mishaps are one of the leading causes of disability in Busia district. If women are seriously disabled, the husband marries another wife and enters into a polygamous relationship. Where men are injured, women do not look for another option.

Safety also has a direct relationship with productivity. Accidents contribute to the decline in the standard of living. In one homestead, in order to raise funds for a victim's treatment, a family sold their only cow, which used to provide milk to the neighbourhood. As a result, children in the neighbourhood lost the privilege of drinking milk.

The study discovered that one of the main reasons for women's reluctance to ride bicycles is lack of safety. Many women gave fears of accidents and previous accident experiences as reasons for not cycling. Many preferred to walk rather than cycle, using bicycles only in an emergency. Others preferred to push loads on a bicycle rather than to ride it.

RECOMMENDATIONS

- The definition of safety in rural travel should be broadened to take into account accidents while walking. Further investigations need to be carried out with the aim of collecting data on rural travel accidents in order to provide evidence to policy makers. More systematic documentation would help gain support from policy makers for rural transport issues. A gender analytical perspective has helped reveal that the accident burden is disproportionately shouldered by women, despite the fact that they are more safety-conscious than men.
- Standards ought to be implemented on bicycle safety.
- Many cyclists feel that safety programmes are directed at drivers of motor vehicles and not them. It is important to change this perception. Radio programmes on safety are rarely listened to by rural people. Community policing programmes could raise the issue of safety at the rural level.

- Communities should be encouraged to rehabilitate and maintain community-level transport infrastructure on a self-help *bulungi bwa nsi* basis. Government should complement community self-help efforts, particularly by providing support for adequate drainage on access routes.
- Communities have little knowledge of first aid. This and the absence of medicines at district health centres encourage the use of traditional healing, which may not always be appropriate.
- There is a need to review bicycle designs to enable both safer carrying of larger loads and their increasing use by women.
- Women's groups should be mobilized to promote safety at the local level.

7

BRIDGES: THE IMPACT ON TRAVEL AND MARKET ACTIVITIES

NKONE RIVER BRIDGE, MERU, KENYA

P.G. Kaumbutho

Karia is an administrative area in Egoji Division of Meru Central district in Kenya. The Karia community has a culture deeply rooted in both commercial and subsistence farming activities. The history of the community goes back to the arrival of colonial Christian missionaries early in the twentieth century. Christianity – the influences of the Presbyterian Church of East Africa to the south, and the Roman Catholic Church to the north; government-set development trends, such as the cooperative movement in coffee and tea farming; and the environmental location of Karia on the eastern slopes of Mount Kenya next to the forest – all have had an impact on day-to-day activities and the status of the people.

Karia is located on the slopes of Mount Kenya in an agriculturally promising area of deep, iron-rich, volcanic soil. The area is capable of producing a wide range of forest products, such as timber, charcoal, firewood, honey and horticultural produce. Benefiting from the resources of the snow-capped mountain, each valley has a permanent fresh stream or river. Colloquially in Karia, as in the whole of Egoji Division, going 'to the valley' is synonymous with 'going to fetch water'. The hilltop location of Karia greatly influences access and general travel to and from the area. Means of transport are very restricted. This has been especially true in the last decade, when, as with many other services, government efforts in infrastructure provision and management have come to very little.

It would appear that as soon as the government had constructed the elaborate Thuci–Nkubu road (see Figure 7.1) all services into the interior

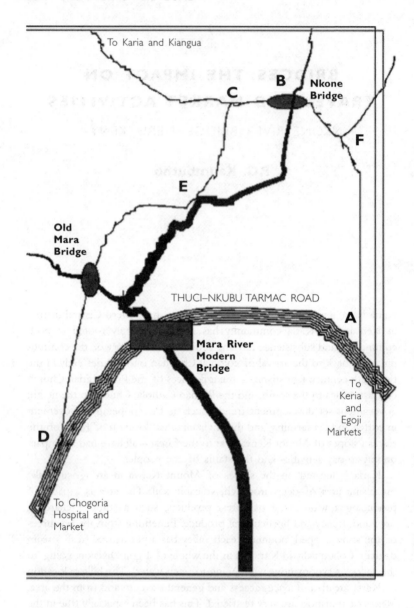

FIGURE 7.1 Nkone Bridge and the Thuci–Nkubu road

rural access road system were forgotten and left to local initiative. Trade and other livelihood efforts shifted to locations near the tarmac. The tarmac road became a gateway through which the community could gain from developments in the rest of the area and the country at large. But in Karia, an area of falling coffee and other important agricultural yields on erosion-degraded and fertility-depleted soils, the road has not motivated development.

Simple but highly important items of infrastructure such as the Nkone Bridge have been abandoned by central government, with a direct and negative influence on rural development. The Nkone Bridge and the road it serves form the shortest and most efficient route out of Karia and neighbouring Kiangua for agricultural produce and other merchandise.

During the rains, Nkone is liable to be swept away by the river water, which swells twenty- to thirty-fold during a storm. The bridge provides vital access to schools, hospitals, information, worship, trade centres and other locations and activities important to the livelihood of the community.

THE STUDY

At the time of this study, a Meru-based body, the Rural Infrastructure Development Organization (RIDO), had approached the International Labour Organization Advisory Support, Information Services and Training office in Nairobi looking for financial and technical assistance to rebuild the Nkone Bridge, which had been swept away by the rains. The ILO had in turn involved the Kenya Network for Draught Animal Technology and the Intermediate Technology Development Group. The community had on several previous occasions provided labour and money and involved other stakeholders such as the District Engineer in efforts to rebuild the bridge. These efforts had been greatly frustrated, more so during the El Niño rains of 1997/8. A permanent solution was urgently sought. From the intensity of the community's search for help it was clear that the bridge and the road it served were of great importance and concern.

Aim and scope of the study

The study was undertaken with the aim of assessing and reporting on how the Nkone River Bridge had different impacts on access to transport and other services for women and men of the Karia region. The study sought to understand the gender-based dimension of the village transport problem in Karia and to provide information to any individual or organization willing to assist the community with its improvement agenda.

The research was conducted through intensive visits to the Karia, Kiangua and other areas. Various stakeholders, including farmers, teachers, schoolchildren, priests, youth and women's groups, were interviewed, as well as members of interested or support organizations. The bridge site was visited several times. A particularly useful visit was with the Nkone Committee and RIDO management. These were the people who had actively participated in the bridge repair with the support of a local mason, the Catholic Church, local administration and the district engineer.

Interviewers attended two quite different meetings: one called by the coffee factory, where all participants were men; and another called by the district officer, the Church and other leaders. The latter was held during a market day, in the market compound, with a loudspeaker. The choice of day and location seemed a way of reaching the majority, who were women. Women would normally be expected to receive reports of deliberations from the many meetings through their husbands. Women are apparently involved in meetings only when they are of general community nature and when donations are being sought from everyone. Otherwise they would be expected to attend meetings of their own women's groups, of which every village has at least one. Women's groups are not expected to deal with *serious* issues, but only with minor development ones!

A participatory rural appraisal was conducted at this second meeting. Through the various discussions and opinions expressed it was possible to assess the value the community attached to a functioning Nkone Bridge and the road it serves. Vivid experiences about the bridge were articulated, which ranged from struggles to get to hospital and even deaths of patients, to marketing produce and the difficulties of getting children to school.

Attempts to reach the district engineer were in vain, though the current incumbent was new and not the one involved in the development assistance work that had taken place at Nkone previously.

During a tour of the location with Father Njeru, who was in charge of the local Catholic parish, it was possible to see the many access problems of the Egoji area. Father Njeru's impressive development programme had worked in a participatory way with communities to assist not only Nkone but also Mbara in the Mweru/Mworoga area. Mbara, like Nkone, had a bridge that was swept away and in urgent need of reconstruction. An early morning visit to Mbara made it possible to interview men and women farmers on their way to the farms, and to learn about the efforts of the community. These interviews captured well socio-economic and other characteristics such as the daily roles and chores of men, women and children.

THE STUDY AREA AND ACCESS SITUATION

Nkone River Bridge

Nkone River Bridge was originally constructed as part of the infrastructure for the old colonial Embu–Meru road. Owing to age, runoff and changing water-flow patterns, the bridge was unable to stand the pressure of the water passing under it, and gave way. The community has repaired the bridge several times. Their most intensive effort was in November 1996, when culverts were replaced. These were easily swept away soon after. The bridge was rebuilt by the community in 1997. Owing to cheap construction coupled with poor workmanship, the bridge was again washed away by the heavy El Niño rains of November 1997 to March 1998. At the time of writing the bridge has a recently built foundation and a temporary wooden walking surface.

Access and the Karia community

Like many other parts of Kenya the interior roads of Meru district are in need of repair and maintenance. The Keria–Karia road, on which Nkone Bridge is located, barely 500 metres from the Thuci–Nkubu tarmac road, is a particularly important gateway to an area with great economic potential. During the rainy seasons, which occur twice a year, and last for over three months each, Karia is virtually inaccessible, and the damage caused in each season makes the area inaccessible long after. The inadequate response to road repairing by government and other stakeholders drastically affects crop harvesting and marketing.

Transport means available to the Karia community are dominated by women and children carrying loads. The variety of intermediate means of transport (IMTs) available is minimal. Some men use bicycles, a few push wheelbarrows; occasionally one will see a pack donkey or ox cart; in addition there are a few motorcycles and other vehicles, though trucks are rarely seen.

Almost all roads are virtually impassable by small cars even during the dry season. During the rains, the only usable roads may be the ones in the tea-growing area, where the Kenya Tea Development Authority (KTDA) has attempted to make them all-weather in order to aid tea collection.

Much of the agricultural produce goes to waste during the rainy seasons. The value of milk is drastically reduced.

Nkone Bridge as a gateway

Figure 7.1 illustrates the access situation and the locational importance of the Nkone Bridge. There is a steep climb to Karia from three main access routes. From point C on the figure the route to Karia and Kiangua is more or less a gorge, between the hilly areas above point E and point B. The road itself has an average gradient of 30 degrees, rising to 60–70 degrees at some points. Another general rise is above point F. This topography makes Nkone Bridge, on one side, and Old Mara Bridge, on the other, weirs at the collection points of two large water catchments. It contributes to the behaviour of the river flow, which can grow into a source of destructive energy during the rainy season.

Road DECBFA on Figure 7.1 is part of the old winding road used before the construction of the new tarmac Thuci–Nkubu road. Section DA, which is a part of this new road, was constructed with British aid and opened for use in 1986. Since the construction of the tarmac road neither the 1945-built Old Mara Bridge nor the Nkone Bridge has received any maintenance. During this period, the Nkone Bridge has been swept away several times while the Old Mara Bridge has not been damaged. However, the Old Mara now has gaping holes and other signs of dilapidation. The Nkone is the more favourable route for vehicles since they cannot use the seemingly stronger Old Mara due to the road having been swept away at point E and a very degraded and slippery section EC. The road at E cannot be expanded away from the river since the farmer owning the land above will not allow excavation through a rock that protects his whole farm from being swept down-slope in this landslide-prone area. The route to Karia through route AFBC is relatively more user-friendly to travellers on foot and on vehicles as long as it is dry and the Nkone Bridge is in place.

Travelling from Karia through Nkone to the tarmac at Keria market is the shortest and most straightforward route. The Keria–Karia route is about 3 kilometres long. The alternative routes to the tarmac are through Kinoro (about 15 kilometres) and through Kabeche and Chogoria (8 kilometres). Travel through Kinoro to the tarmac is at least ten times longer, with sections as rough as the Keria–Karia section. The Karia–Kiangua route is also as rough as anywhere on the Keria–Karia route, though it may be considered passable due to attempts by the KTDA to fix it. The route through Kabeche and Chogoria has a very steep climb into and out of the Mara River upstream gorge. Most vehicles cannot travel across this gorge even in dry weather. No vehicle would try it in wet weather, when even walking on its slopes is an impossible task. Fixing the Karia–Chogoria road would be very expensive due to the Mara gorge. If fixed, however, this would be the logical route to get a sick person to Chogoria General Hospital.

Inhabitants of Karia and Eastern Kiangua use Nkone as a gateway to their homes and farms. It is the only accessible route for incoming farm inputs, building and other materials, stationery and other supplies for schools, shops, churches and other institutions. Nkone is an outlet for agricultural, horticultural, forest and other products heading for markets and an efficient access route to information, administrative, spiritual, medical and other services. Keria, Egoji and Chogoria town centres are all located on the tarmac road, with Keria being the most readily accessible in terms of distance. Egoji and Chogoria are easily accessible on public transport once one is on the tarmac road. These towns are channels of information and services from the rest of the district and the country at large. People's mobility is highly influenced by whether or not it is a market day or a weekend. Many women see market day as the day to catch up on information, their popular day out. Men, on the other hand, consider every day, and especially evenings (when weather allows), as a time to catch up on information.

During the rains the tarmac road and Keria market can appear to be a long distance away because of the steep and slippery roads and depending on whether or not the Nkone Bridge is in place or not. Karia is hardly 3 kilometres from the tarmac (at Keria) through Nkone Bridge but local people will say that the estimated distance between Keria and Karia is 8 to 10 kilometres. Older people in Karia opt to stay home. Men who leave Keria market for home after dark do so in teams, throughout the year. Women make sure they are home long before dark on market days. During the rains and after dark, many opt to stay downhill for the night.

Often farmers are unable to get inputs to farms due to the transport problem. Men will often send women and children to Keria market to divide, say, an 80 kilogram bag of fertilizer among them for portability. They see this as the means of transport whenever some IMT or vehicle is not available, even when the women and children have to do several trips. The other option is to catch the one or two Land-Rovers available to bring the load uphill (when they can), but the charge for transport can easily double the price of the inputs. This is understandable considering that even the owner of the Land-Rover often opts to walk home to save on the wear and tear on the vehicle.

Karia people have to cover longer distances or take more time on the damaged roads to reach essential services such as hospitals, health centres, churches, banks, maternity facilities, administrative offices and markets. At the Nkone Bridge site people interviewed became emotional as they re-iterated incidents where women have given birth at the bridge, unable to cross the river to Chogoria Hospital on rainy nights.

IMPACT OF THE NKONE BRIDGE ON THE DAILY CHORES OF KARIA WOMEN AND MEN

Women have an overloaded diary compared to men and implement al-most all the economic activities of the community (see box). While men may be involved in planning and some of the heavier tillage work, women prepare seedbeds and plant; they weed, harvest and take produce to the market. A survey of the market at Keria showed that the majority of traders are women. There are few men in the market, and they handle only those goods that sell quickly and fetch larger returns, such as live animals and hardware.

In cases where farms were located a distance away from households, women prepare to be away all day. They are forced to wake up earlier to complete their other chores, prepare lunch and make arrangements for their husbands to be comfortable during their absence.

It was apparent that men carry out what they described as 'well-defined and tangible' jobs or chores, such as bringing fertilizer from the market, fetching the veterinarian, attending community and other meetings, and arranging transport to collect building materials or farm produce.

The 'well-defined and tangible' jobs or chores for Karia women were organizing cooking and food for the family, caring for livestock (including feeding, milking and general welfare), home and house care, 'minor' com-mercial ventures such as marketing kitchen-garden produce to neighbours, and transport of small loads, animal feed, firewood and water.

Men definitely stayed away from the tasks which are described as 'miscellaneous', particularly those relating to children, such as helping them with their homework and school projects, care of their clothes and dealing with problems of friends and adolescence. The safety of children crossing the river after the Nkone Bridge had been swept away was not considered a concern of the men.

The women further cited worry and anxiety over their children, who risk crossing swollen streams to reach school, church or market. They said they have to work in turns to supervise the safe crossing of their children. Recently two adults had drowned while crossing Nkone. Following such

A typical day for a Karia woman

6 a.m.	Waking up and preparing breakfast Waking the children up and preparing them for school Preparing breakfast and warm water for the husband's bath Taking or sending the children to school (depending on age) Starting domestic household chores
8 a.m.	Farm work Feeding the animals (usually zero-grazed) Fetching water and firewood Nursing younger siblings Tending cash crops such as coffee and tea
1–2 p.m.	Preparing and serving lunch
2–5 p.m.	Back to work in the fields Fetching firewood and water Locking up the animals and milking Preparing dinner
7–9 p.m.	Feeding the family Cleaning utensils Putting children to sleep
9 p.m. on	Miscellaneous night services to husband
Midnight	Falling asleep exhausted

A typical day for a man

7–8 a.m.	Waking up and taking breakfast
8 a.m.–noon	Some work in the fields and mostly in the cash crop farm May leave for town centre to chase business or attend a meeting
1–2 p.m.	Lunch
2–4 p.m.	May or may not go back to work
4–9 p.m.	Socializing with friends (probably still or back in town centre), later dinner and retiring to bed

a bad experience, parents are obliged to step on stones in the rivers and throw the children across in turns. This is usually done by the mothers, since taking children to school is mainly the woman's responsibility.

In the Karia community rainy and dry seasons make a major difference to people's lives. The chores conducted by men and women change drastically between the seasons. Whenever the normal routine is broken, it affects the accepted gender division of labour. Women and children bear the greater brunt of the new 'miscellaneous' tasks that arise. For example, if the Nkone Bridge was damaged, men could no longer hire transport for the fertilizer and nor could they transport it on their backs or heads. Such chores were immediately passed to women and children. Loads that would otherwise be ferried on bicycles, motorcycles, pullcarts or even motor vehicles were now left to women and children.

During the rains, small streams swell into fast-moving rivers due to flash floods. Crossing points become impassable. The roads are swept away or cut into deep gullies by run-off water. Soil erosion peaks, with tonnes of soil carried away in a matter of minutes. In such circumstances people take longer detours to avoid the attendant dangers. Although everyone is inconvenienced, women suffer more by covering longer distances on alternative bush routes with heavy loads on their backs and at times babies strapped on their chests. Owing to time lost, they get to their destinations late and forgo other important tasks in the process. They also delay many other domestic chores, which no one else will do.

CROP MARKETING

To a great extent men leave their womenfolk and children to struggle alone with transporting crop produce to the selling centres. Children have dropped out of school partly because parents need their labour for transport and other tasks. This is particularly so when conditions are unfavourable, such as when harvesting coffee and tea in the rain. Since only small loads can be carried, there are chances of the harvest being wasted in the fields. For several crops, middlemen exploit the transport situation by buying farm produce at very low prices. The community often prefers to sell at throwaway prices than lose everything in the fields.

According to the Leaf Manager of Kinoro Tea Factory, farmers in Karia area have to be served from the Kiangua side because there is more tea in that area and the number of collection centres in Karia is small. However, he agreed that if the Nkone road and bridge were fixed, tea from the buying centres located even as far as Kiangua would be collected through Nkone. He confirmed that it was a struggle to collect tea during the rainy season, more so for growers on the Keria–Kiangua road, and that tea produced is often lost due to the impossibility of collecting it. Collection vehicles often fail to arrive in Karia at all. In the 1997/8 El Niño rainy season, tea farmers served by Kinoro produced 20 million kilograms of green tea leaf. Out of this, they lost about a fifth (around 4 million kilograms) because of poor roads.

TABLE 7.1   Tea production along the Keria–Kiangua road, 1997/8

Buying centre	No. of growers	Green leaf production (kg)
KR 18 Kiangua	525	588,987
KR 21 Ruiga	254	525,235
KR 22 Githumbi	115	409,228
KR 29 Karia	267	280,145
KR 48 Karau	216	390,292

The Leaf Manager estimated that it would take about Ksh 666,000 per kilometre simply to pour hardcore (rough quarry waste) on the tea roads, as is common practice, and that a decent *murram* (compressed) job would need Ksh 1.5 million. The factory received Ksh 3 million a year from tea *cess* (tax) and has some 130 kilometres of road to maintain inland from the Thuci–Nkubu tarmac road.

Table 7.1 shows the importance of tea farming in the area under study. In tea farming, men mostly plant and prune the tea. They may also help apply fertilizer. Women and children do the plucking and the delivery to collection centres, where they have to sort it for grading. The KTDA agreed that upgrading of the road and bridge would boost production of these centres and generally shorten distances covered to the factory and even to the buying centres for many of the farmers.

The Egoji Catholic parish expressed a great need for a workable solution to the Nkone Bridge situation. The parish had put in considerable managerial and financial effort given the capacity available. They, like other users, needed the Keria–Karia road, which they use to reach parishioners for spiritual counsel as well as for involvement in agricultural and other development efforts. Many of their parishioners are utterly isolated, not only during the rainy season but also in dry weather. Some areas that are hardly 10 kilometres off the tarmac take the whole morning to reach during the rainy season. Areas which would take five minutes to cross by car take several hours as alternative routes are sought and used. Priests often opt to walk to such areas of worship, including Karia and Kiangua.

The parish considered repair of the Nkone and Mbara bridges to be priority projects and had helped raise Ksh 200,000 for this purpose, which paid for the labour and the stone. Some of the money was lost because of mismanagement by an undependable contractor who had earlier built the culverts at both bridges which had been swept away. Father Njeru believed that the foundation put in place at Nkone was now good enough and what was needed was metal to reinforce the top lining (a temporary wooden one had been installed and was currently in use). He felt that half a million shillings (around US$ 8,000) would cover the remaining work.

Any future community-based bridge- and road-work would be handled as before. The church and its associates, including the Local Government Office, would seek funding and any external technical advice, as well as provide a dependable contractor. The community would provide labour, including hot meals from the women. The local District Office of Ministry of Public Works would provide the machinery (without petrol) and technical advice.

Several members of the community insisted that all monies must be controlled and accounted for by the church or its designated representatives. They lacked confidence in the so-called 'committee members', who they felt had not been transparent.

CONCLUSION

It is essential and urgent that the Nkone Bridge and road are fixed. After the devastating effects of the El Niño rains of 1997/8 many farmers are already giving up on their capacity to produce food cash crops. The potential the Karia community has for agricultural production is enormous, but there are no other economical or logistical options open to it in terms of roads out. Travel through Kinoro to the tarmac is at least five times longer with sections as rough as Keria–Karia. Travel through Chogoria would be shorter than through Kinoro but it would be three times longer than Keria–Karia and would traverse a near impossible hill that many vehicles cannot climb even in dry weather.

The study shows that women and children suffer the most due to the absence of the Nkone Bridge and a serviceable road across it, connecting Keria (on tarmac) to Karia and Kiangua. Men are inconvenienced less. Since they abdicate their responsibilities to women and children whenever conditions are difficult or unfavourable, their inconvenience lies mainly in inaccessibility, lost time and opportunities. Men would prefer to have improved motorized transport services and capacity to own and use IMTs such as hand- and animal-drawn carts, pack animals, motorbikes and bicycles. While these IMTs are available in very small numbers in Karia and Kiangua, the introduction of some, such as bicycles, would be discouraged by the sloping topography. However, such assistance to men does not seem a priority for the community.

Fixing the bridge and road would more readily assist women, directly influence their ability to use their time efficiently, and reduce their work-load. The community would directly gain, as goods could then be trans-ported with ease into and out of otherwise difficult areas. The Nkone Bridge is important also because it will help save the lives of men, women and children, increase economic activity, and remove isolation. It will give the Karia community a better chance to develop sustainable rural liveli-hoods, encourage travel and information exchange for the community, boost crop and produce marketing, including better access to farm and other inputs, reduce the price of food and supplies at farm level, and increase the returns from cash crops such as coffee, tea, forestry, and horticultural products through reduced transport costs.

8

FEEDER ROADS AND
FOOD SECURITY

DARFUR, SUDAN

Suad Mustafa Elhaj Musa

Sudan is the biggest country in Africa, with an area of 2.5 million square kilometres. It borders nine African and Arab states and has a population of about 28 million (1993 census). The population consists of a wide range of multiracial ethnic groups and tribes, including the indigenous African of the southern regions, the Nubians of the riverain valley and Kordofan region, and many others. Half of the population are Muslim Arabs, who occupy most of the northern, middle and western parts of the country. The last five decades have witnessed mass migration of West Africans, who have added to the total population of Sudan.

Darfur was the biggest state in the country. The current government has re-divided Sudan into 26 political regions and Darfur has been re-divided into 3 regions, namely the North, South and West Darfur.

Darfur is located in the western part of the country, neighbouring Chad, Central Africa and Libya. It lies on the edge of the Sahara desert and falls within the arid or Sahel zone of Africa. Frequent drought and desertification in the 1970s and 1980s drastically affected the natural resources of the region and the sustainability of the livelihoods of the people. The rural poor have been the first to suffer distress, poverty and insecure livelihoods. Men have migrated out of the area and women have been left behind to look after children and to make the best of a deterio-rated environment. Although recently some improvements to the environment have been observed, the impact of the previous decades seems difficult to eradicate in the short term.

JEBEL SI RURAL COUNCIL

North Darfur region comprised 26 rural councils (localities) in 1995. At the western part of the region is the Jebel Si Rural Council. It covers an area of 6,300 square kilometres and has a total population of 65,000 people in 13,000 households and distributed among 47 village councils. Surrounded by a chain of mountains, most of the interior part is hilly and rocky, crossed by a few seasonal rivers and adjacent plain or wadi areas. Very remote and inaccessible, the area depends on annual rains from June to October for agriculture and for water storage. The population is almost exclusively of the Fur tribe, mostly small-scale agro-pastoralists practising rain-fed terraced subsistence agriculture.

The isolation of the area has provided an excuse for depriving the whole population of any kind of services or support. Education services were introduced to the area in early 1945. But the difficult terrain makes it hard for pupils and teachers to reach schools. Since independence in 1956 little or no effort has been made to provide social services to the area. The mass migration that was brought on by the environmental changes and drought has made the local people think about their future prospects and demand services necessary to meet their basic needs. As a result, a few primary schools and health units have been established. There are 23 schools in Jebel Si Rural Council with poor equipment, buildings, teachers and stationery. Out of 19 health units, only 1 was performing at more than 25 per cent efficiency.

The economy of the area depends on rain-fed agriculture and herding of small numbers of animals, mainly goats. The topography of the area gives little opportunity for ploughing a large area using traditional manual tools and restricts plot size to very few feddans (acres). As the area is mountainous, cultivation in the majority of the village councils is possible only by building terraces. Millet, sorghum, okra, tomatoes, sesame, watermelon, groundnuts and sorrel (karkedah) are the main crops grown both for family consumption and for sale. Millet is the main staple and cash crop food. Sorghum is another alternative, which is often mixed with millet or grown separately in small areas.

Men and women practise subsistence farming. The land tenure system traditionally provides equal access to women and men – women have their own farms and so do men. The sexual division of labour in agricultural production is clear. Ownership of produce and the control over it is entirely in the hands of the respective producer. Women's produce always quantitatively exceeds that of men. The women's farm is the largest and the most important because the household consumes the products of this farm throughout the year. The produce of men's farms is used for generating cash to meet other household needs, such as clothing, meat, sugar and soap, and for social obligations and personal expenses. Women own 95 per cent of livestock in the area. Men may own one donkey or camel and very rarely cows, goat and sheep. Men feed their donkeys from their own farms and have no right to use the women's livestock unless they get their permission.

Polygamy is widely practised: men are allowed up to four wives. Women need to depend entirely on themselves and their children since their husbands cannot afford to maintain more than one family.

In years of good harvest, Jebel Si was famous for its farming and was regarded as a main source of grain for the adjacent big towns of Kebkabiya and Kutum. These big towns in turn feed Elfasher town, the capital of North Darfur region. The situation has changed in recent years due to the successive droughts, which have led to frequent starvation since the 1980s. However, Jebel Si Rural Council still represents one of the high potential areas for millet production, the main staple food for people throughout Darfur.

Annual household income is difficult to assess. The meaning of income itself takes different forms and there is no unanimous understanding within the community. When the people in Jebel Si have good rains, they can expect a good harvest and can earn from their farm products. When this is not the case, no income is expected unless they migrate or sell their livestock. Beside crops and livestock, wood and grass collection, charcoal making, daily labour and remittance make up the livelihoods of a household. There is no single secured income source in most of the area. Petty trading makes a minor contribution to the household economy.

The frequent droughts of the 1980s have changed the local climate of Jebel Si and affected its micro-environment. In the 1970s Jebel Si was densely forested, and highly productive with plentiful wildlife. Deforestation has increased dramatically in the last two decades and desertification has been creeping over the area. Local people, who were dependent on forests and farms for their food and income, have lost such sources and become vulnerable to the deterioration of the environment. This is reflected in frequent harvest failures, water shortages, a depletion of livestock and a lack of basic social services. The lack of adequate means of transport that could help people travel to access services in other adjacent areas has increased their vulnerability.

A baseline survey carried out by the international NGO Oxfam in 1995 confirmed the following:

* a recurring pattern of drought every 10–20 years leading to severe food shortage and famine;
* a gradual decrease in food production from the 1960s leading to Jebel Si's present situation as a food deficit area;
* severe environmental degradation, with large-scale loss of tree cover;
* heavy out-migration, particularly among men;
* a high level of female-headed households (45 per cent);
* major sources of household income coming from agriculture, livestock, wood and grass selling and remittances;
* literacy levels of 30 per cent for men and 3 per cent for women.

THE ROLE OF WOMEN IN FOOD PRODUCTION

The traditional division of labour has assigned Jebel Si women the task of caring for children and older people. This, together with social reasons that prevents them from working in the towns, restricts women's freedom to travel. Women are left behind to maintain their reproductive roles and to increase their involvement in production and managerial responsibilities that fill the gap that has been created by men's migration.

Women constitute 70 per cent of the labour force in Jebel Si. Out of these, 80 per cent are involved full-time on their own holdings in subsistence agriculture and marginal cash cropping. A few work on farms or as unskilled labour, for example in building sites in Kebkabiya and Kutum town. Their daily wages range between 300 and 500 Sudanese pounds (US$0.20).

As we have noted, as many as 45 per cent of the households are female-headed: that is, headed by women who are divorced, separated, widowed, unmarried, or those whose husbands have migrated from home (within the country or abroad) in search of employment. Those who are married to polygamous husbands are also considered as female-headed households. Because the land tenure system enables women to have separate farms, women have the right to decide on how to allocate the land and what to grow to optimize family welfare. Women are therefore considered as the mainstay of agriculture. In their farms, which are regarded as the household farms, women accomplish 85 per cent of all farming operations. Men plant grains and crops for cash purposes. Women have the responsibility for providing grains to the households and marketing cash crops such as okra, tomato and sesame to gain income for their personal needs. Although men claim that the income obtained from selling their farm products is utilized in meeting household expenditure, women claim that men use their income for their own expenses and that they often have to depend on their own income. Food processing for storage for family consumption and for sale is also a task specific to women.

All pre- and post-harvest farming operations are carried out using traditional tools. Land cultivation is done by hand, predominantly using the hoe. Only 3 per cent of women have started using art ploughs, a donkey-drawn plough, which has been adopted only to a limited extent in the area.

FOOD SECURITY AND THE TRANSPORT SITUATION

During the last decade, people's awareness about their villages' isolation and the implications for the sustainability of their livelihoods has increased and has become a matter of concern among the community. As all the people are farmers, they view the situation as linked to food security. During times of good harvests the area lacks an effective storage system that could help maintain food security in case of failure of the following year's harvests. During a good harvest, because local farmers have no contact with the outside world, they lack the information necessary to bargain for good prices. Traders from outside the area offer low prices for their produce. Women, as the main producers, are often the victims of such under-pricing. During scarcity or harvest failure, grain traders do not target Jebel Si to sell their produce. They realize that the poverty of the local people would not allow them to afford the high grain prices. This deprives the area of food supply.

Male migration has left the women to deal with the problem of lack of food. Women have no transport and no information about how to access food and wage labour in other surrounding towns. Consequently, many children and old people have died. Epidemic diseases (such as malaria and diarrhoea) have spread and malnutrition affects many of the children, only 13 per cent of whom in the area are immunized. When the nearby big town wants to intervene or when the humanitarian agencies bring food and other relief items, they are constrained by the inaccessibility of the area to trucks, vehicles and sometimes even donkeys. The delays in reaching a village are always at the expense of the poor, who starve and die.

The situation is aggravated by the fact that government services in the Jebel Si Rural Council are poor or non-existent. At the time of this study there was only one medical dispensary in the area. Under the government's policy of decentralization, local government authorities are expected to raise most of their own resources for development programmes such as health, education and water supply. The Jebel Si Rural Council has little money to maintain these services, particularly at a time when it is trying to establish its own offices and administration. Inaccessibility has also constrained decision-makers, local authorities and the government officials visiting the area, which is why it was not considered in development planning.

The poor communities of Jebel Si were encouraged to approach Oxfam's Darfur office for support and help. The inaccessibility of the area became visible during the baseline survey when Oxfam staff had to walk or sometimes use donkeys to enter 90 per cent of the internal villages, which delayed the survey.

The process of carrying out the baseline survey also showed the local people the underlying causes of their underdevelopment and vulnerability. It further strengthened the process started earlier by the local people of reviewing their situation, seeking solutions to their problems, particularly those of women in maintaining food security. Accordingly, they identified a feeder road as their priority and agreed that it should be addressed simultaneously with mobilization of people, local resources and sustainable livelihood issues. Though Oxfam does not usually intervene in the construction of infrastructure, which it considers to be the responsibility of governments, this activity was justified as part of rehabilitation work and as a means of alleviating suffering and poverty. This led to the implementation of the Jebel Si Development Operational Project by Oxfam GB.

COMMUNITY MOBILIZATION

The Jebel Si Development Operational Project started with the formation of local committees with equal gender representation. The community then agreed to launch a process of road clearing in order that Oxfam vehicles could reach the remotest interior villages. The committees organized a big community mobilization involving all the villages (212), during which they cleared the roads using manual tools as a first stage. While men removed stones, women provided food and drinking water, while Oxfam provided sugar as a complementary item – this was inaccessible for the community because of its scarcity and high price. The project continued for two months, and eventually many areas that had been inaccessible became accessible to small vehicles such as Land-Rovers.

During the second stage, road-constructing machines were procured and eventually 85 kilometres of road were made passable for trucks and for hand-pump drilling and installing machines. More interestingly, people, especially women, feel more relaxed when walking on these roads. These roads connected 24 inner villages and made it less difficult to reach other severely remote ones. Because of the poor resources of Jebel Si, Oxfam contributed two-thirds of the total cost and, together with the committees, lobbied the government, which contributed the remaining one-third. The community contributed unskilled labour, food and water.

Government policy controls the overlapping of NGOs working in the same area and seeks to distribute support opportunities between needy areas. Accordingly, Oxfam has been the only NGO working in Jebel Si. Through working with Oxfam, the community developed skills of collective action. This was reflected in the work done by the community in building schools, health units, community centres, and in further road-clearing and initiatives towards halting tree cutting in Barday village. Women's contribution has been found to be 60 per cent in all development activities. These activities have strengthened the potential of the local people and their participation. The development committees have been transformed into local societies with their own initiatives to address the people's needs, to strengthen their position and to put forward their case to the decision-making bodies. The Barday are an example of a local society that developed strong bargaining power. They are well recognized in the whole Rural Council and facilitate training for other village councils' committees.

THE IMPACT OF FEEDER ROADS ON PEOPLE'S LIVELIHOODS

Research was conducted in three villages located at different positions from the feeder roads and in Ed Elnabag, which represents the centre of the Jebel Si Rural Council, where officials have established their offices. The villages display varying degrees of remoteness: Roga, the village that is most remote, is located in the eastern part of Jebel Si Rural Council; Birgie is in the north; and Barday is the main village to the south, across which the main road passes.

Basic social services

Provision of basic social services in the three villages has improved following the construction of the feeder roads. Table 8.1 shows the difference in provision before and after road construction.

TABLE 8.1 Service provision in each village before and after road construction

Services before	Services after
Barday (population 1,200; 437 households)	
School built from local material.	School built from permanant material.
Small weekly local market (100 persons).	Agricultural and animal husbandry extension and services; nursery for seedling distribution.
Quranic school.	Big market with more than 2,000 persons, trucks, outsiders, various trade activities; women become active petty traders.
Unused traditional wells.	Agricultural products sold at profitable prices.
Local traditional administration services for justice and security.	Movement between villages becomes easier.
Inactive cooperative.	Awareness raised on trade, prices and bargaining.
Kindergarten and women's literacy class.	Community centre with women trained in soap making and credit management.
	Ministers, planners and local authorities start visiting the area and talking to people about local development; women's organizations also visit. Paid trips for extension purposes.
	Child immunization recorded as the highest in the area's history.
Birgie (population 650; 222 households)	
School built from local material.	School built from permanent material.
Small market (200 persons).	Big trucks enter the village, varied goods and market has increased in size (3,000 persons).
One grinding mill.	Construction of a health unit; provision of equipment and drugs through drug revolving fund.
Traditional wells.	Women extension services with female extensionist.
Local traditional administration.	Agriculture and animal husbandry extension services.
	Installation of rain gauge.
	Hand pumps and extension of sanitation.
	Anothering grinding mill.
	Community centre, kindergarten, women's literacy.

Services before	Services after
Roga (population 420; 150 households)	
Local traditional administration.	Agriculture and animal husbandry extension services.
Quran class.	Women's extension services (literacy class, kindergarten and awareness-raising activities by women extensionist).
Traditional wells.	Accessible health services: child vaccination, sanitation and birth attendance.
Small market.	Increased size of local market; increased number of outsiders; almost all people practise trade; women become active petty traders.

Time saving

The burden of some domestic activities of women in the three villages in terms of distance and time spent before road construction and after was compared (see Table 8.2).

Shortage of water was the main problem as most of the water sources are depleted and the environmental changes have increased the depth of water table. Even when wells are located within villages, it takes many hours to collect a can of water. In Barday village, women fetch water at night (11 p.m.) and come back at 6 a.m. every two days.

Because of the limited number of flour mills, women take many hours to grind their grain. Often, though, they don't have money to pay grinding fees and use the traditional manual hand mill (*murhaka*). There was only one mill among the three villages, in Barday, although recently two more mills have been installed, one each in Barday and in Birgie. Roga still lacks a flour mill and a health centre. The lack of services in Roga is attributed to its remoteness, although it is the most productive village in Jebel Si Rural Council.

The Health Centre in Barday has been equipped and provided with drugs through a drug revolving fund that enables it to service a large number of people, especially women and children. The flow of medical drugs is being facilitated by the existence of the roads, which help in their delivery and distribution. Moreover, people who were either depending on traditional medicine or had a taboo about using medical drugs have

TABLE 8.2 Women's burden before and after road construction: distance travelled and time spent on different tasks

Village	Water source km (hr)		Flour mill km (hr)		Health centre km (hr)		Main market (nearest)		Fuelwood collection km (hr)	
	Before	After	Before	After	Before	After	Before	After	Before	After
Barday	1–6 (2–8)	3 (2)	12 (6)	5 (4)	12 (6)	2 (2)	Barday	Barday, Kagiro and Edenabag	4–8 (3–8)	5 (2–5)
Birgie	1–4 (2–8)	2.5 (5)	2–12 (5–10)	2–6 (2–6)	12 (12)	12 (12)	Birgie	Birgie, Mella and Edenabag	4–8 (3–8)	4–8 (3–8)
Roga	1–6 (2–6)	1–6 (2–6)	8 (10)	8 (10)	30 (full day)	30 (full day)	Barday	Barday	4–8 (3–8)	4–8 (3–8)

changed their attitudes. This is evidenced by the increasing demand, which is recorded to be four times greater than the capacity of the Health Unit. The Barday Health Unit has contributed significantly to combating diseases that mainly affect women and children.

Other benefits

Although the main objectives of the road were to facilitate marketing of agricultural produce, women have also benefited from access to government services, for example vaccination and education, and by the ability of Oxfam workers to reach the area.

Local market development

Women and men have developed bargaining power in selling their products at a greater profit than before. As many as 90 per cent of women in the three villages have gained more income from their products and are able to meet other family and personal requirements that they could not before. Both men and women have become aware of the demand for agricultural products. Consequently, all women and men farmers have attempted, with difficulty, to increase the size of their agricultural plots in order to increase production. In Barday village, which is located at the side of the road and where there is the main weekly market, 30 per cent of the women have ventured into petty trading such as providing tea and coffee, cooking food (for example *kisra*), and selling fresh vegetables and milk products. Some women from other villages also engage in similar activities. However, in Roga and Birgie, because they are away from the roads, women spend most of their time in fetching water, grinding or looking after animals. Therefore, women in Barday have more income than those in other parts of Jebel Si, where no road connections have yet been made.

In Barday, the number of trucks and small vehicles attending the weekly market is estimated to be between 12 and 15, compared with none before. An estimated 350–500 outsiders and about 1,500 local people attend the market, of which women comprise 35 per cent. While most of the women attend the market to sell their products and for petty trading activities, a small number attend merely to enjoy themselves. Barday village has developed tangible signs of progress towards sustainable livelihoods.

Increased revenues

The local Rural Council authorities report a substantial contribution from the road development to official revenues. The roads raise between 3 million and 5 million Sudanese pounds a month, which is equivalent to about US$1,200. Because Jebel Si is resource-poor, the local authorities give priority to paying schoolteachers' salaries. The revenues collected are still not enough to cover the salaries, let alone rehabilitation of services or any kind of support to the poor.

Remittances

An additional benefit is that men who have migrated to Khartoum or other big towns have started sending remittances using trucks that directly enter the area. A man from Birgie who was working in Khartoum for a long time bought a truck and returned to work in his home, making round trips between Khartoum and Jebel Si Rural Council.

Health and education

Some 90 per cent of the area's health units that were inactive have started working, and the drugs that are purchased through the drug revolving fund are made accessible at affordable prices to all people. Child immunization has now improved and Jebel Si recorded 70 per cent in the last vaccination campaign carried out by the state government. However, Roga village continued to record only 13 per cent.

A total of 80 per cent of the respondents said that the services provided (wells and hand-pumps) have an effect on reducing women's burden of fetching water, giving them more water for domestic work. Women are able to clean their children and wash their clothes using cheap soaps that are made by them as part of Oxfam income-generating training for women in the area.

Eye diseases and diarrhoea, which had been continuously attacking children, have now begun to disappear because of cleanliness, the availability of drugs and vaccination.

The focus on literacy and education in the form of literacy classes for women and the rehabilitation of schools, accompanied by intensive extension by Oxfam staff in collaboration with the local authorities, has facilitated the development of new attitudes towards girls' education. For the first time in the history of the area, no single girl has been kept from school in Barday village for domestic reasons or due to early marriage. The numbers of girls enrolled in Barday School at the time of the 1995 Oxfam survey were 12, 7, 5 and 3 for the classes from the first to the fourth grade respectively (no girls were enrolled in the fifth and sixth grades). At the time of the present study (1998/9)the number of girls in the same school in the first and second grades were 30 and 25, respectively, 18 of whom are from other roadside villages. A similar result has been obtained for Birgie village. With support of the committees and local traditional administration (Sheikh), a message was disseminated that parents and mothers in particular were not allowed to keep girls from schools for domestic reasons or due to marriage before completing the sixth grade, by which time a number of literate girls will have graduated.

Teachers indicated that they were often unable to reach the schools because of lack of adequate roads and transport. The roads have contributed to solve the problems of teachers, equipment and communication, and they are happy to stay on for at least two years in an endeavour to help the people and change their attitudes towards local development and girls' education. They also think that their presence will encourage visits by the education authorities, which would be a good opportunity to expose them to the level of the poverty in these villages and to attract their attention for collaboration and support.

The area is being exposed to outsiders, who either come occasionally to the market or stay for some time (government personnel, Oxfam staff, women's organizations and relatives). Such interaction will lead in the long term to a new socio-cultural environment that may have a positive impact on local development. The men who have migrated because of isolation and poverty have now started returning with positive views about local development and investments. They know that they can travel and come back more easily to participate in local development activities.

People's dependence on millet or sorghum caused them to suffer during times of shortage. The lack of an alternative survival mechanism in Jebel Si Rural Council was one of the most threatening factors to the sustainability of people's livelihoods, women's in particular. People have started developing knowledge about uses of other products that are locally produced, the use of which has been constrained by traditional beliefs. For example, there is a traditional belief that it is bad for pregnant women and for children to eat eggs. Chicken and milk, the most easily available food items, are not consumed by most women and older people. Women extension workers have encouraged women to try different types of food, especially for children and for school pupils. People (mostly men) have complained that the women have started including other food items in their meals. It is found that the traditional food from millet (porridge) is now supplemented in 50 per cent of the families, with a positive effect on people's health, especially that of the children. Training on food processing for women carried out by Oxfam and the Intermediate Technology Development Group has had a great impact on broadening the awareness of women in how to use local items to cook nutritious food. Techniques of preserving and canning food items that are produced in large quantities during the production season have also been disseminated among women. Some women in Barday and Birgie markets have been seen to trade in pasta, which initially was in poor demand but is now used all over Barday and Birgie for children. Men as well as women in the three villages have welcomed this and emphasize the necessity to develop new ways of using the available produce as survival strategies to escape food shortage and famine and to improve health.

In the past the forest constituted the main source of income for most of the people in the three villages. The roads have enabled alternative income opportunities. Local people have realized the importance of forests to sustainable livelihoods and have acknowledged that they themselves have contributed to their poverty by cutting down trees. The communities in the three villages have decided to stop further cutting and to broadcast seeds in the areas of previously dense forests. In the three villages, the communities have already attempted to construct community forests.

Jebel Si people, and women in particular, are especially vulnerable to harvest failures, and in 1997 the area was identified as among the most affected areas and one needing urgent relief. The past experience of Jebel Si villages with relief distribution was that the inaccessibility of the area to trucks had caused unaccountable delays in the arrival of relief and its distribution. In most cases, donkeys were used to deliver food grain to the interior villages, though some villages are even inaccessible by this means. The delays were forcing people to become part of the internally displaced and leave their homes to where they could access food. The worst effect of the delays was the death of children and of older people who could not travel or wait without food for very long. In 1997, because of the feeder roads, the Save the Children Fund and other local and international NGOs succeeded in bringing some food to the area. A successful and timely distribution was achieved in Jebel Si, recording an unprecedented distribution result. Trucks were moving from Khartoum directly to Jebel Si villages. Fewer people had to move away because of the availability of food grain supplied by grain traders, remittances received from migrants, and support provided by people from neighbouring towns.

Gender and community organization

Apart from delivering services that meet some of women's practical needs, the feeder road has enabled Oxfam and other like-minded local organizations, especially women's organizations, to access the area. Their interventions are mainly concentrated on providing extension services to women, capacity building for committees, and upgrading women's skills for income-generating activities. The subordination of women to men has been addressed through equal representation of women in the village committees. This involvement of women in the village committees has been the major way in which the strategic gender needs of women have been addressed. These committees are being assigned an active role in promoting local development. They are considering the different opportunities and resources within and outside the area of Jebel Si and are developing strategies that could maintain food security and escape unpredictable hazards. Women, as permanent residents who undertake all the responsibilities of migrated men, have been targeted as recipients of training and skill-promoting activities so that they will be able to achieve their targets independently of their absent menfolk.

The village committees have been formalized and registered and are being recognized at the official level as representative of the local people. They have acquired the right to address the needs and any emergent problems in the Rural Council. Some influential women were traditionally known to represent women's views and participate in decision making (*hakamat*). The representation of women on the committees is a process of widening their participation and enabling other less experienced women to enjoy opportunities for decision making. This has fostered significant changes in the community among both men and women. Women's position has been enhanced and promoted through their equal participation and their aspirations have been raised as they become keen to know what is going on in their villages and to give their opinions to their representatives who attend meetings.

Women have learned the importance of organization and participation in local affairs. The roads enable women representatives to travel to meetings and return to their villages the same day, which was difficult for them before. Women in the area now have greater access to information and are able to identify their needs and to explore ways to address them.

CONSTRAINTS AND DIFFICULTIES

The changes described in the study cannot be attributed solely to the feeder roads. Alleviation of suffering, distress and poverty is a multidimensional process. The severe poverty and historical isolation of Jebel Si means it is very vulnerable to unpredictable disasters. Feeder roads can only help facilitate the presence of other processes. Even though feeder roads in Jebel Si have made a significant contribution to the area's rehabilitation, women and men are still not always able to attend meetings from their villages because poor transport (by donkey or on foot) makes this very time-consuming.

Since the construction of the roads in 1996, no official effort has been put into their maintenance, and it has been left to local people to maintain them manually. Moreover, the 1998 rainy season has washed away a large part of these roads. The local authorities, which collect revenues from trucks passing through the main roads, do not allocate any portion for maintaining the service and instead rely on the poor community to carry out the work. The attitudes of the authorities have a negative influence on the poor and exacerbate their vulnerability. Women, because they play the role of food provider, suffer food insecurity because of the need for continual provision of food, which leads them to use their reserves and to spend their small income in feeding the working men.

Men and women find it impractical to use donkeys and prefer to walk, particularly in villages as remote as Roga. Wild monkeys also threaten women when passing through some pathways. Government policy has closed the School Boarding Houses that used to accommodate pupils from distant villages. Because of the lack of adequate roads, pupils cannot arrive in school on time and this has made many families abandon the idea of getting their children enrolled. Girls are particularly victimized by such policies because mothers are not willing to let them walk long distances, especially the little ones, who could easily be targeted and hurt by wild animals. Therefore, those girls who are enrolled in schools are often from the village where the school is located.

Apart from using donkeys in the inter-village movements, no other means of transport has ever been attempted in the area. Carts, bicycles, cars or any appropriate transport technology that could suit the topography of the area are non-existent. Because the land is rocky, it is even difficult for donkeys, which is why the majority of women prefer walking rather than riding on rocky pathways. Some severely remote villages have not witnessed any outside visitors and the women extensionists find it quite hard to travel in such rocky and mountainous land. The consequence of the lack of means of transport in the remotest villages is deprivation of any sort of service.

CONCLUSION AND THE WAY FORWARD

Darfur region suffers from unfair distribution of resources from the national level because of its isolation, underrepresentation and weak voice at decision-making levels. Isolation has contributed to the poverty of the region. It has been exacerbated by the natural disasters of drought, harvest failures and famines that have been striking the region in the last decades, especially the rural areas. Men are forced to migrate to other parts of Sudan, leaving women to bear the most difficult task of securing food for the community as a whole. In the Darfur region Jebel Si Rural Council is the most isolated. Men migrate; children and older people are sick, malnourished or die of hunger. Who should bear all these problems? Women – simply because they *are* women.

Oxfam appreciated the role of women as producers and recognized their role as breadwinners. It contributed to the construction of 85 kilometres of feeder roads, connecting 45 interior villages. These roads facilitated the delivery of formal and informal services to the Jebel Si Rural Council. Though the feeder roads were not sustainable, the impact achieved on people's sustainable livelihoods over a short time shows that there is a close link between feeder roads and the sustainability of the livelihoods of poor people, women in particular. As the main gate to delivery of other basic services, feeder roads represent a priority for rural people in this area.

As one of the first studies to be carried out on rural transport in Sudan, this research can be said to provide some indications of what can be done in other isolated rural areas in the country that have been marginalized by development planners.

9

OFF-ROAD AREAS: A GENDER PERSPECTIVE ON TRANSPORT AND ACCESSIBILITY

WOMEN TRADERS IN GOMOA, GHANA

Gina Porter

Marketing is a major responsibility for women in coastal Ghana. In many districts they face considerable difficulties in getting their goods to market, particularly when they are resident away from the paved road. Feeder roads and tracks deteriorate rapidly in the rainy season and settlements only a few miles away from the tarred road can become relatively inaccessible. Many traders will not visit such settlements during this time, and consequently prices are depressed. Women must head-load their produce to the nearest motorable road if they are to obtain better prices.

The objectives of this research were to explore the following questions: What were the current organization and cost of transport services in off-road areas? What were the particular needs and difficulties of women traders (and to what extent were they transport-related)? Was there potential to develop women-run/owned transport services, given that most transport is owned by men? And what was the potential for various types of intermediate transport use and its implications for women's trading activities?

The research was conducted in May and September 1998 in Gomoa district, Central Region. It aimed to pick up seasonal contrasts and changes in perceptions related to variation in rainfall and associated road conditions and crop production techniques. But in 1998 there was remarkably little rain in the district even by the end of September, a condition locally attributed to the global impact of El Niño.

The work included an initial survey of current transport services in selected off-road settlements, and participatory techniques to assess the needs and difficulties of traders and the potential for women-owned or women-run services. Findings of the initial work were fed back to participating villages and more studies took place focusing on transport problems in the midst of the maize harvest period. A series of separate focus-group discussions on the potential of intermediate means of transport (IMTs) was held with women and men, using a set of photographs. This chapter focuses on the work conducted with women.

THE STUDY AREA

Gomoa, in Central Region, is one of Ghana's poorest coastal districts. It is located mainly in the coastal savannah belt. The climate is characterized by a bimodal rainfall distribution and a mean annual rainfall of between 70 and 90 centimetres along the coast and between 90 and 110 centimetres in the northernmost area, where savannah gives way to semi-deciduous forest.

Gomoa is principally an agricultural district. The main crops grown are maize (often the major cash crop), cassava (grown both as a food crop and generally, to a lesser extent, as a cash crop), peppers and tomatoes (both the latter grown as a cash crop and, in the case of green pepper, sometimes as an export crop). According to the District Development Plan (May 1996), there is a high potential for grain production and the development of large-scale production of pineapples and pepper. This potential is constrained by unreliable rainfall, lack of credit for farmers, fluctuation in agricultural prices, high input costs and poor roads. Labour shortage is also a problem in many areas: youths have migrated out of Gomoa to the forest zone to engage in cash crop cultivation. Labour migration is encouraged by the relatively underdeveloped state of agriculture in Gomoa and labour shortages help perpetuate low productivity. Communal labour parties (*nnoba*) for agricultural work are still common in this area and shifting cultivation without any fertilizer is widespread.

Central Region has a relatively good road network compared to northern Ghana, for example, but the condition of the roads is very poor. In a recent survey of road conditions in Ghana, only 2 per cent of all roads (including earth and paved) in Central Region were considered 'good', compared to 67 per cent 'poor' and 31 per cent 'fair' (Wilbur Smith Associates, 1998). Road network maps show Gomoa district to have a high density of 'gravel' roads, which on inspection are found to be indistinguishable from earth tracks. In the rolling topography of Gomoa, the gravel surface is rapidly lost during the rains, and gulleys appear.

The condition of local roads and paths is of particular concern to women in Gomoa since they are the principal agricultural produce traders, travelling extensively both within and outside the district to market their own and their husbands' produce, and returning home with other items to sell in their village area. In addition to trading, most women are involved in farming (sometimes on their own account, sometimes in conjunction with their husbands) and a host of household activities, including head-loading water and fuelwood and most of their own and their husbands' produce from the fields to the village.

Four villages located off the paved road were selected for detailed study: Adabra, Lome, Sampa and Abora. The villages are described below. All are primarily Fante villages with some families from other parts of Ghana.

Adabra

Adabra is located in northeast Gomoa, in a region of moderately good rainfall and mixed gravel/sandy loam soils. Adabra's farmers grow maize, cassava, pepper, yam and some tomatoes and groundnuts for sale. Maize and cassava are the principal crops. The farmers have ample land and most also have sufficient labour.

Adabra is approximately five miles from the nearest tarred road. The tracks that connect it to the tarred road were badly eroded in May of the study period, with many potholes. The road out of Adabra is sometimes impassable, in years of heavy rains for long periods, notably in June and July. Local chiefs have made requests to the district administration for assistance with road improvements in the area. The road contract was reportedly awarded at one point but the contractor absconded before the road was built.

Thirty years ago Adabra was an important market centre. Nowadays the village is relatively small and the thatched roofs and general lack of infrastructure indicate the poverty of the inhabitants. The villagers regret the loss of the market and blame it on the deterioration of local roads. In May, local women complained about the cost of taking goods to the main market centre at Kasoa 15 miles away, saying that they had insufficient funds to pay transport fares, even when the road is motorable. They were forced to head-load their produce. Even if they had funds for transport, all the vehicles passing through the village are full.

By September there had been a remarkable change in perceptions of accessibility in Adabra among both men and women. The local roads had been graded in June, there was limited rainfall since then, and the main harvest, though lower than normal due to low rainfall, had brought sufficient money into the local economy to enable most women to pay the fare to Kasoa. The frequency of vehicles passing through the settlement had also increased. The change in conditions at Adabra emphasizes the need for seasonal studies of transport and accessibility since perceptions can change substantially between seasons.

Sampa

Sampa is located in western Gomoa, north of the Accra–Cape Coast road in an area of clay/gravel with moderate rainfall. It is larger and rather more prosperous than the other off-road settlements studied, and has some substantial buildings, including the chief's palace. A wider range of crops is cultivated here: tomatoes, oranges, palm oil, sugar cane and pepper, in addition to maize and cassava. Maize, cassava and oranges are all produced in sufficient quantities to attract regular visits from local wholesale dealers.

Sampa is situated about 5 miles from the main road: the first mile from the main road was once tarred (reportedly in 1956!) but is now badly eroded. The remainder, apart from a small section at Sampa Junction, is untarred with corrugations. Along steeper sections of the road there is severe gullying and the road becomes very narrow. It is impassable after heavy rains. The road was last repaired in 1995 when the children of a local chief paid for a grader in order to make the road motorable for their father's funeral. In May, the current chief had been to Accra to request assistance from the Minister of Roads and Transport and had been promised help 'at some time in the future'. In September the situation has been somewhat improved by the grading of roads in the vicinity, though the road out of Sampa itself was still bad.

It is usually easier to find transport by taxi rather than *tro-tro* (minibus) from the junction to Sampa because for *tro-tro* owners, given the condition of the road, there are often too few goods and passengers at Sampa to make their journey worthwhile. Two women produce-dealers bulk much of the local produce in Sampa and take it to market because many other women cannot afford the fare, particularly if they have only a small amount of produce to sell. They mostly travel to their closest market centre, Kyiren Nkwanta, five and a half miles away. Some also visit the markets at Mankessim and Kasoa along the main Accra–Cape Coast road.

Lome

Lome and its associated temporary farm settlements are located in an area designated in Gomoa district administration maps as a 'potential agricultural region'. The area has moderate to good rainfall in a bimodal distribution and soils are a mix of gravels and sandy loams.

Lome is just under four miles from the nearest tarred road along a narrow graded track with some corrugations and other signs of erosion. Associated with the main, fairly large settlement at Lome are about twenty temporary farm settlements where Lome farmers have practised shifting cultivation for around forty years. Access from Lome to these temporary farm settlements is by footpath only. Farmers at temporary settlements sleep in barns (*osan*) during the farming season, returning only at the weekend to the parent settlement. Men and their wives occupy the temporary settlements: about twenty farmers or so may be based in each. Women return to Lome when there is less work for them to do.

Lome women spend a great deal of time after harvest carrying crops between the temporary settlements and the parent village. Maize is the principal crop. Cassava is too bulky in its unprocessed state to justify head-loading to Lome. Farmers say that if they had a corn mill at the temporary farm, they could grow cassava and process *gari* (dried and grated cassava meal). Women head-load maize daily to Lome in the harvest season. There used to be barns at intermediate points, but these are no longer utilized because of theft: nowadays barns are either in Lome or at the temporary settlement. Some farmers remain in the temporary settlement after harvest to guard the maize crop and to grow tomatoes, garden eggs and pepper in the minor season. Tomatoes are carried back to Lome every four days, peppers preferably within one to a maximum of three to four days of harvest.

Women take produce beyond Lome to local markets, notably Dewurampong (4 miles away) and, to a lesser extent, Swedru (about 13 miles away). Lome's own market (on Tuesdays and Fridays), patronized by dealers from Swedru and even Accra, declined due to the movement of nearby settlements to the tarred road and the consequent expansion of the Dewurampong market (also held on Tuesdays and Fridays). Though there is some talk of reviving the market at Lome since vehicles do not always come to the village to take its women to other market centres, this seems unlikely without careful planning and concerted action on the part of the local inhabitants.

Abora

Abora is located just south of the main Accra–Cape Coast road in an area of somewhat difficult clay soils and relatively low and sporadic rainfall. The improved 110-day maize variety is cultivated in this area: it grows well but is susceptible to weevils. Cassava is grown for home consumption and recently a number of farmers have started cashew production. Fuelwood, sold in local markets to fish smokers, is a major income earner for women. Abora is the smallest and poorest of the four settlements and is poorer than many other Gomoa villages. No one, for instance, owns a grinding machine – women have to take their maize to the settlement at the tarred road for grinding; there are no stores or kiosks; and the physical infra-structure is very limited.

Abora is only 2 miles from the tarred road and provides evidence of the difficulties that even settlements a short distance from good transport can experience. It is located on a rough narrow track which is totally impassable in periods of heavy rain and for up to three days afterwards. The village elders have made the decision to move to a new site three-quarters of a mile closer to the main road in order to ease their access problems. The fact that the settlement has few facilities makes the deci-sion to move feasible, though the relocation will occur over a long period since villagers do not generally have the funds to build new houses.

THE CURRENT ORGANIZATION AND COST OF MOTORIZED TRANSPORT SERVICES

Motorized transport services from and to off-road villages are extremely restricted and mostly dependent on vehicles coming in from the paved road, rather than on transport based in the villages themselves. Vehicles are privately owned and often owner-driven or driven by a relative of the owner. The most common vehicles operating to the villages are *tro-tros* and passenger cars used as taxis for the transport of passengers and goods. Motorcycles and mopeds are remarkably rare. There are motor-cycles on sale in Kumasi and Accra but many of the customers are Ivorians.

Adabra and Sampa have no vehicles. Lome has a *tro-tro* owned by a man in Swedru, and Abora has a taxi owned by a woman trader in the village. A man in Adabra, a farmer, owns a car which he bought three years before the survey period from the proceeds of his cassava and gari production. A year later he had enough money to purchase the engine. At first he operated it as a taxi from Adabra (driven by a brother), but the road was so bad that he decided to move it to a base near Accra.

Taxis generally charge higher rates than *tro-tros* over the same distance. Transport charges are higher along unpaved roads, and when road conditions are very bad drivers will not take their vehicles along such routes. Some vehicle owners who regularly run on off-road routes have to replace (second-hand) tyres every month. A tyre for a passenger car can cost up to 200,000 cedis when purchased new. On local market days services to off-road villages in the market's vicinity are better than average: the driver may arrive at the village, load the vehicle with goods the evening prior to market or very early on market day, pick up his passengers and bring them back from the market at the end of the day. All the drivers encountered have been male. Large trucks do not generally visit these off-road settlements.

On Kaoa market day there are usually plenty of vehicles passing through Adabra, particularly now that the road has been graded, but sometimes all the vehicles are full before they reach the village. On non-market days there are occasional vehicles passing through to Swedru, and in the harvest season mammy wagons and *tro-tros* are brought in by outside traders for the collection of maize. It costs 700 cedis by *tro-tro* from Adabra to Kasoa market (a distance of about 15 miles, of which 5 are on untarred road) and 1,200 cedis per sack of cassava.

In September of the survey period, only five out of fifteen women in Sampa had used motorized transport in the past seven days, mostly to travel to their local market at Kyiren Nkwanta, even though this is the season when much maize is sold. On the evening before market days in Kyiren Nkwanta four or five taxis or *tro-tros* may come to Sampa to load their vehicles. They set off for market with the traders at dawn and bring them home again when their goods are sold. There are a number of different cars that may or may not come. On non-market days only two or three vehicles will visit the settlement at most, and usually it is necessary to walk to the road junction about a mile away to find a vehicle. It costs 600 cedis per person and 1,000 cedis per minibag of maize to travel to Kyiren Nkwanta by *tro-tro* (about five and a half miles all along poor, unpaved road) and 1,000 cedis per passenger by taxi. The journey to Mankessim, about twenty-four miles away and including five miles of unpaved road, costs more: 1,000 cedis by *tro-tro* and 1,200 by taxi. The majority of women in Sampa, however, do not have sufficient money for transport and walk to Kyiren Nkwanta market regularly with their own and their husbands' produce. Some even head-load cassava, the heaviest crop grown. They return with smoked fish and other items for sale in the village. They say it takes about one and a half hours when carrying a load.

Sometimes women who travel to more distant markets are unable to find transport to take them home. Women who expect to be away overnight need to ask their husbands for permission. Occasionally, absence without permission may result in a suspicious husband following his wife 'to see what she is doing'. Husbands do not like the inconvenience when their wives are unable to return home and are not available to prepare the evening meal.

In Lome the village's *tro-tro* is used for a wide variety of journeys and has no regular route. On Dewurampong market days, six to ten vehicles, mostly *tro-tros*, come to Lome to pick traders up and a further three to five arrive on Swedru market days (Monday and Thursday). On Sundays two vehicles leave Lome but do not return in the evening. The cost of travel to Dewurampong, the closest market, four miles distant and almost all along unpaved road, is 300 cedis per passenger by *tro-tro* and 400 cedis by taxi. The *tro-tro* fare seems to be affordable by almost all the women residents. A minibag of maize will cost 500–600 cedis by *tro-tro* and 700–800 cedis by taxi.

The taxi in Abora works from the paved road and merely makes an early morning run to the road and a late evening run back to the village when the driver has completed his day's work. Other transport only comes to the settlement if someone from outside has reason to make the journey to Abora, such as dealers who come to purchase crops. Even on local market days Abora's own traders travel to the paved road on foot. It costs 200 cedis to travel by *tro-tro* or taxi the two miles to the nearest market centre at Apam Junction and about 3,000 cedis per load (depending on size). There is no motorable road, merely a narrow four-mile-long footpath to the coastal market centre and district headquarters at Apam, and consequently only pedestrian traffic in this direction. Since Apam is a major fish-smoking centre and market for fuelwood, traffic along the footpath is heavy.

NON-MOTORIZED TRANSPORT USE

Apart from pedestrian head-loading, which is ubiquitous, non-motorized transport is remarkably rare in Gomoa. Bicycles mainly and handcarts have been acquired within the last decade and are wholly owned and operated by men, purchased with cash from farming or hunting. (Gomoa is an area where small game is still common and hunting widespread.) Few women have ever ridden a bicycle. Some younger women have done so within the village centre 'for pleasure'. Men do not generally lend their bicycles to their wives. Handcarts are mainly found in the district capital, Apam, and are hardly encountered in the rural areas, though two of the study villages did have carts.

The cost of non-motorized transport is an important constraint on its purchase, since it is generally obtained for cash. A basic bicycle of Chinese/

Asian manufacture (such as the Phoenix brand) costs from 120,000 to 150,000 cedis, and a new bicycle tyre, which may last less than six months on poor roads and tracks, costs around 12,000 cedis. Second-hand tyres can be obtained much more cheaply from vulcanisers but are reckoned by those with sufficient funds to be a bad investment since they are very rapidly worn out.

In Adabra, six men own bicycles, and in September of the study period none except the one belonging to the primary school headmaster was being used. There is no bicycle repairer in the village. The headmaster mends his bicycle himself. In Sampa there are only three bicycle owners, all men. They hire out their bicycles to other men, at 200 cedis per five minutes, who use them to travel to nearby settlements. Lome has about ten bicycles, mostly the standard Chinese/Asian makes, again all owned by men. Two men had recently purchased mountain bicycles with gears, which were much admired, though one had already broken. Some of the bicycles seem to have been purchased with the thought of renting them out to young boys in town. A hunter/farmer has a sturdy Raleigh bicycle with a double crossbar that he never hires out, which may explain why it is in such good condition. He purchased the bicycle for cash five years before the survey period in Swedru and paid 80,000 cedis for it. Bicycle prices had risen substantially over the last few years. He buys second-hand tyres at 4,500 cedis per tyre from Swedru (sending money with any of the drivers who come to Lome) and has to change his tyres every two months. Fortunately, Lome has its own bicycle repairer who repairs the spokes when they break. The owner uses his bicycle every time he goes to his farm and also for riding to the paved road and onwards to nearby centres such as Afransi and Apam Junction. He carries small quantities of goods, on his head and on the bicycle, but observed that cycling with a load was difficult because of the potholes in the footpaths. During harvest, he employs head-loaders, mostly women, rather than use the bicycle.

Abora has three bicycle owners: one man, a hunter; one schoolboy, whose brother in Takoradi purchased it for him; and the only woman cycle owner encountered in the district. The hunter, who has a Phoenix bicycle, purchased it new two years ago for 105,000 cedis cash, travelling to Accra to make this purchase. He uses the bicycle to transport game to the village and to the roadside for sale. He loans it out daily without charge to his male friends. When it breaks down he makes simple repairs himself, but otherwise must take it to the nearest mechanic, located at Apam Junction. He had recently seen a three-wheeler tricycle on television and had an ambition to purchase one.

The woman cycle owner, an Adventist Relief Agency 'motivator', was purchasing her machine, a Chinese 'Hero', at a total cost of 130,000 cedis on instalments through her work, She had the bicycle for one year at the time of the first interview but for two months it had not been in use due to loose bolts, a broken pedal and a split inner tube. She did not have the 12,000–18,000 cedis repair cost and had not received assistance from her employer for the repair. She blamed the damage to the bicycle on the fact that she loans it out often to friends and to the village children (at no charge). In September the bicycle was still broken.

Most other women in the villages cannot ride or cannot afford to buy bicycles, though some have occasionally borrowed a husband's to ride in the village ('for pleasure'). In Lome, the chief's niece, a major trader in her forties, described how she had ridden a bicycle to the next village, 'just for fun'. Husbands do not usually loan their bicycles to their wives, though it was unclear why. The hunter/farmer with the Raleigh bicycle said that he loans his bicycle to his wife and she rides it occasionally to a nearby farm but 'because she has a child on her back she cannot take it very far'. He admits that she would like to use it more but argues that he needs it himself.

In Adabra, one man owns a small four-wheeled hand cart which he purchased from a local manufacturer in Accra and which he rents out to men and women at between 1,500 and 3,000 cedis per day, depending on load and distance. People use it mainly to transport crops to neighbouring villages and from their farms to the village. The cart cost 150,000 cedis and third-hand tyres from the vulcaniser cost between 8,000 and 10,000 cedis per tyre. They had been changed several times since the purchase of the cart eighteen months earlier. Nonetheless the owner was pleased with his investment.

Lome has two small handcarts, with solid wooden wheels and rubber treads pasted on, that were made by the owner, a mason/farmer, about a year before at a cost of 55,000 cedis. Like the man in Adabra, he hires the carts to men and women who use them to take their maize the four miles to the junction for a charge of 6,000 cedis for a full load, or from their farm to the village at a charge of 2,500 to 5,000 cedis, depending on the distance. Only people without relatives to carry their produce pay to hire the carts. Relatives are simply given a small portion of maize for their assistance. The main use of the carts is for transport of construction material during house building. The owner or his brother always accompanies the cart when it is hired out. There are no hand carts in Sampa or in Abora.

THE NEEDS AND DIFFICULTIES OF
WOMEN TRADERS

Issues relating to the difficulties and needs of women traders partially depend on the economic status and other specific characteristics of the women concerned. Both wealthier and poorer women frequently cited as a difficulty the lack of capital for expanding trading activity. Poorer women lacked money for transport fares to visit local markets and the wealthier women to visit larger, more distant markets. Although women are the principal produce marketers, they are less able to afford transport than their husbands. Husbands have larger areas of land to farm and are expected to give their wives transport money to sell their produce, but they do not always do so. Many poorer women make long journeys to market on foot with heavy loads. Others travel with their loads by *tro-tro*, and pay the driver once the goods are sold.

Another common problem for traders, small and large businesses and roadside and off-road residents is that of defaulting creditors and long delays in repayment of credit. Small-scale trading frequently involves extension of credit. In off-road villages, where poverty is greater, credit transactions are extensive and complex. When there are long delays in payment or default by a creditor, even though the sums involved are small, it can have extremely serious implications for a number of people.

Many of the larger-scale women traders resident in off-road areas are also at risk of losing money by default in their activities as bulkers of agricultural produce. They usually buy from small producers/traders who cannot afford transport to local markets and in the local marketplaces sell the produce to larger dealers, many of who come from the major cities. These transactions often involve regular 'customers' to whom some credit may be extended, though usually part of the payment for goods is made in cash. Sometimes defaults involving large sums of money occur with little chance of redress.

Women in off-road settlements face the problem of drivers arriving late on market days to pick up them and their goods, and the loss of sales from such delays. The market may already be well advanced by the time they arrive, and it may not be possible to sell all the produce before the customers disperse. Most customers may have already made their purchases from more punctual traders. In the wet season, when drivers are unwilling to venture along difficult stretches of road, transport may not arrive at all, and produce will be lost. Fresh cassava in particular deteriorates after about four days. Therefore women generally organize a vehicle before uprooting the cassava; however, if the vehicle does not arrive the cassava has to be processed into gari, because it is very heavy and difficult to head-load over long distances. Processing gari requires a substantial amount of firewood and not all women are skilled in its production. In Adabra, where a lot of cassava is produced, every woman in the village makes gari, but in Sampa only about six women are specialist gari processors.

Other losses have included tomatoes, which should normally be marketed within two (or preferably one) day(s) of picking and will certainly rot after four days if already soft when picked. In Sampa, sugar cane evacuation has also been difficult at times, resulting in losses due to deterioration in crop quality. A male farmer in Sampa had harvested his cane on Sunday and Monday having arranged for a driver to collect it on Tuesday to take it to Kyiren Nkwanta market that day. The driver failed to turn up so he went to the junction to find a car but all the drivers there had customers. He managed to sell a little of the cane in Sampa, but since no one in Sampa makes *akpetshie* (local gin), sales were few. By Friday the cane had started to go brown. He managed to sell the remainder but at a much lower price. Losses of this nature are fairly frequent in the village.

Though not all trader problems are transport-related, access to transport figures significantly among the difficulties described by women traders in the off-road villages studied.

THE POTENTIAL OF IMTs FOR WOMEN AND WOMEN'S TRADING ACTIVITIES

Intermediate means of transport (IMTs) use is relatively low in Ghana. Officials in Accra and Cape Coast pessimistically perceive IMTs as unlikely to be acceptable in the coastal areas in comparison with northern Ghana for 'cultural' and topographical reasons and because of the large quantities of goods which have to be transported (Porter, 1998). The results of the small study of IMT acceptability among women in the four off-road study villages in Gomoa are, however, more encouraging.

Photographs of five different types of IMT were shown to a group of eight to twelve women of varying age and economic status in each of the four villages.[1] The women were asked to comment on each of the pictures and then to rank them according to their potential value for use in the village by women. The five photographs were selected to illustrate a range of transport options and were shown in varying order. The photographs shown were:

- the 'kencart', a large-mesh two-wheeled handcart, shown pushed by a woman;
- a tricycle cart, shown piled high with goods and ridden by a man;
- the wheelbarrow, shown by itself laden with what appears to be crop residue;
- the bicycle, shown with a longer than usual flat rear metal carrier and a man, presumably the owner, standing by;
- a shoulder pole, shown with a heavy load being carried by a man.

No pictures were selected to show IMTs involving animal traction since there is little tradition of large animal husbandry in the coastal zone.

Women in all the villages favoured the 'kencart'. They saw it as being a really valuable means of transport for crops from field to village and also onwards to nearby markets. In Adabra, the existing handcart is often in use every day at harvest time, and there is reportedly need for more carts. In Abora women thought the kencart would be useful for moving produce from farms to granaries in the village, and for taking firewood to Apam along the footpath. Women in Lome thought the kencart would be suitable for farm-to-village transport of crops, and even to take crops to the paved road, but they pointed out that there was a stream that had to be crossed to reach many of the more productive farmlands and when this was in full spate it would be impossible to negotiate with a cart. Some women suggested that where paths were too narrow for the cart, it could be parked at the junction with the nearest broad track and would still ease women's work considerably. In these villages it is the men's responsibility to weed and maintain the paths. In the two villages that do not currently have carts, women suggested that the paths could be easily widened to allow passage of the cart. In Adabra and in Lome, where handcarts are being used, access was considered a problem.

The tricycle cart was generally the popular second choice, especially with older women. They saw its potential, like the kencart, for both farm-to-village and village-to-market transport. Women who did not know how to ride could put their goods in and find someone to take it. In Abora, where there is no grinding mill and women walk two miles along the road to Apam Junction to grind their maize two or three times a week, the tricycle was seen as particularly useful.

There was less interest in and comment on the wheelbarrow, though the dealer in Sampa did say that if her car didn't come she could put her goods in it and take it to the junction herself.

The bicycle attracted considerable debate. Its long carrier was admired but only the women in Lome ranked the bicycle above the kencart or the tricycle. Both younger and older women in the other villages felt it had restricted load-carrying capacity, was difficult to ride on uneven farm paths and required tying the load as opposed to simply putting it inside. In Sampa women considered the bicycle impractical for journeys to market, particularly with cassava, because 'bicycles cannot carry a heavy load'. The paths to the farms were also considered too rough for bicycle riding, though 'some young women might use it to go to the farm, but it is men who could use it more than women'. One woman trader from Sampa said, very firmly, that what she needed was a motorcar, not a bicycle! – a view strongly expressed by many men. In Lome, the women thought the bicycle could be used to travel to Swedru if no transport arrived or to go to the next village or their farms. Women did not anticipate any opposition from men if they had bicycles to ride, but many (especially older women) were rather uncertain as to whether they would be able to learn to ride. In Lome it is possible that the views of the group were somewhat influenced by the Chief's niece, who had obviously enjoyed tremendously her one experience of cycling. In Abora women said that children could use the bicycle if they themselves could not ride it. Patience Sam, the woman cycle owner, appears to be a useful role model: a number of young girls have learned to ride her bicycle. She says that when women see her on it they 'admire me and fancy it and at times are surprised; old ladies even encourage me'. It is possible that if women obtained bicycles, for instance through a loan scheme, these would be commandeered by men. Women's ownership would have to be firmly established and a training programme made compulsory so that women were confident about riding bicycles.

The carrying pole was immediately and strongly ridiculed by the women, who thought that 'carrying is better than tying your load to a stick'. They could not imagine any benefits from distribution of the load in this manner and said they would never use anything like it. It did, however, stimulate a discussion on the difficulties of head-loading. In all the villages, pain and discomfort from head-loading was acknowledged. Women said that head-loading is very damaging to the neck – 'you get neck pains, it even goes to the waist' – and that they buy a rub and massage their neck when it is particularly painful. Other women complained of chest, waist and head pains as well as neck pains from head-loading. The common remedy was to buy 50 cedis' worth of paracetamol, then go and sit down somewhere and chew them. Some women described how they prepare an enema from herbs collected from the bush and a little pepper and ginger and use this when the pain from head-loading is particularly severe.

THE POTENTIAL FOR WOMEN-OWNED/RUN
MOTORIZED SERVICES AND IMTs

Only one middle-aged woman in the study has become a transport owner through dint of careful saving of her earnings from grocery trading. The taxi-car she owns was obtained locally for 3.5 million cedis on a 'work and pay' arrangement and is driven by a friend's son. When she has paid for the taxi in full, her ambition is to sell it and buy a minibus. She knows of no other woman who owns motor transport, but this did not deter her from purchasing her vehicle, which she decided to buy because of the problems of reaching the market from Abora. She is clearly an exceptional case: most women in Gomoa have little likelihood of ever accumulating sufficient funds on their own to purchase even a cart or a bicycle.

At the same time there is a fairly widespread concern among the women in all the villages that groups would have difficulty in sharing any motor vehicles or IMTs purchased on a group basis. Some women argued that one person would take the machine, while others thought that if they all agreed then it would be workable.

In the poorer villages, even joint purchase was considered to be beyond women's means. They simply could not envisage ever having sufficient money, even if all the women in the village joined together to purchase a vehicle. No woman in the village has, or knows any other woman who has, a bank account, though they all belong to a woman's Susu credit group, organized by one of the village women, which starts from January and pays out in December for the Christmas celebrations. Women pay in differing amounts and take out according to what they paid in. The woman taxi owner and woman cycle owner in Abora were both viewed as remarkably fortunate.

The concept of joint action is to some extent accepted in Sampa, which appears to be a richer settlement without any Susu groups. Women tend to save individually and a few women have bank accounts. There is the 31st December women's group[2] in town, to which many women belong. There might be an opportunity for some of the better-off women in Sampa to purchase a market vehicle collectively; or, alternatively, it is possible that individual women would have sufficient funds to follow the example of Abora's taxi owner, and might consider this option if made aware of the success of that enterprise.

This suggests that in many villages poverty or lack of experience with group enterprises may inhibit development of women-owned/run motorized transport services and that substantial groundwork would be necessary to ensure the success of any such arrangement. In some villages Susu groups operate and group-based work parties for communal village tasks and for agricultural work (*nnoboa*) are still common. It may be possible to explore and develop ways by which such activities can be extended into group transport initiatives.

CONCLUSION

This chapter has reviewed a range of access-related issues in coastal Ghana with particular reference to their impact on women. Women have the principal responsibility for marketing in this region and were keen to discuss their trading and transport problems. It is clear that access to motorized transport services from and to off-road villages is often extremely restricted and more costly than comparable journeys along paved roads. Traders are regularly disappointed by the late or non-arrival of vehicles on market day, particularly in the wet season, when the roads become impassable. They lose money by their late arrival at the market or through the deterioration of the crop, notably cassava.

IMTs are currently rare in rural Gomoa and almost wholly male owned and operated. The more widespread use of IMTs could assist off-road women in moving crops from farm to village and onwards to local markets, and the majority of women were extremely interested in the photographs of IMTs provided for discussion, even though few saw opportunities for obtaining such equipment themselves, because of their low incomes. They were mostly negative about the concept of group purchase.

NOTES

1. A similar exercise was conducted with groups of men but it is not reported in detail here. The exercise will be repeated in future fieldwork with different groups in order to check these preliminary findings.
2. The 31st December women's group is officially an NGO, but because its president was the wife of Jerry Rawlings, Ghana's former head of state, it is widely perceived in Ghana to be an extension of government.

10

ROAD REHABILITATION:
THE IMPACT ON TRANSPORT
AND ACCESSIBILITY

SOBA DISTRICT, KADUNA STATE, NIGERIA

Mohammed-Bello Yunusa,
E.M. Shaibu-Imodagbe and Y.A. Ambi,
with Aminu Yusuf and Binta Abdul Karim

The assumption that there is a positive relationship between transport infrastructure and development has informed policy interventions in Nigeria. Transport is considered to have a serious impact on agricultural development and is expected to facilitate faster movement of persons, livestock and goods and services at low cost, saving time and financial resources that could be used for other developmental purposes. In Nigeria, Amadi (1988) established a causal relationship between rural road construction and agricultural development by showing that in some rural areas of Anambra state, road construction led to the expansion of markets in terms of greater frequency of market days, increase in the number of buyers and sellers and growth in the volume of transactions. This led to an expansion in farm size and adoption of improved agricultural production techniques. The development of other important infrastructures, particularly electricity and pipe-borne water, also contributed to the increase in both agricultural and non-agricultural business enterprises and to higher levels of income and employment, and reduced the level of rural–urban migration in the area (Amadi, 1988). A more critical appraisal of transport investment in economic and social development sees it as playing a permissive and responsive rather than a proactive role (Howe, 1997a).

A few years back, the Kaduna state government decided to renovate the road linking Soba and Ikara towns and restore the flow of services that might have been lost due to the poor state of the road. There has been no evaluation of the impact of this project. How have the transport needs of the rural population been affected by the reconditioned road?

What economic changes have taken place after the rehabilitation? Has it affected the cost of transportation? Has it affected the distribution of the transport load among members of the household? What is the distribution of the socio-economic benefits of the road along gender lines?

This study aims to examine these questions and to assess the routes and means of transport available to members of the communities before and after rehabilitation of the road; to understand the transport needs, problems and potentials in the communities before and after renovation; and to identify various services and employment opportunities that have reached the communities due to the rehabilitation.

This study can assist policy makers, national and international organizations, NGOs and, in particular, the Kaduna state government to assess the impact of road renovation and to identify how the state government could address some problem areas in order to maximize the welfare effects of the road.

THE STUDY AREA: LUNGU

Lungu is located in Soba Local Government Area (SLGA), which covers approximately 2,955 square kilometres. The area has a tropical climate characterized by two distinct seasons. The rainy season extends from May to September, while the dry season covers the period of October to April. The cold and dusty harmattan wind from the northeast prevails in the area from November to January. Mean annual rainfall is 1099 milimetres, while the lowest temperature during the hot and dry period between February and April is between 102 and 104 degrees Fahrenheit. SLGA is a region within the Northern Guinea Savannah Zone. It is characterized by woodland vegetation with a well-developed grass layer. The natural vegetation has been reduced to farmed parkland occasioned by the economic benefits of tree planting.

The 1991 census puts the population of SLGA at 187,277 people, comprising 95,741 males and 91,536 females. Administratively SLGA of Kaduna State was created in 1989 out of the former Zaria Local Government Area, and further reduced in size in 1991. Presently, SLGA comprises two districts, Soba and Maigana, with Maigana as the administrative headquarters. Each district is headed by a District Head, appointed by the Emir of Zazzau, under the traditional system. The District Heads report to the Emir of Zazzau, while Village and Ward Heads are answerable to the District Heads. There are 16 village heads under Maigana and 17 under Soba.

Lungu is located about midway down the length of the rehabilitated

Soba–Ikara road. The road directly touches on the settlement. 'Lungu Taka Lafiya' village was selected for the survey because of its relatively large size, the heterogeneous nature of its population and proximity to the renovated road. Data were collected through a survey of 125 randomly selected respondents and supported by secondary data from official documents.

ROAD RENOVATION, ACCESSIBILITY AND HOUSEHOLD NEEDS IN LUNGU

Access to medical facilities

The bad road condition affected most villagers' access to medical services. The nearest cottage hospital is at Maigana, which has inadequate facilities and barely trained personnel. Maigana is about 20 kilometres away from Lungu through Soba. A small number of villagers use the private rural clinic for normal ailments, and use local chemists and traditional medicine within the community for treating such endemic diseases as malaria and typhoid. They had no problems of access. But for other villagers, the bad state of the road resulted in problems such as premature delivery and sometimes death due to the very uncomfortable means of transportation to the hospital. After the road's renovation all the men and most of the women agreed that most of these problems were no longer significant. Several women still felt that the renovation of the road had not improved the state of medical services available in the community, because the community still lacked a well-staffed and equipped health delivery institution.

Women were mainly responsible for taking the sick to the hospital before the renovation of the road. After the renovation, men, especially heads of the households, were increasingly involved in taking the sick to the clinic, probably because of improved transportation to a bigger hospital at Maigana, but women continued to have the main responsibility and to bear a higher proportion of the burden of looking after sick members of the household.

Transporting children to school

Before the road's renovation most of the children used to go to school (Arabic or Western) on their own. Men sometimes escorted the children when they were unwilling to go or were too young to find their way. Few women took children to school.

The bad road condition affected the transportation of children to school, particularly those in secondary or higher institutions of learning outside the village. Several families, however, did not send their children to school at all. Since the road renovation more children go to school on their own. The proportion of men escorting children to schools has declined, with a corresponding slight increase in the proportion of women taking children to school. Since most children attend school in the village, the impact of the road has been minimal.

It is the duty of men, particularly household heads, to educate children (in both Quranic-Islamic and Western schools), and as such the male head of the household has greater responsibilities in managing children's school affairs. This accounts for the high involvement of men in this activity.

Collecting water for domestic needs

Water transportation is mainly by foot (62.9 per cent). The use of donkeys, bicycles, ox carts and motorcycles is rather limited. A little over a fifth of the villagers indicated problems of cost and time in collecting water.

Before the road was renovated, water collection was the responsibility of women and girls. Only 17 per cent of men collected water. Women collected water for cooking, washing and drinking. Men were involved in water collection for commercial reasons (as water vendors), or during drought periods when local resources dried up. It is common for men to collect water in households that practise purdah, households that have no wells or households in which there are no children to be sent for water collection. In these households the men either collect the domestic water or buy from water vendors in the village. With the renovation of the road, the involvement of men in water collection declined and the proportion of women involved in water collection marginally increased. It is possible that road renovation led to an increase in the movement and activities of the men, leaving women and children to attend to domestic tasks.

Transportation to the farms

The population of Lungu is predominantly agricultural. Movement of inputs and farm produce to and from the farm depends on its distance from the village. Most of the male farmers (73 per cent) had problems of getting to their farmland due to the bad state of the road. Most of the women do not own farms and do not travel to the men's farms due to purdah or seclusion. However, the 22 per cent of the female respondents (about 17 per cent of the total) who are active farmers also experienced transportation problems to the farms. An added problem for those who own farms (and this excludes a majority of the women) was that poor transportation due to bad road conditions also created a scarcity of hired labour.

Access to grinding mills

The deteriorated road condition had a significant effect on villagers' access to grinding mills. They were spending a lot of time travelling to the mills to process their food and other agricultural products. The bad road caused loss of produce from accidental spilling, forced villagers to pay high transportation costs, and caused heavy wear and tear on their means of transport.

In a majority of the households, children, mainly boys, were largely responsible for taking food items to the grinding mills. In households where women are in purdah and there are no children to send, male heads of household undertook this task. Very few women travelled to the mills; instead many did their own grinding or pounding at home. This trend has not changed with the road renovation, except that a greater number of adult men are now going to the grinding mills, taking larger quantities of grain for milling outside the village.

Access to markets

The deteriorated state of the road meant that many people were not able to go to the market. A few lost large proportions of their produce because they could not market it and there were no storage facilities. The bad road also affected the time spent in travelling, and resulted in high transportation costs, which increased people's financial burden.

Fuelwood collection

Men and boys are the principal collectors of firewood for the household and the burden of fuelwood collection tends to be heavier on men than on women. Unlike domestic water supply, fuelwood has to be collected from distant locations. As a result it is usually procured by male household heads, who sometimes hire transport to bring the wood. A few women still gather fuelwood for household needs.

Before the road was renovated, much of fuelwood transportation was by foot (29 per cent), donkey (11 per cent) or a combination of the two (12 per cent). This changed following road renovation, with only 10 per cent of wood transported on foot; 21 per cent used bicycles, ox carts and/or motorcycles and 12 per cent used taxis and buses. The renovation of the road has facilitated the use of these diverse means of transport.

Refuse collection

Household refuse collection is important to sanitation and health. Women are more involved in collecting and disposing of household refuse. In 67.7 per cent of the sample households before road renovation, women collected and disposed of household refuse. After renovation, the number of men collecting and disposing of household refuse increased significantly (62 per cent of households).

The involvement of men in refuse disposal is likely to be related to the scarcity and high cost of chemical fertilizers, which has made most households dependent on locally generated household refuse as a source of soil supplement and fertility management to raise or sustain agricultural output. While women deal with household refuse for sanitation and hygiene purposes, men gather the refuse for farm application as fertilizer. The availability, after the road's renovation, of transportation facilities to deal with refuse in this way has enabled the sudden takeover of refuse collection and disposal by men.

When the road was in disrepair the most common modes of transporting domestic waste were by foot (44 per cent), by foot and donkey (20 per cent) and by foot, ox cart, donkey, bicycle and motorcycle (8 per cent). After the road renovation, the proportion of people who carry refuse by foot declined to 31 per cent just as the proportion of people who transport refuse by foot and donkeys declined to 6 per cent. The proportion of those who transport refuse by foot, ox cart, donkey, bicycle and motorcycle increased to 19 per cent.

SOCIAL AND ECONOMIC EFFECTS
OF ROAD RENOVATION

Social effects

The renovation of the road did not affect religious activities, engagement in social visits and participation in rotating credit associations and agricultural cooperatives. As before, there was greater male participation in religious activities and in agricultural cooperatives, while women engaged in social visits and participated in religious associations and rotating credit and marketing cooperatives. The role of women in maintaining social values and family ties accounts for the high importance attached to social visits. Rotating credit associations are popular among women as a means of saving to raise capital for their various economic activities.

Gains in economic activities

The renovation of the road led to significant gains in economic activities, in employment, in increased sales of farm produce at higher prices, in access to agricultural inputs at lower prices, and in lower costs of storage and processing of agricultural inputs. Only a small number of men and women did not experience any economic gains.

It should be noted that, generally, political activities were less affected by the bad state of the road than due to the political impasse which has prevailed in Nigeria. Religious activities were least affected because most of the religious facilities for both Christians and Muslims are located in the village studied.

CONCLUSION

This study has revealed different effects on the men and women of Lungu Takalafiya village resulting from the renovation of the Soba–Ikara road.

The bad road resulted in high transportation costs, thus making it expensive to send children to school outside the village, and affected access to medical facilities. Few people could afford the private medical facilities available in the village. Once the road was improved, access to medical facilities and schools outside the village increased. There were no major changes in access to water because of the road, possibly because the water towers are not very far away from the village. Participation in religious and social activities, in associations and in politics was not affected by the state of the road.

A better road led to reductions in costs and travel time and in losses to perishable products and to accidental spillage of grain. It also facilitated the use of intermediate means of transport.

Road renovation has had some impact on the gender allocation of tasks. More men are carrying the sick and accompanying children to clinics and schools outside the village, making use of the improved transport services. Men are also responsible for fuelwood collection and for taking grain to the grinding mills outside the village (within the village this is done by boys). The renovation of the road has improved access to fuelwood and to grinding mills and increased the frequency of travel to the markets and the farms. A good road has made it possible for male farmers to move household refuse to their farms at affordable rates. This has meant an increase in the use of refuse as fertilizer. It has also meant that refuse collection, a task once almost exclusively handled by women, is now also the responsibility of men.

11

GENDER NEEDS AND ACCESS
TO RURAL TRANSPORT

TUYA, YATENGA PROVINCE, BURKINA FASO

Amadou Ouedraogo

Burkina Faso is a landlocked Sahelian country located in the heart of West Africa, with a population of ten million. Facing severe droughts year after year due to poor, unpredictable and badly distributed rainfall, it is one of the poorest countries in the world. About 90 per cent of the population are farmers, working mostly on degraded and barren soils, relying on unpredictable harvests as the only means of subsistence.

Yatenga province is located in the northern part of the country – 186 kilometres away from Ouagadougou, the capital city. Drought is particularly severe here and living conditions are harsh. In this area, where people daily fight for survival, the development of transport means and infrastructure does not appear as a priority. Yet the inadequate transport facilities in Yatenga province dramatically affect trade and the distribution of agricultural produce, increase people's workload and unreasonably consume their time.

Women and men do not experience these difficult conditions equally. Gender relations clearly affect control over transport and the need for access to it. The gender distribution of labour is detrimental to women and yet they have no financial autonomy, and have almost no access to and or control over means of transport. There is a striking discrepancy between women's needs for transport and what is actually available to them. The purpose of this study is to highlight this imbalance.

TRANSPORT FACILITIES IN TUYA VILLAGE IN YATENGA PROVINCE

Tuya is a village of about three thousand inhabitants, located 25 kilometres to the north of Ouahigouya, the chief town of Yatenga province. All of the people in Tuya are farmers, exclusively involved in the production of food crops such as sorghum and millet.

It is a very dry area where farming is an extremely hard and unrewarding activity. People live in a permanent situation of food crisis. The rainy season lasts only four months a year – from June to September. The remaining eight months are dry and no farming activity is possible. During that period, a few people get involved in activities such as petty trading, cattle breeding and gold washing. The rest wait idly till the next rainy season to resume their farmwork.

A primary school was established in the village only ten years ago, accounting for the very low rate of literacy, probably one of the lowest in the country. For various reasons, such as poverty, the small size of the school, and the general tendency of parents to send their children to the farm rather than to school, only one-third of the total number of children attend school.

There is no health centre in the village. The nearest centre is 17 kilometres away, but it is in such poor condition that people instead try to reach Ouahigouya, 25 kilometres away. Sometimes it is impossible even to make the shorter trip.

In the village, there are wells but they are used up as the dry season progresses. Usually there is a shortage of water around April and May. The water available is of such a poor quality that it often causes health problems. The wells are up to 2 or 3 kilometres away.

The village does not have its own market. Instead, it is part of a group of villages served by local periodic markets – that is, markets open in turn in different villages at regular intervals of three days. Within this system, the nearest market for the people of Tuya is 5 kilometres away.

The difficult living conditions of Tuya, as in most parts of the province, are made worse by a very poor transport system and bad access roads, making the village isolated at certain times of the year. Tuya is connected to Ouahigouya only by two roads, or rather paths, both in bad condition. At the boundary of the village, those two paths cross a small river, without a bridge. So, during the rainy season, when the river is full and the surrounding areas flooded, the village is totally isolated. It then becomes impossible to have access to or out of the village, no matter what means of transport are used. Some villagers are unable to reach their farms and the neighbouring villages. The only thing to do is to wait till the water subsides, which takes up to two or three days after heavy rains. When this happens, the village school has to be closed for a few days, since children from the neighbouring villages are unable to attend class. Also during this time it becomes impossible for people to reach markets, which affects trade and exposes the people of Tuya to a shortage of basic commodities and other goods. The biggest crisis is when a person falls sick and has to be taken from the village to hospital. A number of people have died in such circumstances just because it is impossible to cross the river or to use the path.

During the dry season, the river evaporates and its sandy bed is very difficult to cross. So for much of the time, this river surrounding the village is an almost impassable barrier. To cover the 25 kilometres from Tuya to Ouahigouya takes more than an hour, threading one's way through the bush and shrubs, climbing huge rocks, and going through mud and puddles in the rainy season. On that path, bicycles and motorcycles, due to their smaller size and greater manoeuvrability, travel faster than cars. No truck has ever ventured into the village.

The isolation of this village places a limit on economic and agricultural activities, affects the rate of school attendance and increases the death rate.

MEANS OF TRANSPORT

The village is isolated not just because of the bad condition of village transport infrastructure, but also because of the absence of adequate means of transport. First of all, no public transport system is available for travelling to and from the village. To travel out of the village, villagers must have a personal means of transport. The means that are generally used are bicycles, donkeys, animal-drawn carts and motor cycles. It is rare to see four-wheeled motor vehicles travel on that road. Owing to the very low purchasing power of the people in Tuya, bicycles and donkeys are the most commonly used means. The most indigent people are left to walk, even for relatively long distances, up to 30 or 40 kilometres. Donkeys, bicycles and carts are used to transport everything (people, goods, crops, animals, other goods) and they are used to carry excessive loads, far beyond their actual capacity.

Though 96 per cent of the male heads of families own bicycles in Tuya, given the polygamous nature of these families and the large family sizes, there is limited availability of bicycles for use by village residents. The same goes for donkeys and carts. Most people in Tuya would also prefer to own motorcycles or to have access to motorized public transport, which they feel would better meet their needs.

In such a context, when one has to cover about 20 kilometres in one or two hours with a means of transport, or when the same trip is made on foot in three or four hours, the notion of time becomes meaningless.

GENDER ACCESS TO TRANSPORT MEANS

In the village as well as in the whole of Yatenga province, the only economic activity for at least 98 per cent of the male population is farming during the rainy season. So, outside that period, for seven or eight months in a year, most men have no other activity. In very rare cases, some men are involved in trading, cattle and poultry breeding. Some of them, especially the youth, get involved in gold washing and traditional cloth weaving. But for the largest proportion of the male population, the activity period for a whole year covers no more than the four or five months corresponding to the rainy season.

Things are totally different for women. A number of tasks, especially tasks related to their domestic responsibilities, are assigned to them exclusively and permanently. In addition to those permanent tasks, they have to take part in farming activities along with men during the rainy season. Women's farming work is not limited to the family farm. Besides working on the collective farm, they have their own farms, where they usually grow groundnuts, beans and herbs used for cooking. All the tasks that fall on women require constant travel over short or longer distances.

Women are always first to rise, last to go to bed, and are intensely active throughout the day (see box). During the dry season, most women get involved in gold washing, a very hard activity that keeps them busy all day long and requires trips of up to 30 kilometres every day. In terms of volume and intensity, women have to bear a much heavier burden than men. Yet no matter how inequitable the task distribution is, no one in the society has ever questioned it, since it is based on cultural values.

Women's activities require constant travel, with distances to cover varying from 2 to 15 kilometres according to the kind of activity. For an ordinary day in Tuya, distances covered by women can be estimated as follows:

- water collection: 2 to 8 kilometres
- travel to market: 2 to 6 kilometres
- travel to farm: 4 to 8 kilometres.

Women's daily activities

- Wake up very early (4 or 5 a.m.) and start housework
- Fetch water from the well
- Take care of children (food, hygiene, health)
- Go to the market
- Cook the meal
- Transport the meal to the farm
- Work on the family farm
- Work on personal farm
- Collect and transport fuelwood
- Come back home
- Fetch water from the well
- Grind grains by hand
- Do housework
- Take care of children
- Fetch water from the well
- Go to bed late (10 or 11 p.m.)

On average, women travel an estimated 16 to 44 kilometres daily. That distance is even higher when, during the dry season, gold washing replaces farmwork. To cover these distances, women have no means of transport. All distances are covered on foot and nearly all activities – water collection, transport of grain, transport of meals to the farm, transport of fuelwood, transport of goods to and from the market – involve carrying heavy loads on their heads.

Women are therefore permanent walkers and permanent load carriers, even during pregnancy, or when they have a baby to carry. When the family owns a bicycle, a donkey or a cart, those means are the exclusive property of men. Because all women's activities are considered secondary, no means of transport is allocated to them. The injustice of this is most striking when, for example, after a day's work on the farm, on the way back home, men proudly ride their bicyles or donkeys, carrying no load, while women walk, carrying loads on their heads and babies on their backs. Even when the husband is not using the family bicycle or donkey, the wife does not have access to it, either because she cannot use it (bicycle), or because the cultural rules forbid her to use it (donkey).

Table 11.1 illustrates the striking gap between men's and women's ownership of means of transport. All means of transport are almost exclusively

TABLE 11.1 Ownership of means of transport according to gender (per cent of households)

	Men	Women
Bicycle	96	0.02
Donkey	63	0
Cart	60	0
Motorcycle	23	0

owned, controlled and used by men. In Tuya village 96 per cent of the households use a bicycle, 63 per cent the donkey, 60 per cent carts and 23 per cent motorcycles. Donkeys and carts are especially used for carrying huge loads. The cost of a second-hand bicycle usually ranges between 20,000 CFA F (US$40) and 50,000 CFA F (US$100). Very few people can afford a brand new bicycle, which costs at least 70,000 CFA F (US$140). As for donkeys, their cost ranges between 30,000 CFA F (US$60) and 60,000 CFA (US$120) depending on age and breed.

Since people's purchasing power is one of the most important determining factors in the acquisition of a means of transport, it is not surprising that women have almost no access to means of transport. Though finance is certainly not the only limiting factor, all women interviewed pointed it out as one explanation. Women in Yatenga province have no financial autonomy as they are not involved in income-generating activities. Their activities are related mainly to house- and farmwork. Many women have no income at all, or only very insignificant amounts (see Table 11.2), earned from petty trading of groundnuts, beans, leaves, and so on, harvested from their personal farms or from gold washing during the dry season. By participating in farmwork, they contribute to increase the family income, which is under the exclusive and strict control of the male head of the family.

In the dry season women engage in gold washing, a poorly remunerated activity that requires long trips and very hard manual work. Despite the fact that the income is insignificant, gold washing requires no financial investment (unlike trading and weaving); it provides women with their only source of cash income for about eight months of the year. The work

TABLE 11.2 Annual income according to gender

Annual income (CFA F)	Women (%)	Men (%)
0–10,000	89*	3
10,000–20,000	8	67
20,000–50,000	3	25
Over 50,000	0	5

* This figure represents the percentage of women with less than 5,000 CFA F annual income. 500 CFA = US$1 (subject to exchange rate fluctuations).

itself is gendered. Men do the actual digging manually. They make big and deep holes looking for nuggets of gold, and they usually find some, depending on their ability to dig deeply and fast. Women collect the mud extracted from the holes, and pass it through a sieve to obtain a fine dust. Water is then added to that dust and stirred up. The fine particles of gold contained in it are visible in the water and can be collected easily. The gold found is sold on the site to traders who travel there for this purpose. Women control the income received from gold washing, but usually they use that money to contribute to the household expenses, especially for meals and children's care. Though men do not claim this money, women rarely use it for their own personal needs.

Family income from farmwork is sometimes used to purchase means of transport, which only men use. Even when a family can afford more than one bicycle, for example, it will not be seen necessary to have one for the wife. Only one bicycle will be purchased for the husband, and the extra money is used for other purposes. More than one bicycle is bought in a family only when there are adult sons likely to use them. In other words, buying a means of transport for women has never been regarded as necessary. Women themselves seem to be more willing to contribute to purchase a means of transport for their husbands or grown-up sons than to consider buying their own.

In our survey we came across one woman who owns a bicycle. She is involved in a relatively prosperous trade buying and selling traditional clothes and is somewhat financially independent from her husband. But this is an exceptional case.

In Yatenga province, financial reasons alone do not explain the fact that men are the only owners of transport means. Gender access to and use of means of transport are, to a large extent, determined by inflexible cultural rules, as is the gender division of labour. One example is the fact that it is strictly forbidden for women to ride a donkey or a horse. This is a strong and persistent custom that nobody ventures to question. To the many questions we asked about this, we got no satisfactory answer. The most common answer was that this custom has existed for generations and that the only sensible behaviour is to comply with it, since it is to be understood as the will of the ancestors and gods. Indeed, nobody ever tries to understand or explain any rule that is said to be imposed by the ancestors and gods. One just abides by such a rule and contributes to its perpetuation. We received a few answers mentioning the fact that riding a donkey or a horse is believed to incur the risk of young girls losing their virginity, not only because of the specific position taken on the back of the animal but also for some mystical and inexplicable reasons. Anyway, such explanations are unconvincing, since the interdiction to ride a donkey or a horse is not limited only to young girls likely to be virgins, but is extended to all women. Yet, though there are no objective or scientific justifications for such beliefs, people take them for granted. The consequence is that women are limited in their means of transport. Even when a donkey in a given family is not being used by anyone, women are still not allowed to use it. This means that women have to walk while a means of transport is available in their family. Women themselves never question this situation, nor complain about it. They accept it as normal, which shows the overwhelming power of traditions even when they become a source of deprivation in people's lives.

The cultural rules vary from one ethnic group to another. For example, while women in Yatenga province are not allowed to ride a donkey, in some other areas in the country brides receive a donkey as part of the dowry, for their own use. In some ethnic groups, meanwhile, women are not allowed to ride a bicycle.

Women are usually the only victims of cultural rules. Cultural rules are rarely unfavourable to men. In this case cultural rules limit women's access to means of transport and no one challenges them.

CONCLUSION

The study shows plainly that access to and control over the existing infrastructures and means of transport are largely influenced by gender. Women in Yatenga province suffer from various forms of injustice that seriously hamper their access to transport and affect their mobility. The first is the unfair division of labour. The second relates to women's unfavourable financial situation. The third is the constraints imposed on women by cultural rules. All this contributes to a vicious circle – not having access to transport prevents women from saving enough time to get involved in income-generating activities; and not getting involved in such activities prevents them from attaining the financial autonomy likely to enable them to afford a means of transport. In other words, women do not own means of transport because of their poverty, and they are poor because they do not own means of transport.

The study also shows that men and women have different transport needs. Women spend more time on transport activities than do men because of their reproductive and domestic responsibilities, and their workload is increased by their low access to transport. And indeed, the time and effort spent by women on transport activities are an impediment to their using time more productively in other activities.

Planners and policy makers should see transport in Yatenga province as a priority, as a basic factor of development. They ought to be aware that women and men have different needs and strive to achieve equality in meeting these needs. Planned interventions should take account of women's interests and perspectives and a more substantial effort should be made to promote women's access to transport. There is a need to support women to increase their financial autonomy as well as to have a clear understanding of local traditions, with a view to encouraging people to be critical towards some of their own beliefs and to convince them to give up unjustified taboos such as forbidding women to ride donkeys. Promoting intermediate means of transport and implementing non-transport interventions such as installing improved water supplies should also be considered.

To attain positive results from those suggestions, there is need to conduct further studies and surveys, especially those based on participatory approaches, so that the beneficiaries can analyse their own situation, express their deepest concerns and specific needs, and ultimately be fully involved in the search for solutions.

12

WOMEN'S EMPOWERMENT AND PHYSICAL MOBILITY

IMPLICATIONS FOR DEVELOPING RURAL TRANSPORT, BANGLADESH

Nilufar Matin, Mahjabeen Mukib, Hasina Begum and Delwara Khanam

The issue of spatial mobility is inextricably linked to the social and economic empowerment of women. Access to transport facilities by men and women is unequal and in many cases discriminatory to women. Restrictions on the physical movement of women define their entitlements to income and employment opportunities and to other services like education and health. Lack of access to safe and secure transport also impinges upon the physical security of women outside their immediate surroundings, reinforcing the cultural restrictions traditionally imposed on them.

In Bangladesh, studies on gender issues in transport are a relatively under-explored area. In our study we analyse the gender aspects of transport in the context of rural Bangladesh, relating rural women's practical need for mobility to the question of their social empowerment.

The study collected qualitative data using methods of participatory rural appraisal (PRA) in villages in two geographical regions, Faridpur and Netrokona. Faridpur is located in the central-south floodplain region of the country and Netrokona in the relatively dry and arid northern zone. In each region, accessibility was the basis for the selection of the villages. Villages that were within 2 kilometres of the paved road were termed 'easy access'. These villages have access to motorized transport. Villages further away from paved roads which could only be reached by earthen tracks and using non-motorized means were considered 'remote'.

TRANSPORT PROVISION IN BANGLADESH

The transport network comprises rail, road, water and air transport. In both urban and rural areas, motorized and non-motorized modes of transport are used such as trains, cars, buses, trucks, auto rickshaws, rickshaws, rickshaw vans, pushcarts, animal-driven carts, mechanized boats, and various forms of country boats (built and operated in the informal sector). Non-motorized modes of transport are the most important component of the transport system in Bangladesh. In 1986 they accounted for 94 per cent of all commercially operated vehicles and two-thirds of the total carrying capacity (Dawson and Barwell, 1993). Most rural transport is dependent on non-motorized means, and pedestrian traffic still dominates.

The construction, development and maintenance of road infrastructure are the responsibility of the government, but the private sector dominates the operation of different types of vehicles. Almost all buses, almost the total truck fleet and over 90 per cent of passenger and cargo vessels are privately owned. The private sector also operates a large number of non-motorized vessels, like country boats, for both passengers and cargo in different regions of the country.

Transport in Bangladesh is largely influenced by the topographical and climatic conditions of the country and is characterized by its seasonality. The country can be divided into the regularly flooded regions of the south and the relatively high non-flooded regions of the north and east.

All-weather roads have to be built high enough to keep them flood-free. Earthern roads, used by a large proportion of the rural population, are submerged during monsoon flooding and remain muddy for a considerable part of the year, accounting for the large expense in improving rural road networks.

In the easy-access rural areas, bus, rickshaw, bicycle, *tempo* (auto rickshaw), rickshaw van and, during the monsoon season, country boat and engine boat are available. Railways may also sometimes connect villages. In remote rural areas, the modes are mostly rickshaw van and, during the monsoon season, country boat or *donga*, a canoe made from the hollow trunk of a palm tree

TRANSPORT POLICIES: ASSUMPTIONS, PRIORITIES AND PROVISIONS

Government planning documents consider the alleviation of poverty and the creation of job opportunities as the main objectives of the transport sector (Government of Bangladesh, 1990). The government strategy proposes extending the existing transport network on the basis of economic viability, improving water transport and promoting private sector participation. The policy emphasizes investment in physical infrastructure for motorized vehicles, and the choice of new projects is determined by economic considerations only.

The Roads and Highways Department (RHD) and local government institutions are in charge of road infrastructure development in both urban and rural areas. The road network under RHD comprises national highways,[1] regional highways[2] and feeder roads.[3] Local government institutions, on the other hand, have the responsibility for construction and maintenance of feeder roads connecting villages and farms to local markets and union headquarters, as well as roads between villages and within a village.

GENDER ROLES IN BANGLADESH

Women's roles in Bangladesh, as elsewhere in the world, originate in traditions of patriarchy, custom and religion that have sanctioned subordination and seclusion of women in both private and public spheres. This social and cultural inheritance interacts with macro-economic and political forces and determines the parameters within which women are expected to operate.

Bangladeshi women face a rigid gender division of labour, where they remain responsible for reproductive activities needed to sustain their families. The domain of productive activities belongs to men. Women's position is inside the home and it is not considered appropriate for them to step beyond the homestead. Women's mobility and movements are considered a significant measure of a family's *izzat* (respectability and honour). Such a clear division of gender role and responsibilities, in both economic and social terms, largely restricts women's mobility. The ideal woman is seen as one who does not leave her home except for socially accepted purposes, like visiting the parental home, attending relatives' weddings, or going on pilgrimages.

But social norms governing women's mobility are not monolithic. Society's acceptance or rejection of women's mobility varies according to the social status, education or age of the women, the means of transport used, and the purpose of movement. In general, women who come from poorer or destitute families face fewer restrictions on their mobility than do more well-to-do women. While there are few social injunctions against poorer, abandoned or destitute women going to trade in the marketplace or to work in road construction or in agricultural fields, women from more well-off backgrounds are expected to limit their employment-related travel to schoolteaching or professional work in an office. In the case of women from upper- and middle-income groups, employment in such 'open', 'public' environments is taboo.

The village studies present a rather complex picture of how the various economic, climatic and cultural conditions affect women's spatial mobility and restrict their access to livelihood opportunities. There are cases where socio-economic and cultural factors have restricted women's access to transport facilities. There are also cases where women have been able to break through the barriers and have established increased spatial mobility as a means to empowerment. In these cases, with minimum aid from outside institutions, successful women, irrespective of their socio-economic status, have confronted restrictive social attitudes that inhibit their mobility. Their experience reveals the potential for change in the rural social culture.

FARIDPUR

Faridpur district is located along the southwest bank of Padma river. Faridpur town is 145 kilometres from the capital, Dhaka. The district comprises 2,072 square kilometres, of which about 5 per cent is riverine. It comprises a total of nine *thanas*, or administrative units. For this study, data were collected from two *thanas*, namely Char Bhadrasan and Nagarkanda.

Easy-access area: Badulya Matbardangi

Means of transport

The village is located in Char Bhadrasan union and *thana*. A 1-kilometre road, recently paved, usable in the rainy season, connects it to the union centre of Char Bhadrasan. Now people can travel in *tempos*, rickshaws and buses throughout the year. The bus fare is Tk 1 up to the union centre, and the rickshaw fare Tk 4–5. The village is accessible by the river. During the rainy season, people make long-distance social or business trips by waterways. It is also convenient to travel to Dhaka by the waterway. It takes only three hours by boat and costs Tk 30 (travel by road costs Tk 60–70). During the dry season, when *chars*, or sand bars, surface in the river, a locally made mode of transport called *tuli* is used, made by attaching a body of a truck to a tractor. Since the village is accessible both by roads and by waterways, it is convenient for traders.

Social context

In the 1991 population census, there were 139 households in the village. The number of households has increased substantially since then but it is not possible to say by how much. The women participants of the PRA sessions categorized the village households into three socio-economic groups: rich (8 per cent), middle-class (34 per cent) and poor (58 per cent).

The rich and middle-class families depend on agricultural land and remittances from migrant members. The poor families own only homestead land and mostly earn their living from petty trading in grocery and work in the transport sector, such as driving rickshaws and rickshaw vans. There are four female-headed households. These women work as road construction workers and as housemaids. Women of other poor households do not work outside their homesteads but are engaged in home-based income-generating activities. Many of them are members of NGO-led groups and have received credit and skill training for activities like poultry and livestock rearing.

Some village women, most of whom are widows or those who have been abandoned by their husbands, work in Dhaka in the garment factories, or as housemaids and construction workers. Others have gone to Dhaka because their husbands work in the factories or pull rickshaws.

Since the construction of the road, men have been more involved locally in income-generating activities and travel regularly to the union centre for work. They have received credit to purchase rickshaws and rickshaw vans. There are 10 to 15 rickshaws, 15 to 20 rickshaw vans, and 10 to 12 bicycles in the village. They are all owned by men. No one in the village owns a bus or a truck.

Women's mobility

A majority of the poor women of the village travel to the union centre in connection with the income-generating activities in which they are involved. Most women walk but some take *tempos*, which cost them Tk 2 for a return trip. For training in Faridpur they take a bus. The fare is Tk 20 for a return trip.

Social restrictions prohibit women from getting onto public transport along with men. Women are pushed aside by men when they use buses during rush hours. It is more difficult for women if they have to carry young children with them. There are only a few seats reserved for women; when these are full the bus conductors do not take them, and the women wait a long time for the next bus. So women often use rickshaws or rickshaw vans, which are relatively expensive.

Agricultural families obtain their fuelwood requirement mostly from crop residues. Women and children collect fuel such as dry branches and leaves from trees and cow dung. The landless families have to buy fuelwood. One *maund* of wood (35 kilograms) costs Tk 40. A household of ten people requires six to eight *maunds* of wood every month. The male members of the family purchase this from the market and transport it using a rickshaw van. According to the women, fuel collection is not a burden as they do not need to travel far, but it is costly to buy.

Women and girls collect water for domestic use. Water collection is not a problem because some households have their own tubewells, and for those who do not the river is nearby and there are tubewells available in the neighbourhood. Women usually walk to collect water; it does not cost any money.

The village women, irrespective of their socio-economic status, often go to movie theatres at the union centre. Women can pay for movies themselves with the money earned from income-generating activities. Young girls mentioned their interest in the circus. They go to the circus in the company of a senior male member of the family, usually an elder brother.

Economic opportunities   Since the road was paved, poor women have engaged more in various income-generating activities. Better transport has made it easier for government and non-government organizations to initiate active programmes in the village and has enabled women to go to

---

Rahima, a mother of four (three daughters and a son), is in her late twenties. Abandoned by her husband, she started out by trying to make a living with stereotypical 'women's' activities: tailoring and embroidering. Predictably, the income was not enough to make ends meet, forcing her to turn to petty trade. She now sells vegetables and rice, which are in good demand and provide a steady income, just enough to keep her and her family in food, shelter and clothes. Rahima joined an NGO two or three years ago to improve her access to credit and training in small business management. She is a somewhat controversial figure because she owns and rides a bicycle. The bicycle is a boon to her, allowing her to travel further to sell her goods, saves her time and the cost of travelling by rickshaw van. While many in the village criticize her for being 'forward' and find it 'shameless' that a woman should be riding a bicycle, her father and sisters defend her on the ground that her husband was a wastrel who left her no choice but to 'bring herself into disrepute' in order to provide for her children and herself.

these agencies at the union centre for training and for credit transactions. Their husbands and other male members help them obtain raw materials and market their products. Widowed and elderly women work as earth workers in road maintenance. Before the road was built, women did not have access to credit and income-generating activities.

Poor women are willing to work in offices or factories if they are located nearby and they can return home daily. They cannot travel too far from home because they have other household responsibilities. Travelling from this village is not a problem as various affordable modes of transport were available, but using them along with men was difficult.

Education   The village does not have a school. All educational institutions are located at the union centre, a kilometre away. Neighbouring villages have primary schools, but because they are submerged during the monsoon the villagers prefer to send their children to the union centre. It takes 20–25 minutes to walk, and those who can afford it take a rickshaw, bus or *tempo*. Rickshaws cost Tk 8 for a return trip whereas *tempos* and buses cost Tk 2. Most girls and boys, however, walk to their schools and colleges. Small children are accompanied by their elder brothers and sisters or walk in a group with other children. The availability of bicycles in some households has enabled schoolgirls to learn how to ride and to use them for travel to and from school. These girls are willing to continue cycling when they become adults and have a job.

Selina is the daughter of a village schoolteacher. Ten or twelve years ago, there was no high school in her village so she attended a high school in the town of Faridpur. She scandalized her neighbours and relatives by riding a bicycle daily to and from school. Her father was frequently warned that this flouting of social norms of modesty would lead to his daughter ending up as a spinster. Fortunately for Selina, on her way to her school on the bicycle, a police officer fell in love with her and now she is happily married to him.

Medha pensively recalls that, as a child, she so much wanted to go to school. However, there was no school close by, her family was too poor, and society did not consider it important for a girl to study. Now that there is an adult literacy centre in the village, she is partially able to fulfil her dreams and learn how to read and write. Medha has three daughters, all of whom go to school. She vows to allow her daughters to continue their education as far as they want. She wants them to have office jobs after they finish studying. She wants to see her dreams fulfilled through her daughters.

More girls than boys from this village go to high school as girls receive free tuition, scholarships and other government support. Boys work with their fathers as agricultural labourers or in business. Security on the road has not been a problem for girls travelling to and from schools and colleges.

Two adult literacy centres were established in the village recently under the government programme for mass literacy. Villagers were enthusiastic about these centres. Adults who did not have opportunities to go to school are now able to learn how to read, write and count. Since these centres are located in the village, the villagers are spared long travel. Women studied in the afternoons, men in the evenings.

Health   Because the village is near and well connected to the union centre, it is not difficult to see a doctor or visit a hospital there. For severe illnesses, the villagers sometimes go to a hospital at the district centre. Women pay for their own treatment from their own income; sometimes their husbands also pay.

Remote area: Mridha Para

Mridha Para is a remote village in Bhawal union in the district of Faridpur. The village is located across a big field, around half a kilometre across, at the far end of a one-and-a-half-kilometre-long herringbone brick road that runs from the union centre. This is the only way to reach the village. During the monsoon, the field is submerged and has to be crossed by boat. The road links the village to a big market called Salta Bazaar.

Means of transport

Country boats and rickshaw vans are the only modes of transport. There are only three bicycles and three rickshaw vans in the village, but during the five to six months of the rainy season the only means of communication are the country boat and *donga*. Rich families have their own boats and the poor use the *donga*. Most people grow palm trees in their homesteads for the purpose of *donga* construction. In the rainy season, villagers, particularly women, hardly go out. Children are in danger of drowning and often, especially girls, do not go to school. There is hardly any work for men. Government health workers do not come to Mridha Para, so infant immunizations cannot be completed, and health and family planning services do not reach the village. Most NGOs are reluctant to operate their credit programmes as they know that the village remains isolated for half the year. Women have almost no employment and income opportunities. Bad communication also prevents them from attending training programmes.

Social context

The village comprises seven neighbourhoods. Information was collected on 60 families. Women categorized the families into four socio-economic classes: rich, middle, poor and landless. There are 3 rich families, who own land ranging from 10 to 20 acres; 7 middle class families, each owning land from 3 to 10 acres; 25 poor families, owning land up to 3 acres; and 25 'landless' families, owning little or no land.

The rich families are very influential and form a village elite who make all the decisions for the village. The poorer villagers are usually not allowed in their houses or to use their tubewells. The poor in the village grow food that lasts for three to four months a year. They survive by selling labour and taking jobs outside the village. The landless group hardly eat two meals a day. Most of the time they work in different places outside the village. There are about 10 to 12 female-headed households in this group. Four of them beg in the village, four have left the village to live with their parents, and the others have gone to Dhaka to work either as housemaids or as garment workers.

Two NGOs have their development activities in the village. Almost all the poor households have become members of these groups. Two men have also borrowed money to purchase rickshaw vans.

Women's mobility

Women in this village are not involved in any income-generating activities and are not permitted to do any agricultural activities in the field. They cannot rear livestock or poultry as they do not have access to veterinary services. The society has very restrictive rules for women, and they are not allowed to move outside their homestead. Despite these conservative attitudes, some women are working in garment factories in Dhaka and some work in India.

About a decade ago, a number of women went to India looking for better jobs. After a while some came back because they found it difficult to adjust to a new country. They faced serious sanctions for having violated the norms of purdah, which required them to stay village-bound. The village elite and leaders decided that all of the returnees would be treated to a public shaming, which took the form of twenty-five lashes with shoes (*juta mara*) – the ultimate form of public humiliation.

Women do not travel outside home to collect fuel. They usually use domestically available dry leaves, branches and cow dung. Men collect fuel from agricultural fields. During the jute harvest, women dry jute stems and store them for use as fuel.

Most of the families have their own tubewell for water. Because the village is so remote, if a tubewell breaks down, it takes a long time to repair it. Women then have to ask their neighbours for water.

Women of this village do not go to marketplaces. They wait for the vendors to come to them and depend on their husbands or other male members to help them get their essentials as well as items like cosmetics and ornaments. Women's social visits are also rare. They do not go anywhere for entertainment. They only visit their closest neighbours and listen to religious preaching.

Economic opportunities   There are no income or employment opportunities for women. A majority of women were reluctant to face social

---

Santa became destitute after the sudden death of her husband, a rice trader, seven years ago, left her with five sons. When her husband was alive, it was relatively easy for her to manage her family and she had never felt the need to work. Things changed drastically after widowhood. She had to send her three elder sons away to work as domestic servants in other people's houses. Even so, it is a struggle to make ends meet and take care of her two younger sons. She herself works as a domestic servant and, when the opportunity arises, takes up employment in 'earth work' – that is, in digging and hauling earth at road construction sites in her village. An object of pity in her community, she lives in constant dread of social repercussions were she to do anything in the least way unconventional. She avoids going to the market and sends her sons or her elderly mother or one of her brothers, who is a rickshaw van driver, to do the shopping. While willing to become associated with an NGO, she has neither the time nor the membership dues needed to become a member of a NGO-sponsored women's group.

Moni was separated from her husband fifteen years ago. She and her two children, a son and daughter, live with her father. He is old and works as an agricultural day labourer. Moni has never been to school. She sends her son to the local primary school but does not think it important to educate her daughter. Economic necessity forces her sometimes to lend a hand to her father working in the agricultural field – once a taboo for women. Three years ago she became a member of a local NGO and got a loan to raise goats. Moni likes to play it safe. As long as it does not involve working outside the homestead, she is willing to take up any other form of income-earning activity. She fears social repercussions and does not want to compromise her chance of marrying off her daughter.

sanctions for working outside their homestead, despite their poverty. They expressed a preference for better job opportunities for their husbands and other male members of the family.

Health   Women try to tolerate any illness as long as they can. Their husbands see a doctor in Salta Bazaar, and get medicine for them. They are taken to the hospital at the *thana* centre or the district centre only if the illness becomes life-threatening. They receive hardly any visits from health workers. Traditional birth attendants help in childbirth. If there are complications, the rich can afford to go to a hospital but poor women often do not have this option. As women do not have independent income, they depend on their husbands to bear the cost of their treatment.

Education   There is no primary or high school in the village, and, because of difficult access, children cannot go to schools in the neighbouring village or at the union or *thana* centres. Only 50 per cent of all children go to primary school, and do so only six months in a year. Only 3 per cent of the girls have studied beyond the primary level, with social attitudes also acting as a serious barrier for girls to attend schools in neighbouring villages.

NETROKONA

Netrokona is located in the relatively dry northern part of the country, adjacent to the Garo hills. The total area of the district is 2,810 square kilometres, of which less than 1 per cent is riverine. The district has about 9 square kilometres of forest. The district has 10 *thanas* and 86 unions. Our study villages are located in Durgapur *thana* and cover four unions, namely Chandigar, Birisiri, Durgapur and Kakairgara.

The majority of the population in these villages are Bengali but there are Garo and Hajong neighbourhoods as well. This ethnic feature has considerable social influence on the culture of the entire area as Garo and Hajong women are known for their relative freedom of movement compared to their Bengali counterparts.

Easy-access area: Majhiali

Means of transport

The village is located along a brick road constructed in the mid-1990s. Rickshaws, rickshaw vans and bicycles travel on this road all the year round and there is the occasional bus or *tempo*. There are about 40 rickshaws on the road, 25 of which are owned by the villagers, bought with credit from NGOs. Women took credit to purchase these rickshaws for their husbands to operate. There are 8 to 10 bicycles used by men.

The road remains usable throughout the year and there are no seasonal variations in transport cost. The village does not have access to any waterway. According to the villagers, even though the poor cannot afford to use any means of transport, the road has made it easier for them to walk to the places to which they want to go.

Social context

Majhiali is a village under Chandigar union in the district of Netrokona. According to the villagers there are 185 families living in the village. Only 10 rich families own land up to 4 acres; 25 families own about 2 acres. The large majority have very little or no land.

The rich families can support themselves throughout the year with the produce of their land. Some members of their families are also engaged in office jobs in the village or outside. The middle-income group can support themselves with the produce of their land for half a year. They are also engaged in trading. The herringbone brick road has made it convenient to travel to different marketplaces in the district.

The poor families are mostly casual labourers and rickshaw or rickshaw-van pullers. A large number of women have become members of a local NGO. This has enabled them to access credit and to start income-earning activities. There are ten widows. Most of them live with their sons or father, who provide for them. Only two widow families have to fend for themselves. These women work as housemaids.

Women's mobility

Women in this village enjoy considerable freedom of movement. Nearly all women, the poor as well as the better-off, are engaged in various economic activities. Both Bengali and Garo women are engaged in agriculture and as vendors and traders in the marketplaces. They go to the NGO office in Durgapur to get credit and training. They also go to Durgapur market, which is 4 kilometres away, to purchase essentials. Many travel as far as Dhaka and the neighbouring district of Mymensingh to purchase and sell goods. Women mostly trade in saris, soap, oil, cosmetics, toys for children, spices and processed food items. Women traders frequently travel to twelve villages and markets covering a distance ranging from 3 to 10 kilometres. Poorer women have less access to far-off markets as they cannot afford the rickshaw costs.

Men who are involved in trading also travel to the surrounding markets and villages. They mostly trade in paddy, vegetables, grocery and livestock.

Women gather their fuel from agricultural fields, and collect dry leaves and branches as well as cow dung from in and around the village. Hardly anybody buys fuel. Water collection is also the responsibility of women. Since there are very few tubewells in their village and those are privately owned, not all villagers have access to tubewell water. The village is located in the drier northern zone of the country, so there are not many ponds or canals. During the rainy season, women collect rainwater for domestic use, but for drinking water they still have to depend on tubewells. Water collection is a problem for poorer women who do not have tubewells. They have to travel to houses where people are willing to let others use their tubewells.

Both men and women go to marketplaces to buy household essentials. They usually walk to Koran Khola Bazaar, which is a kilometre away. In this village women do not face any social problems or criticism if they go to the market or travel to any other places such as the adjoining district. However, it is the middle-income and poorer women who walk to the market, not the women from richer households.

Economic opportunities   Poor women have access to credit from NGOs and do various economic activities such as rice husking, livestock and poultry rearing, and selling textile items and processed food or cosmetics from door to door. Women in the village are very willing to work but they find that the transport cost is too high for them. They feel that a bus service running from their village would be affordable. In a rickshaw the cost is Tk 3 per kilometre whereas by bus it is Tk 1.

Education   The primary schools are between 1 and 4 kilometres away and the nearest high school is 4 kilometres away. Children walk to school in groups. About 80 per cent of the boys and girls of the village go to the primary school but only 25 per cent of the girls make it to high school. The reason is the distance. It becomes expensive if the girls use rickshaws to go to school. However, as the road is now brick-laid and does not become so muddy as it previously did, more girls are going to high school. There is one adult literacy centre in the village, which accommodates thirty women at a time.

Health   Discrimination in terms of health care is not very pronounced. Given the presence of an NGO run by a doctor, villagers have come to accept that both women and men have an equal right to treatment and

Sultana is a woman of 45. At the age of 13, she was married into a well-off farmer's family. After two to three years of her marriage her husband took another wife. Shortly after, the new wife left, but he went on to acquire two more. These successive marriages drained the husband's resources, while he continued to have children with Sultana. She has three surviving children. Finding it difficult to make ends meet, Sultana borrowed Tk 300 from her father and started selling spices, pickles and snacks door to door. She did well but realized that selling saris and clothes was much more profitable, and switched over to selling clothing. She has done well and even managed to buy some agricultural land. Her husband now lives with her and works on her land.

Topoti, now 48, became a widow ten years ago. Her husband was an agricultural day labourer and left nothing for his family. Her son used to work as a day labourer too but did not earn enough to take care of his mother and three sisters. Topoti started work as a maid in other people's houses. Working as a maid was drudgery and Topoti soon fell sick. When she went to see a doctor, the doctor suggested that she take up selling bread from door to door. She started with only Tk 30 as working capital and made a daily profit of Tk 10. She was frugal and forced herself to save Tk 1 or 2 every day and soon had TK 100 in savings. This she used to diversify into other processed food. She also widened her search for customers and travelled to other villages to sell her products. She is now an established vendor, has successfully married off three daughters, and is no longer dependent on her son. When asked if she had faced any negative attitudes to her trading activities from the village, her reply was, why should she care about society when she did not expect it to feed her?

Nilima goes to a college which is 16 kilometres from her village. It is not possible for her to walk the distance and a rickshaw would cost her Tk 40 every day. Although her father is quite well-off, it's difficult for him to pay this. As a solution, she opted to buy a bicycle. Her father agreed and her brothers, who work in the army, taught her how to ride. Naturally, she had to face intense criticism from the village but she ignored it. Riding the bicycle to college every day saved not only money but time as well. It has made it possible for her to run errands for the family, who now turn to her whenever they need something from the pharmacy or other shops. Nilima thinks that she has been able to set an example for other women and has been able to change society's attitudes towards women riding bicycles.

good health. If the illness is not that serious, they walk to Chandigar Bazaar, 2 kilometres away, where there is a village doctor. In the case of more serious illness, they go to the doctor in Durgapur or to the hospital in Birisiri. These places are 5 and 6 kilometres away, respectively, and cost Tk 30–40 for a return trip by rickshaw.

Social visits and entertainment   The major social visit and also entertainment for a woman is to go to her parental village. If it is in the region, women usually walk, or, if there is a road, they take a rickshaw. Women cannot justify spending Tk 30 on the rickshaw fare for entertainment in Durgapur, 5 kilometres away, but they watch television with their neighbours.

Remote area: Bhabanipur

Means of transport

This is a village located in Durgapur *thana* of the District of Netrokona. It is situated 7 kilometres away from the *thana* centre. From the *thana* centre there is one kilometre of paved road, a damaged culvert where the paved road ends, and after that a 1 kilometre earthen road that leads to a hilly spring called Someshwari. After crossing the river and travelling three kilometres on a herringbone brick road to a village called 'Tin Hali', an earthen road goes up to Bhabanipur village another 3 kilometres away. In Bhabanipur people mostly walk or use bicycles. There are some rickshaws. There are 20–25 bicycles in the village that are used exclusively by men.

Social context

There are in total 65 households dispersed around the village, belonging mainly to the Garo and Hajong ethnic communities. There are some Bengali houses too. The Garo population is predominantly Christian, the Hajongs are Hindus and the Bengali families are Muslims. The village lies at the end of the Garo hills bordering India, and the villagers regularly travel between India and Bangladesh to gather forest products for sale.

In Garo and Hajong society, women, both rich and poor, work outside the home and have access to means of production, like land. Garo society is matrilineal and inheritance is passed from mother to daughter. This has given women much more power and control over their lives compared to their Bengali counterparts. Women are freer in their movements and social restrictions experienced in other villages are much less evident.

Villagers categorized the households into three socio-economic classes: rich, middle class and poor. Eight rich families own land ranging from 5 acres to 8 acres. They are better educated and are involved in various trading activities between India and Bangladesh. The middle-income households own land ranging from 1 acre to 3 acres. They cultivate their own land and work on other people's land as sharecroppers. They can support themselves throughout the year by agricultural activities alone.

There are 41 poor families and some of them are female-headed. Some own land up to half an acre but most are landless. They work as agriculture day labourers and do petty trading in forest goods and other essential items.

Women's mobility

Since the women here are mostly engaged in income-earning activities, they have to travel quite a distance. They take their harvest to various marketplaces located at distances ranging from 3 kilometres to 8 kilometres. The usual load that they carry on their head ranges from 20 to 40 kilograms. If it is heavier, they take a rickshaw. They also head-load timber. Timber collection is a women's job, and women walk as far as 7 kilometres for timber collection.

Men usually travel by bicycle. Those who do not have a bicycle or cannot afford a rickshaw have to walk.

Fuel collection is women's responsibility irrespective of their ethnicity. They usually use the by-products of the timber they collect for sale as their fuel. Collection of water is also women's responsibility and is time-consuming. There are only five tubewells in the village and that is not enough. The tubewell water is so iron-rich that it is undrinkable, so women have to collect water from a spring in the hills.

Women say that the improvement of roads and communication needs to be addressed. They find it particularly difficult to travel for work and business purposes and feel insecure if they are to travel a long distance alone. It takes about two hours by foot to the *thana* centre, which is 8 kilometres away, and one and a half hours by rickshaw. Men do not have any major problem as they have access to bicycles.

Employment Women are willing to work and there are no social or cultural barriers to their employment. But employment opportunities for the poor are limited to agricultural labour or petty trading in timber and other forest products.

Education Children go to different schools, which are located at distances ranging from 2 to 12 kilometres. Most of the time they walk, and if they take a rickshaw it costs Tk 20 to 30 for a return trip. There is no discrimination against girls going to school. Girls are usually more interested in continuing their education. Two girls from the village study in a college and also work as agricultural labourers. Despite the remoteness of this village, the literacy rate is around 30 per cent. There are a couple of NGOs that have adult literacy programmes.

Health The nearest hospital is at the *thana* centre or at Birisiri, which is 12 kilometres from the village. There are hardly any facilities in the village for birth delivery and it is almost impossible to take a pregnant woman at her advanced stage to the *thana* centre. However, government health workers visit the village regularly for family planning and immunization of children. Some primary health care and sanitation are provided by the NGOs.

Social visits and entertainment Women of the village go to the church or temple within a distance of 1 kilometre. They also walk to their parental homes in and around the village. Occasionally, they go to cinemas in a group in the *thana* centre.

TRANSPORT PROBLEMS: WOMEN'S PERSPECTIVE

Table 12.1 attempts to capture the transport problems as presented by women in the communities studied. Some problems were found to be common to women of different positions, while there were other problems specific to particular social categories of women.

MOBILITY AND ENTITLEMENTS

Physical mobility is rarely recognized as a fundamental aspect of women's human rights. Yet it is a precondition for women's ability to activate – enable – their other rights and entitlements, whether to political participation, employment, education or health. Therefore, recognition of women's right to mobility has traditionally been a point of contention, and negotiation, in the history of Bengali society.

For social acceptance or rejection, the means of transport used is also important. Mobility is less resented if the transport is owned by the family or where a woman's modesty is not violated. For example, availability of rickshaws or of women's bus services has always helped to ease the restrictions.

The purpose of mobility is the other factor shaping social attitudes. Society's reaction seems to vary according to whether the purpose of a women's travel is socially approved. Women's movement out of the homestead boundary is thoroughly scrutinized. Social approval for employment-related travel is reserved for 'respectable' professions or jobs with a 'high' income. The large number of women workers in the garment sector shows social acceptance of a form of employment that is unconventional but brings in a profitable earning.

TABLE 12.1   Transport-related problems

Women in easy-access villages	Women in remote villages

Women in easy-access villages

- Question of security in travel restricts girls' education and women's social visits.
- Absence of separate and low-cost transport facilities for girls and women.

Women in remote villages

- Inadequate access makes it difficult to arrange marriages for girls.
- Social norms regarding mobility are more restrictive for women.
- Women feel isolated because they cannot make social visits, such as visits to parental homes.
- Accessing health facilities is difficult and expensive.
- Government and NGOs find it difficult to access remote villages.

Women in riverine flood plain region (Faridpur)

- Preference for education is given to boys as it is expensive to travel, particularly to high schools and colleges.
- Social restrictions prevent women from travelling to centres of employment.
- As women's needs are least prioritized, access to health services is almost fully denied to most.
- Absence of a separate and affordable transport system for girls and women reinforces social barriers against mobility.

Women in dry and hilly region (Netrokona)

- Inadequate job opportunities for women due to difficult transport.
- Expense and insecurity of travel to educational institutions make them inaccessible for girls.
- Absence of separate and affordable transport facilities for women.
- Despite absence of social restrictions, travelling to distant services and social visits is difficult and expensive.

Poor women

- Available transport is expensive.
- Absence of separate and appropriate transport and travelling facilities for women and girls.
- Difficult for a girl to continue education after primary school.
- Inadequate employment opportunities: most local jobs are low-paid, low-status menial jobs.
- Prohibitive expenses to visit parental home.

Rich women

- Mobility of women and adolescent girls is linked to family honour.
- Given the transport problems, women require stronger justification to access high schools or jobs, e.g. prospects of good marriage.
- Absence of proper transport facilities for modest women.

- Access to development programmes for women is lower in remote villages.

Adult women

- In the absence of convenient transport facilities, e.g. preferential seating in buses, it is difficult to travel with children.
- Walking long distances carrying children is tiresome.
- Inadequacy of transport leads to inaccessibility of appropriate jobs and health services.

Women

- Mobility of women is linked to family honour/respectability.
- Violation of male social norms leads to harsh social punishment and humiliation.
- Access to sources of income for own expenditure and that of the families is restricted.
- Social visits, including visits to the parental home, are difficult, leaving women totally isolated.
- Visits to places of entertainment are restricted and can only be made with a male guardian.
- Lower access than men to education due to expense of transport and security on the road.
- Lower access than men to health and sanitation facilities.
- Absence of appropriate transport facilities for women, e.g. separate buses, toilet facilities, etc.
- Travelling with children is tiresome – no bus shade under which to wait and long waiting hours due to only few reserved seats for women.

Adolescent girls

- Lack of appropriate and affordable transport facilities to high schools and colleges.
- Walking to educational institutions is tiresome due to bad roads and weather.
- Walking long distances on roads is not secure.
- Social restrictions on riding bicycles.
- Absence of roadside toilet facilities.

Men

- Inadequate transport facilities make it difficult to access better work opportunities.
- If roads are not good, it is difficult to ride bicycles, rickshaws or rickshaw vans.
- Inadequate relief and help during natural calamities.

Thus women's right to mobility is not a natural right in Bangladesh: women have to acquire it. Well-planned provision of transport facilities can largely help to achieve this right. Mobility of women is restricted not only by social barriers but also by the cost, the inadequacy and the inappropriateness of available transport facilities.

Political participation

The lack of physical mobility restricts women to a limited view and vision of the world by denying them exposure to competing ideas, social priorities and perspectives. With restricted access to markets and public places where important networks are formed, alliances forged and public policies debated, women lack the worldly wisdom, the intuition and 'savvy' needed to understand and effectively participate in political processes. Now that Bangladesh has moved towards a system in which one-third of elected offices at the local government level are reserved for women, physical mobility has become all the more critical if women are to be effective as public representatives and members of the electorate.

Income and employment opportunities

Roads and vehicles do not necessarily create income opportunities for women locally but they increase their opportunities to find jobs in higher employment areas. The easier it is for a village to access a town, the greater the opportunities for jobs and incomes. Whereas men can afford to travel far and stay away for a considerable period, women need to travel shorter distances and return home at key times of the day to attend to critical household chores. *Efficient* transport, by reducing the time distance, can increase women's options for employment and income.

From this perspective, reconsideration is necessary of the policy favoured by government and NGO women-and-development programmes of promoting home-based self-employment opportunities such as handicrafts, sewing, embroidery, livestock and poultry rearing. This accommodates the transport problems and the social restrictions that prohibit women's mobility, and allows women to earn an income and make significant contributions to their families' wellbeing. But women's own empowerment remains a distant target. They remain dependent on male family members to manage their enterprise; market-related transactions of buying the inputs and selling the outputs are done by men. Consequently, the control of the cash income, to a large extent, has to be shared with the men. These development programmes reinforce the existing discriminatory gender allocation of space that cuts women off from the world of markets, and perpetuates male dominance over household decision-making (Dawson and Barwell, 1993, p. 74).

Education

As a result of improved communications, girls from well-off families are able to attend high schools and colleges away from the villages, whereas girls from poorer households in remote villages are often unable to attend even primary schools. Although social resistance against girls' education still persists, parents are well aware of the importance of education for their daughters not only for good prospects in marriage but also for economic independence. The village studies provide us with a picture of change. In the easy-access village in Faridpur, women attending adult literacy classes expressed their regret at not going to school when they were young and wanted to continue the education of their daughters as long as they could afford to do so. They hoped that education will one day help this new generation of women to become self-reliant. In the Netrokona village of Mahjiali, when the earthen road was upgraded with a brick surface, making walking and rickshaw travel easier, girls started going to the high school even though it was 4 kilometres away.

In the remote villages, girls face a number of barriers, such as lack of appropriate transport facilities; long walks to school, especially in difficult weather conditions; negative social perceptions about girls' education; as well as insecurity (sexual harassment) during travel. Lack of appropriate toilet facilities on the road was expressed as an important transport issue that hinders women from attending educational institutions.

Health

Access to health services is particularly strongly correlated with access to transport. Poorer women from the easy-access villages mostly use government health care facilities, which cost less than private facilities. Richer women, however, often go to private facilities, which are less crowded. They can afford to call the doctor for home visits if needed. During childbirth complications, women in these villages are able to acquire the necessary medical assistance even though most of the deliveries are still performed at home by trained birth attendants within an easy access distance.

In the remote villages, the situation is different. Women, when sick, mostly rely on male family members, who travel to the health centres with

a description of the symptoms of the illness and bring home medicines as prescribed by the doctors. In the case of serious illness, the patient is carried in on a bamboo stretcher on the shoulders of two to four men. The problems of transport, and the associated cost, prompt women to suppress their ailments and stoically bear things as long as possible. Child-birth also involves considerable risk. The traditional birth attendants are the only help available, and nothing can be done when complications arise.

CONCLUSION

The case studies provide sufficient indication that rural women's mobility needs are substantial. Here a distinction is made between women's mobility needs and their transport burden. Mobility needs refer to women's requirements to be able to participate in political processes, income-earning opportunities, education and health services. The transport burden, by comparison, refers to transport-dependent tasks that are related to women's reproductive or domestic work functions. Although time-consuming and characterized by drudgery, women's transport burden in Bangladesh nowhere compares to the situation in Africa. Marketing of produce and fuel collection are often done and shared by men; and collection of water, though an exclusive female activity, has been privileged by geographical conditions: that is, the presence of rivers and ponds in close proximity; and large-scale installation of hand pumps due to the high groundwater table.

In Bangladesh, the gender aspect of rural transport relates more to the social, economic and political empowerment of women than to the easing of their burdens. While it is important to address the accessibility needs of rural women, it is not enough to stop there. Given the restrictive socio-cultural conditions that limit women's empowerment, it is critical to respond to women's mobility needs. These require policies and interventions that aim to expand the physical world and orbit of women, and thereby women's command over the political and social processes which determine their lives.

NOTES

1. Roads connecting the national capital with divisional headquarters, old district headquarters, port cities and international highways.
2. Highways connecting different regions with each other which are not connected by the national highway system.

3. Roads connecting important growth centres/markets, including *thana* headquarters and places of socio-economic importance, with the paved road network, as well as roads connecting union headquarters and local markets with *thana* headquarters.

13

CYCLING INTO THE FUTURE:
THE PUDUKKOTTAI EXPERIENCE

TAMIL NADU, INDIA

Nitya Rao

Pudukkottai district is one of the most backward districts in the southern Indian state of Tamil Nadu. More than 85 per cent of the population live in rural areas, but lack of industrialization and low levels of rainfall make the majority dependent on dry land farming for their survival. Barely able to take a single crop in a year, they live in conditions of abject poverty. Pudukkottai was one of the districts with the lowest literacy rates in the state, and the gender gap, at 24.3 percentage points, the highest.

THE LITERACY CAMPAIGN

In July 1991, Pudukkottai district was selected for the total literacy campaign – a mass campaign for the eradication of adult illiteracy and promotion of basic education. Initiated by the National Literacy Mission, the total literacy campaign was based on the principles of people's participation and voluntarism. The Pudukkottai Mavatta Arivoli Iyakkam,[1] a registered society that comprised members of the government, NGOs and interested members of civil society, led this campaign.

An initial door-to-door survey found that of the 290,000 illiterate people in the 9–45 age group in the district, more than 75 per cent were women. If the campaign was to be successful it needed to address itself specifically to the needs and problems of the women in the district. The women's component of the programme was consciously and meticulously planned and implemented, made possible to a large extent due to the initiative and enthusiasm of the District Collector (the top bureaucrat at the district level) – a woman!

Teaching started in October 1991 and continued until June 1992. Over 26,000 volunteers, young boys and girls, were mobilized and trained as teachers. Women's Committees were formed at the *panchayat*, block and district levels. These Committees were involved in a variety of activities that helped motivate women learners to write their own petitions and solve local problems, handle conflict situations, and organize campaigns such as the 'Back to School' Campaign.

From the very beginning the National Literacy Mission promoted mobility alongside literacy, numeracy, functionality and awareness. This was inspired by an earlier rural development programme, the Development of Women and Children in Rural Areas (DWCRA), which had organized women into groups and introduced them to cycling as a practical, business skill to help them with purchasing and marketing for their enterprise. The success of the DWCRA programme prompted the idea of cycling as a mass campaign for women. Cycling for women became a popular slogan and thousands of women were taught to ride the bicycle. Songs were composed and promoted through cultural troupes and events.

> Learn to ride the cycle sister
> Set in motion the wheel of life sister.
> See the little boy riding high,
> You too can learn and ride by,
> Cars, ships and planes, are now piloted by women,
> Those days are gone, when the drivers were only men.
> So learn to ride the cycle quickly,
> And begin a new story.
>
> (Song from the cycling campaign for
> women, translated from the Tamil)

There were two reasons for promoting cycling for women. First, increased mobility would help women address some of their major transport needs, making the performance of daily tasks more efficient. Second, and at that stage more important, was the social, cultural and psychological rationale. It was felt that the self-confidence gained from learning a skill such as cycling would provide women with a sense of freedom, motivate them to learn more about the outside world, evoke a desire to gain access to information, and also encourage literacy – if they could learn cycling, then reading and writing too were not impossible! And over time it could also help to change the unequal gender relations in society.

THE CYCLING CAMPAIGN

All those who had bicycles in the villages (mostly men) were asked to spend a few hours every day teaching the women. Men who taught women cycling were given recognition for contributing to the process of development and change. Women also pooled money once or twice a week, collectively hired bicycles, and helped each other learn. Schoolgirls taught their mothers. Training programmes started with an hour of cycling in the morning. The campaign organized cycle demonstrations for women, conducted competitions and distributed prizes. The district administration threw challenges to the women. One village where an old woman learned to cycle was rewarded with a bore-well (Athreya and Chunkath, 1996). Within a few months more than 50,000 women in the district learned to ride a bicycle. A new song was composed, the first two lines of which ran as follows:

> We have learned to ride the cycle brother,
> And rotate the wheel of our life.

To make this whole process possible, however, bicycles had to be made available in the area. The Indian Bank financed more than 1,500 women's cycles in the rural areas. The loan of Rs 1,200 had to be repaid

Marikannu, who is 39 years old, lives in Thoppupatti village and works in the gem-cutting centre there. When the electricity at the centre failed and the women had to stop work they called the volunteer and asked her to teach them to cycle. In a cycle race organized in their block, Marikannu received the first prize – a women's bicycle! She has been using it ever since for a variety of tasks: collecting water, taking flowers to the market for sale, dropping people at the bus-stop two kilometres away, taking grain to the grinding mill 3 kilometres away, delivering messages, dumping rubbish in the fields, and so on. Marikannu's workday begins at 3 a.m., with milking the cows, then cooking, cleaning, taking the rubbish to the fields, collecting flowers for sale. She leaves for the town by 6 a.m. After returning around 10 a.m., she works in her own fields, or takes part in agricultural labour work, returning home only in the evening. By the time she finishes cooking, running errands for others, and so on, it is almost 10 p.m. and time to retire. Her husband, a party worker, used to help a little with household chores but now he doesn't at all. Nor does he interfere in decisions regarding household expenses and maintenance. Single-handedly Marikannu manages her own household, and at the same time assists her parents, who live close by, and other neighbours. The number of errands she runs for others has increased since she started cycling. The time saved on her regular tasks is thus used for helping others.

in 24 equal instalments of Rs 50 each. Most of the women who took bicycle loans at this stage were government extension workers or groups of women engaged in some business enterprise. They had a regular source of income, and were able to repay the loans. The availability of bicycles itself made many women learn to ride them.

Even at that early stage, the impact of cycling was visible on the lives of several women. They gained self-confidence and met some of their practical needs. As the sight became commonplace, women on bicycles were no longer the butt of male jokes and men had to accept 'mobile' women as a reality!

At this point there were still very few women cyclists. A cycling tour by 11 girls across the district three years later, in 1995, organized by *Samam*, the women's network within the literacy programme, helped to remotivate many women to learn or resume cycling. More songs were composed and discussions were held on several problems relating to women, from alcoholism, dowry and infanticide, to the relative equality in rights of men and women. It appears that it was after this second motivation that the use of bicycles came to occupy a more permanent place in the routine of women's lives.

This chapter explores the impact of the introduction of bicycles on women's lives since the campaign began in 1991. How far has this intervention sustained itself and contributed towards empowering women? Have the bicycles also been able to meet women's transport needs, for both their productive and reproductive activities? What has been the impact of women's increased mobility on their self-esteem and confidence, on gender relations in the community? Has providing bicycles to women been a sustainable intervention? In particular, has women's investment in bicycles continued and do they have control over the use of these bicycles?

PROFILE OF VILLAGES

The author and her team of researchers talked with 49 women using bicycles, their husbands, shopkeepers, bankers and other villagers in 12 villages in Pudukkottai. The villages included those with a frequent bus service in the village, those with a frequent bus service located at a distance of 1 to 3 kilometres from the village, those with about four buses a day, and those with low access, namely one or two buses in a day. A summary of their characteristics is given in Table 13.1.

Most were scheduled- or backward-caste villages, and most of the population were engaged in agriculture or agricultural labour. In

TABLE 13.1 Characteristics of villages in the study

Category	Name of village	Distance to bus stop	Bus service	Cycle shops	Bicycle ownership	Main occupation	Other services (school/market)
Well connected	Seegampatti	In village	Frequent	Yes	Low but increasing	Stone quarries, agriculture	1 km
	Parambur	In village	Frequent	No	High	Gem cutting, labour, trade, agriculture	In village
Medium access	Malaikudipatti	In village	Frequent	No	High	Gem cutting	In village
	Pudhur	In village	4/day	No	Only the rich	Agriculture, wage labour	1 km
	Mullur	In village	4/day	Yes	Increasing	Agriculture, wage labour	6 km
Low access	Agarapatti	In village	2/day	No	High	Agriculture	2 km
	Maguthupatti	In village	Infrequent	Yes	Low	Wage Labour	7 km
Frequent service outside the village	Vadugupatti	3 km	Half hour	No	–	Gem cutting	In village
	Vaguvasal	2 km	Half hour	No	High	Labour in town	1 km
	Thoppupatti	2 km	Half hour	Yes	High	Agriculture, wage labour	1 km
	Seranur	1 km	Half hour	No	Low	Agriculture	1 km
	Ayipatti	1 km	Half hour	No	High	Agriculture, wage labour	2 km

Seegampatti, villagers were employed in the nearby stone quarries. In Malaikudipatti, Parambur and Vadugupatti, a significant number were engaged in gem cutting.

Some villages were in very close proximity to schools, health centres, the ration shop, the post office, the bank and markets. For others, these were a bus ride or bicycle ride away in nearby villages and towns. Several villages had a water supply in terms of drinking-water pipes or bore wells, but for many water had to be fetched from sources at least a kilometre away. Bicycle ownership varied in the different villages: in some almost every household had a bicycle; and in others very few, though the number seems to be increasing. Four villages had bicycle shops which hired out bicycles to women and men. There were no women's bicycles in any of the villages or in any of the shops.

WHAT SORTS OF WOMEN RIDE BICYCLES?

Out of the 49 women we spoke to, only 3 did not know how to ride a bicycle.

The majority of the interviewees were scheduled- and backward-caste women earning their living through their labour. Half of them were barely literate and the others were educated up to middle school. The women engaged in gem cutting were more literate than others since literacy was a criterion for selection for training in artificial gem cutting and polishing. Most were in the 20 to 30 age group, and had children and families to look after (see Tables 13.2–13.4). The workload on these women is heavy. Apart from earning an income they also have complete responsibility for household maintenance tasks, from fetching water, fuel and fodder, to cooking, cleaning and washing. In the rural context each of these tasks involves several activities. For instance, cleaning involves collecting all the garbage and waste from in and around the house, and dumping it in the fields, a kilometre or more from the house.

An activity and time profile exercise conducted with eight couples revealed that while both the men and women spent six to ten hours a day on paid work, the women spent a similar amount of time on household maintenance and childcare tasks. Men spent less than two hours on domestic tasks and got three to five hours of rest and leisure. Women averaged less than two hours of rest and had a working day that stretched from twelve to eighteen hours.

TABLE 13.2 Age, caste and educational profile of respondents

Age	No. of women	Caste	No. of women	Education	No. of women
Under 18	8	Scheduled	10	Neo-literate	20
19–22	19	Backward	34	Primary	4
23–28	15	Most Backward	5	Middle	11
29–35	4			High	13
Over 36	3			Graduate	1

TABLE 13.3 Occupational status of respondents

Occupation	No. of women
Agriculture	18
Stone quarrying	1
Gem cutting	18
Agricultural labour	4
Teachers	3
Tailoring	1
Cattle-rearing	1
No work	3

TABLE 13.4 Family size of respondents

Size of family	No. of respondents
1–2	4
3–5	27
over 6	18

Ramayi, who is 18 years old, unmarried and living with her parents, does a range of tasks in her house, such as collecting fuel, fodder and water and going to the rice mill. As her family does not own a bicycle, she either borrows one from a neighbour or in an emergency hires one from the shop. For collecting water, she usually borrows a bicycle from the neighbours, bringing one pot of water for them in addition to her own. When she hires a cycle from the local shop, she combines a range of tasks such as going to the mill, the bank or post office and shops. Once when her classmate was very sick, she took her directly to the hospital from her school on a hired bicycle. She then rushed to the village to inform the girl's parents. The entire family is so grateful to her even now that Ramaji's sense of self-esteem is high; she feels herself a useful and wanted member of society.

CYCLING TODAY

All women who had access to bicycles, whether their own or that of a husband, father or brother, were using them for a range of tasks related to their productive work as well as domestic responsibilities. The most common uses appeared to be fetching water from the well or tank, taking paddy to the rice mill for grinding, collecting fuel and fodder, going to the hospital in an emergency, going to school, and social activities. A few women use a bicycle for their productive work, such as going to the market to sell flowers, to purchase gems from and sell them to the contractor, or working in a government plant nursery.

Only 4 of 49 women had their own bicycles (see Table 13.5), even though the households to which they belonged owned bicycles. One woman owned a moped.

Women were willing to use hired bicycles not only in emergencies but also for use in paid work or when they are able to plan together several household tasks that are located at a distance. Hiring a bicycle every day was too expensive, but they have planned out their work in a way that they could hire a bicycle once or twice a week for a couple of hours and complete several errands. For most of their daily household chores, however, they prefer to use the bicycles belonging to other members of their household, or borrowed from neighbours.

Ownership of bicycles is highest among households in the low-access cluster of villages where the value of bicycles as a mode of transport is well recognized. But none of the women interviewed in this cluster had a bicycle of her own. Though all the women in the low-access cluster

TABLE 13.5 Who owns the bicycle?

Owner	No. of households
Father	7
Brother	4
Husband	11
Neighbour	2
Own cycle	4
Hired cycle	15
Don't use*	6

* Includes three households where women don't know how to cycle; and three that own bicycles but where women have no access to them.

complained that access to bicycles was difficult for them as the men used them for travelling to their workplace, it is in this cluster that we find a majority of women using bicycles for their daily chores.

In the well-connected cluster, mainly roadside villages with fairly good service provisioning (except for Seegampatti, which has a bus service but no other facilities), the usage of bicycles is low. In these villages they are mainly used for social and emergency purposes.

While almost 30 to 50 per cent of the persons hiring bicycles are women, women's bicycles can rarely be found in any of the shops. The women have all got used to riding men's bicycles, and in fact now feel that these give them better balance while carrying a load. Riding a men's bicycle in a sari, the common dress of women in rural Tamil Nadu, isn't exactly an easy task as there is always the danger of the cloth getting entangled in the wheels of the bicycle. Though exposing their legs by raising the sari for safer riding could be considered a sign of impropriety, the women no longer seemed bothered about this, the convenience of cycling outweighing all other considerations.

Women used the bicycles most for fetching water from the well or tank. The next most frequent uses were going to the fields and to the mill for grinding paddy (see Table 13.6). The distances covered for each of these activities range from 1 to 5 kilometres, and each takes anything from half an hour to three hours to complete. While fetching water normally takes up to half an hour, collecting fuelwood takes the longest

Pichayi works in the childcare centre in her village, Mullur, so doesn't use her bicycle much for work. When her supervisor visits the village, however, she does expect Pichayi to take her around to the neighbouring centres on her bicycle. Her mobility has meant her involvement in several additional tasks such as surveys, organization of functions and meetings, collection of food for the children under the government's nutrition programme from Vanthangudi, 7 kilometres away from Mullur, and so on. She finds that now she saves a lot of time in daily tasks of collecting water, going to the fields, taking the paddy to the mill, and so on, and this allows her to engage in numerous other activities. She is the major decision maker in her household. Her husband is quite happy with this arrangement as his workload has reduced. Pichayi bought the bicycle on loan from the bank and she has already repaid this.

Marikannu is also from Mullur. She begins her day early in the morning by taking a bicycle from her brother's cycle shop to fetch water. She then takes the afternoon food for her father, who works 5 kilometres away in Pudukkottai town. On her return, she collects all the waste and takes it to the fields, then drops her mother at the bus stop two kilometres away. Her mother runs a shop, so goes every day into town in order to purchase goods for the shop. She also picks her mother up from the bus stop. In addition to this, she takes the grain to the mill for grinding once a week or fortnight and does any other chores that may come her way. She has endeared herself to many in the village due to her willingness to perform small errands for them.

time, often up to three hours. Most of the tasks involve carrying up to 30 kilograms load but the trip to the grinding mill often involves a sack full of grain weighing nearly 50 to 60 kilograms. 'Carrying people doubles', as a pillion passenger, whether to the school, hospital or roadhead, is also a relatively heavy task. Yet most of the women were able to carry 'doubles' on their bicycle.

Fragile-looking Jayamma narrated the hilarious episode of a Block Development Officer visiting the village and pooh-poohing her ability to carry a sack full of grain to the mill. Annoyed by his disbelief, she promptly asked him to sit on the pillion and took him around the village! He had no option but to believe her then.

There are several other examples, especially of women taking their relatives and friends for medical help in an emergency, and hiring a bicycle if none is available in the neighbourhood. Chinamma of Seegampatti took her sick father to hospital and virtually saved his life. Chinamma's family doesn't own a bicycle, and they have to hire one whenever required. Yet she feels that knowing the skill has itself given her a lot of self-confidence

TABLE 13.6 Activities for which cycles are used

Activities	No. of respondents
Bringing water	41
Going to the fields	10
Mill for grinding rice	7
Collecting fuelwood	5
Going to the shops	5
Dropping somebody up to the road	2
Going to the town	2
Taking rubbish to the fields	2
Going to work	2
Going to the temple	1
Gem-cutting work	1
Going to the school	1
Going to the hospital	1
Taking cattle for grazing	1

and a sense of independence. In addition to getting timely medical assistance, helping in emergencies has gained women a lot of social respect and prestige. It is also a major force for breaking down both caste and gender barriers.

The motivation to learn, even amongst those who don't know how to cycle, is high. Kamalam of Ayipatti, who is 45 and belongs to the Thevar community, was not allowed to learn cycling. She has a lot of work to do every day, from looking after all the work in the fields – digging, weeding, watering – to collecting water, fuel, fodder, and so on, for the home. Her husband has a betel nut and cigarette shop, so leaves in the morning and returns only at night. He is unable to help with any of the household work. But Kamalam wants to buy a bicycle if she is able to accumulate the necessary resources for it.

ISSUES OF ACCESS AND CONTROL

While access to bicycles for women seems widespread, what is more problematic is the issue of control. Because very few women own bicycles, they are dependent on the bicycles of others and have to adjust

Kalyani is from Agarapatti village. Though they have a bicycle at home, her father or brother gets priority in its use. Collecting water and going to the fields have to be done by foot. Kalyani sells vegetables in the market. As this is more than 2 kilometres away, she takes the bicycle for this purpose early in the morning, returning home by 8 a.m., at which time her father or brother is ready to take the bicycle out for his work. If she misses this opportunity, then she has to walk with the load as there is only one bus to the village and that is not always reliable. Earlier she and her mother both used to go to the market for selling vegetables, but with the bicycle she has started going alone, and this has increased her self-confidence and saved her mother a lot of time and effort.

their schedules according to the needs of the owners. If a husband works in the town and leaves early in the morning, then the woman has to get up even earlier to try to finish as much of her work as possible before this time.

While both men and women in the community today perceive cycling as a positive skill, only 12 of the women spoken to had easy access to bicycles (see Table 13.7), and another 10 reported that they could usually access a bicycle when they required it. Just as many women found it difficult to access a bicycle at home. The non-availability of bicycles in the cycle shop or the distance of the cycle shop from the village also made accessing bicycles difficult.

There are, moreover, some social restrictions that still prevent some women from cycling. In some cases, men are scared that their daughters

TABLE 13.7 Problems faced in accessing cycles

Problems	No. of respondents
Father/brother/husband takes the cycle	18
No cycle in the house	8
No cycle available in the shop	4
No cycle shop in the village	5
Don't ride the cycle	2
Have easy access	12

Dhanalakshmi, aged 22, the second of five sisters, lives with her mother. Dhanalakshmi had been the first woman to start cycling in her village. Her father taught her cycling when she was studying in school, a few years before the beginning of the literacy campaign. People at that time used to jeer at her. During the campaign she hired a bicycle in the evenings and taught several other women in her village to ride. After her father's death, much of the burden for running the household and supporting the education of her younger sisters fell on Dhanalakshmi's shoulders, as her elder sister was already married. She used to own a bicycle till two years ago, when she was working in a factory at Pudukkottai. Once she left that job, she sold the bicycle. She needed to raise as much money as possible for a younger sister's wedding. Despite selling off most of their assets, except for a small plot of land, they still incurred a debt of Rs 55,000. She has a lot of work to do, both agricultural and house-hold, but has to do it on foot. Whatever spare time she has, she uses for gem-cutting work. If she polishes about 100 pieces everyday, she can earn Rs 1,250 in the month. As the household runs on her income, she tries to borrow a neighbour's bicycle to finish her household chores quickly and spend the maxi-mum time possible in the task of gem cutting and polishing. This is not always possible. The cycle shop is far away from the village, so she does not hire a bicycle either. She would not be able to afford it on a regular basis, anyway. Even though she no longer owns a bicycle, Dhanalakshmi is happy that she has helped others and is willing to do so in the future if required. She has now initiated a savings group of ten women in her village. They have already saved Rs 600 and propose to start giving credit according to needs of the members of the group.

Chandana Mary is a traditional gem cutter from Maguthuppatti village. Her husband scrapes and cuts the stones and she polishes them. In addition, once a week she goes to Illuppur, about 8 kilometres away, to collect the stones and return the polished ones to the contractor there. The bus service is infrequent, so she usually hires a bicycle for about four hours for the round trip at the rate of Rs 1.50 per hour. She also has to complete all the household chores – fetching water from the pipeline 1 kilometre away, getting provisions from the ration shop 3 kilometres away, going to the mill, the school, the doctor and so on. Her husband, meanwhile, spends all his day in the workshop. She has discussed the purchase of a bicycle several times with her husband, but, as he doesn't need it, he is not willing to make the investment, and asks her to hire one when she needs it.

or wives may lose control and get hurt if they ride in crowded places; in others, women's work is just not a priority for men. Even though bicycles can greatly reduce the time and labour inputs for women in several drudgery-ridden tasks that are essential for daily household maintenance and provisioning, these tasks are unpaid and have no cash value. So the

TABLE 13.8   Decision makers on household expenditure

Particulars	No. of respondents
Father	17
Husband	16
Mother	4
Self	4
Brother	2
Joint	6

owners of the bicycles, usually men, do not see them as critical for women in performance of these tasks.

Even where the gender allocation of tasks means that the woman does most of the work outside the village (as in the case of Chandana Mary – see box) and needs a bicycle, it is the man (father or husband) who controls decisions regarding major household expenditure. Even though women are engaged in productive as well as household tasks, decision making on expenditure in a majority of cases continues to be vested in the men, women making decisions only on petty expenditure on daily consumption articles (see Table 13.8).

INVESTMENT IN CYCLES AND CYCLE SHOPS

Except for 1996–7, when there was a sharp decline in the number of cycle shops sanctioned for loans by the District Rural Development Agency, the number of cycle shops steadily increased, indicating a growing demand

TABLE 13.9   Financing of cycle shops by the District Rural Development Agency

Year	No. of shops financed	Loan amount in Rs
1994–5	208	911,641
1995–6	225	1,063,465
1996–7	130	65,000
1997–8	282	1,276,765

TABLE 13.10 Cycles sales figures for 1997–8 in Pudukkottai

Name of shop	No. of men's cycles sold	No. of women's cycles sold
A.V.M. Cycle Mart	700	250
Supreme Cycle Mart	650	200
Anand Cycle Mart	400	120
Devan Cycle Mart	350	125
Total	2,100	695

for bicycles in the rural areas and the profitability of setting up a cycle shop as an income-earning enterprise (see Table 13.9). With changes in employment patterns and lifestyles, the isolated and self-sufficient village economy is a feature of the past. In the current economic scenario, mobility and transportation are integral parts of people's lives. A cycle shop is now considered as a facility available in the village. The trend is also corroborated by the willingness of the women respondents to hire bicycles when the need arises.

Bicycle sales figures of four leading shops in Pudukkottai show that despite the very low number of women's cycles in the individual households or in cycle hiring shops, the sale of women's cycles is almost 30 per cent that of men's cycles (see Table 13.10). The demand for women's bicycles comes from the large number of girls who are seen cycling to schools in the district and block towns. This trend is definitely indicative of the likely higher usage of cycles by women in the next generation.

IMPACT OF CYCLING

What is the impact of cycling on women's lives? Does it only have social value, or has it actually contributed towards meeting their transport needs?

What seems to emerge as the primary impact is women's perception of independence in terms of all their roles in the household and community – the productive, reproductive and community managing roles (Moser, 1993). The second and related impact has been in terms of an improvement in both their self-confidence and their self-esteem (see Table 13.11).

Assessing the impact on gender relations is more complicated. On the positive side, women cycling has now come to be accepted as a normal phenomenon; jokes and kidding have stopped. Rural girls learn to cycle along with the boys. Husbands are encouraging their wives to learn cycling.

TABLE 13.11 Women's perceptions on impacts of cycling

Impacts	No. of respondents
No dependence on men for daily activities	17
Can move alone for both work and social responsibilities	16
Self-confidence and courage	9
Helpful in emergencies	4
Can help others	1
No impact	2

Shopkeepers of cycle hiring shops now hire out their cycles to women where once they used to hesitate.

On the negative side, for almost 40 per cent of the women, workloads had actually increased. Tasks that the men would do formerly, such as marketing, taking the children to school, or any other household chore that involved travelling distances, have now shifted to women. Bicycles, however, have helped them to complete their tasks faster and more easily. Their efficiency has improved, as before they had to do the household chores by walking and, where it required travel outside the village, by bus. Most of the women felt that the bus service was insufficient and irregular and did not fully serve their needs. Women with goods to sell were not allowed in the buses during peak hours so had to travel either very early in the morning or late in the evening, both of which meant losing time. Using a bicycle saves women time, so despite taking on extra burdens they still seem to have time for leisure!

More than the change in the gender division of roles and responsibilities has been the change in social status and esteem for the women. Small jobs such as taking a neighbour to the hospital or dropping an old man to the bus stop a few kilometres away have earned them both gratitude and social respect. This change appears to be real. The inevitable next step would be a fairer balance between men and women in terms of distribution of work as well as the ownership and use of bicycles. Women are already reflecting and thinking about these issues, something they could not have dreamt of doing a few years ago.

Poomgothai, a 23-year-old scheduled-caste woman, was working as a volunteer in the literacy campaign. She had mobilized several women for an event to inaugurate a library and reading room in a village 4 kilometres away. However, when the bus failed to turn up, she, along with five other girls, decided to hire bicycles to reach the venue on time. Both her enterprise and her commitment to the cause of literacy and post-literacy were greatly appreciated by all.

Vellaiamma, an 18-year-old woman in Pudhur, was alone at home one day when there was an urgent message for her father. He was needed immediately to deal with an emergency, but he was in the fields. Vellaiamma quickly borrowed a neighbour's bicycle, took her father the message, and then transported him on the bicycle to where the problem was.

Meenakshi of Agarapati can never forget the day when her mother fell critically sick and the two of them were alone at home. She borrowed a bicycle, rushed her mother to the hospital, and thus managed to save her life. Neither can **Hridaya Mary** of Mahudupatti, who saved the life of her five-year-old daughter. Or **Mallika**, whose brother fell sick while they were at school. The headmaster asked her to take him home, but instead she first took him to the doctor and then home.

Amuda of Vadugopatti had hesitated to learn cycling when she was a child and did so only during the literacy campaign. Once when her friend was unwell and there was nobody around from her family to attend to her, Amuda herself took her to hospital. This has endeared her to her friend's parents.

Joyce Mary of Mahudupatti, aged 17, was just leaving for school when her mother received a message from her grandmother, living 3 kilometres away, and needed to go there urgently. Joyce hired a cycle, completed the round trip of 6 kilometres in less than 45 minutes, and then took the bus to school. If her mother had waited for a bus it would have taken her another two hours to reach her grandmother's house.

Meenakshi is a gem cutter in Malaikudupatti. Her younger sister used to go to school at Illupur, 5 kilometres away, by bus. One day she missed her bus, so started crying. Meenakshi hired a cycle and took her to school. It is now possible to see an increasing number of girls going to school by cycle, some single and several doubles. This was not a very likely scenario in Pudukottai even ten years ago.

ON THE ROAD TO SUSTAINABILITY

The increased social acceptance of women cycling is reflected in a recent initiative of the University of Tirunelveli in Tamil Nadu that encourages all women students to learn cycling. The campaign has been launched in all the colleges affiliated to the university in the three southern districts of Tirunelveli, Tuticorin and Kanyakumari (Muthahar, 1998). The motivation, as expressed by the vice chancellor, Dr V. Vasanthi Devi, has come at least in part from the Pudukkottai experience.

The women in Pudukkottai have repeatedly stressed the usefulness of cycling for improving the efficiency of their work and reducing the time taken to complete their tasks. While empowerment may have been the objective of those who taught them the skill, for the women cycling has become an efficient, cheap and easy way of meeting their daily transport needs, the bulk of which are invisible and relate to unpaid household or social tasks. They do not expect that transport planners will ever fully be able to address their needs through public transport.

Though most of the women learned cycling during the literacy campaign, it was only two to three years later that it became widespread. While many women still do not own bicycles or even control their use, their access to and use of bicycles, either owned by other members of the family or hired, has definitely increased.

While the increased mobility of women has in several instances increased their workloads, this is offset to a large extent by the increase in their self-esteem and self-confidence, and the social recognition and respect they have gained as members of the community. With other social relations changing, it could also mean a move towards more equitable gender relations in the future.

Though investment decisions in assets such as bicycles continue to remain largely with the men, there seems to be a silent change in favour of investing in women's bicycles. Accepted by the people, particularly women themselves, as an integral and necessary part of their lives, the use of bicycles by women seems to be a phenomenon that has come to stay in Pudukkottai.

NOTES

Nitya Rao was assisted by a survey team that included K. Kumaresan, I. Alphon Stella Mary, I. Arockiarani and V. Maheswari, members of the local literacy team in Pudukkottai. The data collection was coordinated by R. Rajakumar and N. Kannammal. A few key interviews as well as the focus group discussion were conducted by the primary researcher.

1. Pudukkottai District Literacy Society.

14

WOMEN, WATER AND TRANSPORTATION: MAPPING THE INTERPLAY

BANASKANTHA, GUJARAT, INDIA

Poorni Bid, Reema Nanavaty and Neeta Patel

In July 1998, the Self-Employed Women's Association held a participatory workshop and carried out several discussions with its members in Banaskantha district in Gujarat, India, about how the availability of water and transportation circumscribes the conditions under which they lived. In this chapter, we show how these women in Banaskantha described the interplay of water and transportation in their lives.

SEWA: A BRIEF BACKGROUND

The Self-Employed Women's Association, also known as SEWA, was founded in 1972 as a trade union for poor women working in the informal sector. Today, SEWA's membership exceeds 150,000 in the state of Gujarat, India, comprising a wide range of occupations. These women have no fixed employee–employer relationship, cannot rely on steady wages and other benefits available to workers in the organized sector, are often illiterate, have no assets or working capital and are vulnerable to exploitation by employers and to fluctuations in the market and economy.

SEWA seeks to improve the working and living conditions of these economically active women through the twin strategies of struggle and development. The key to these strategies is organizing women into functional trade-based groups such as trade unions, cooperatives and savings and credit groups that are owned and managed by the women, and that aim towards financial and managerial self-reliance. Through organizing, the women have been able to promote their own economic and social development, increase their bargaining power with employers and government officials, increase their incomes and assets, obtain social services such as health care and childcare, and become self-reliant, economically and in decision making.

SEWA has also promoted campaigns on issues identified by both women and village leaders as those that affect large numbers of people – that affect them deeply and are continually brought to the attention of the Association.

One of SEWA's most important campaigns focuses on water. The Water Campaign is being carried out in North Gujarat (including Banaskantha), where the availability of water for both drinking and agriculture is a major problem.

BANASKANTHA

The district of Banaskantha is located in the north of Gujarat, bordered to the west by the Rann of Kutch and to the north by the Thar Desert. It is an arid, landlocked region with 1,375 villages and 5 towns. Banaskantha derives its name from the Banas River, which originates in the Aravalli mountain range to the north, and runs through the district into the low-lying alluvial plains of the surrounding deserts. While the Banas River is dry and fails to provide water for most of the year, it floods the villages bordering the deserts during the monsoon season.

Banaskantha's total population of 1,667,914 is predominantly rural. The main occupations are agriculture and dairy production; 58 per cent of the population are cultivators while 19 per cent are agricultural labourers. Agriculture is mainly rain-fed and frequent droughts coupled with few natural resources have made agricultural work sporadic. In 1989, 1,534 families from 60 villages in Banaskantha migrated out of their villages in search of work. SEWA's activities helped reduce that number to 324 families in 1994.

Most of the women in Banaskantha are self-employed, surviving on wages from whatever work they can find throughout the year. About 40 per cent are cultivators and another 40 per cent are agricultural labourers. About 10 per cent work for less than six months a year.

SEWA's rural development activities in Banaskantha focus on water resource planning and management. In the early 1980s the Gujarat Water Supply and Sewerage Board, in cooperation with the Dutch government, launched the Regional Water Supply and Sanitation Programme, which aimed to supply safe drinking water through pipelines to 120,000 people in 72 villages in the Santalpur *taluka* (sub-district) of Banaskantha district. Construction of the pipeline was completed in 1987, and during the following year the scheme was extended to 110 new villages. At that time, SEWA was invited by the government of Gujarat to implement the social and economic development components of the Santalpur Rural Water Supply Scheme.

SEWA's goal was to promote long-term sustainable development and to improve the socio-economic status of the stakeholders so that they would be able to gain maximum benefits from the water supply scheme and eventually contribute to the operation and maintenance of their own water resources.

SEWA quickly learned that the water supplied by the pipeline was irregular and the need for potable water was still high in the pipeline area. It would be difficult to implement any economic and social development activities until these problems were sufficiently addressed. As a result, SEWA began designing and implementing projects that would either develop new or revive existing local water resources to augment the water supplied by the programme. This led to the development of the Water As a Regenerative Input Programme and SEWA's involvement in the National Watershed Development Programme.

The women of Banaskantha hold the primary responsibility for collecting and distributing water for drinking and other purposes, and are the main beneficiaries of these activities. They are also the primary stakeholders of any activity regarding the transportation of water.

WOMEN'S ROLES AND RESPONSIBILITIES

Women in Banaskantha take on many responsibilities early in life and continue to carry them throughout their life cycle. Before the age of 10, both boys and girls help with the household chores. After that, families who can afford to, send the boys to school, while most girls remain at home helping their mothers and taking on more household responsibilities. If and when not in school, boys will be sent out to labour for wages or to help in the fields.

As women grow older, they become accountable for a larger number of tasks and their burdens increase. They must fetch water, take care of the children and tend to all the cooking and cleaning within the home. In most cases they are also responsible for feeding and caring of animals, tending to the fields, bringing necessities from outside the village and generating income for the household. Men's responsibilities, for the most part, are limited to generating income for the household.

In a few cases the adult male members of the household may not do anything, leaving the women to run the home as well as to generate income for the family. Occasionally, the male members may share equally in the household and income-earning responsibilities. Saviben, a woman of Datrana village, earns a good income from the embroidery work provided by SEWA. As a result, her husband has taken on almost all the household responsibilities, leaving her free to do her embroidery work. However, more often than not, women take on whatever additional responsibilities they can to promote the wellbeing of their families while men are less likely to share the domestic burden.

There are more significant issues underlying the uneven division of labour. Women were generally silent when asked who made the decisions regarding household chores and responsibilities and needed to be prodded by SEWA staff to speak on the issue. Many said that their burdens fell on them by default. If they don't cook the food, wash the clothes, clean the house, fetch the water, and so on, no one else will. Most men only worry about income-generating labour and don't see domestic labour as their responsibility. Sometimes men become violent and strike their wives if all the chores have not been completed. Within the home, it is mostly men who have decision-making powers.

However, this does not mean that the women of Banaskantha do not have the ability to participate effectively in decision-making processes. The women are deeply involved in all aspects of running their homes and caring for their families and understand how best to provide for them. They are more than capable of making sound, informed decisions with regard to their villages, their homes and their families. Several women had been involved in planning the construction of a new water source to the area. They had participated in all aspects of the planning process, from deciding what source (well, pond, pipeline, etc.) should be constructed, where it should be located, through to maintenance and how the water should be distributed. However, deeply rooted gender constructions often deny women access to decision-making processes that profoundly affect their lives.

WATER RESOURCES IN BANASKANTHA

Clean, safe drinking water is a basic necessity for life. This is where Banaskantha's troubles begin. The whole of Gujarat suffers from an acute water shortage that affects more than 70 per cent of the villages each year. The villages of Banaskantha lack adequate water resources as well as the infrastructure that might relieve this shortage (see Figure 14.1). Studies

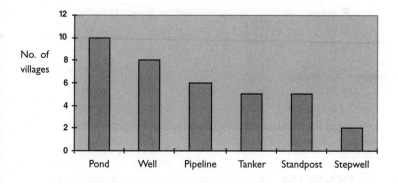

FIGURE 14.1   Water resources in selected villages in Banaskantha

conducted by SEWA estimate the maximum amount of water available for all household use to be 55 litres per day. According to the District Rural Development Agency in Banaskantha, 15 litres is the minimum for feeding cattle alone.

While the government pipeline scheme was intended to provide a constant supply of clean water to the villages of Santalpur *taluka*, it is an irregular and unreliable source. In most cases water is available for only a few days of the month. In addition ponds tend to dry up by the time the summer months arrive.

TRANSPORTATION IN BANASKANTHA

Families in Banaskantha travel for many reasons: to the *taluka* centre to buy food, fuel and other basic necessities; to collect water from a common village source; to different locations for their income-earning activities – wage labour, gum collecting or salt farming.

The only formally regulated transport facilities (with set routes and fares) in Banaskantha are the buses operated by the State Transport Corporation. Though they sometimes use the buses, the people of Banaskantha rely heavily on informal facilities for their transport needs. Transportation in the informal sector consists of privately owned jeeps, *chhakdas* and other vehicles, trucks, bicycles, animal-drawn carts (mainly camel and bullock carts) and, perhaps the most important, walking. Aside from

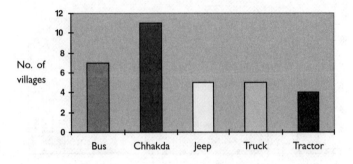

FIGURE 14.2 Modern transport facilities in selected villages in Banaskantha

walking, the most frequently used mode of transport seemed to be the *chhakda* (see Figure 14.2).

Formal transport facilities

The Gujarat State Road Transport Corporation (GSRTC) aims at providing reliable, affordable transport facilities to the population of Gujarat which enable the public, both urban and rural, to engage in social, economic and political activities. A special effort is made to provide transportation facilities to the rural population, and 95 per cent of the villages in Gujarat have a GSRTC bus service. However, in most villages the quality of this service is inadequate. Though the statewide demand for transport service calls for 16,000 buses, the corporation's budget can only fund 9,000 vehicles.

If a village does have a bus service, it generally runs to and from the village and *taluka* or district centre. Each route includes eight to ten villages. While the bus may go directly to some of these villages, other villagers have to walk several kilometres to a main road or a neighbouring village to catch a bus. The buses are relatively infrequent and may often come once early in the morning and return only late in the evening, forcing villagers to sacrifice a whole day's work if they need to go to the town centre. For example, Puriben of Vauva must leave her village at 5 a.m. and cannot return until 6 p.m. if she wants to travel by bus to Radhanpur. Her husband is forced to stay home while she is away. Both lose a full day's work and a day's income.

While the bus fare is affordable to many villagers, the timings and infrequency make it an unreliable and underutilized means of transport. If the bus routes and timings were better planned, the women of Banas-kantha could use the State Transport buses to bring rations from the distribution centre, send their children to school, access needed medical care and obtain raw materials and resources for economic activity. When the women do use the buses for these purposes, they sacrifice valuable time and equivalent income. If not, they walk long distances or pay money for private transport.

A bus route is revised or expanded to include new villages following an application from the village *sarpanch*, elected head of the Gram Panchayat. Once an application is received, the district office sets a tentative timetable based on several factors. First, there needs to be a motorable road to and from the village. This is a problem for many villages. Next, the GSRTC officer considers how and by whom the bus will be used. Commercial and educational needs are often given preference and the existence of other transport facilities is taken into account.

Once the new route has been set, the State Transport runs a trial bus for fifteen days and conducts a feasibility study. The bus must recover the cost of Rs 8 per kilometre. After fifteen days, the GSRTC decides whether or not to continue the route. In many cases the village *sarpanch* or the owner of a private vehicle intimidates the villagers into using their vehicles for transport. As a result, state buses remain empty while villagers are forced to pay more than necessary for their transport.

Women from a few villages have gone directly to the GSRTC to demand better service, but many were not aware that the *sarpanch* could request a new bus route or timetable. In Babra, a village which has no bus service, the women didn't believe that the *sarpanch* would listen to them and submit an application. In Patanka, they have submitted an application but are still awaiting a response. In other villages, where an improved bus service is needed, the women made no mention of approaching either the *sarpanch* or the GSRTC. There is an information and communication gap between the GSRTC and the village women. If women were more aware of the Corporation's policy with regard to revising bus routes, they might make use of it to obtain the services they need.

Informal transport facilities

Because bus routes are restricted, villagers rely heavily on informal, unregulated transport facilities for travel over shorter distances or to destinations other than the *taluka*, and even for travel to the centre if the

Ranbai, a SEWA member and leader, spoke about the state of transportation in her village of Anternesh.

Anternesh has had no government transport facilities for over a year now. The road leading to the village was washed away during the monsoon season and remains in grave disrepair. Nothing has been done to repair the road or make alternate provisions even as the next monsoon approaches.

Anternesh has a *chhakda* that makes two trips a day. It departs at 8:00 a.m. and returns at 1:30 p.m. It departs again at 3:00 p.m. and returns between 6:00 and 7:00 p.m. The fare is Rs 7. Ranbai explained that the *chhakda* usually is crowded beyond capacity, making for an uncomfortable and sometimes dangerous ride. Ranbai uses this transportation four to five times a month to buy goods from the town or to attend SEWA meetings.

If someone is very ill or a woman is going to give birth, he or she must hire private transport and pay whatever is asked. The price may be as high as Rs 300–350.

During the monsoon season, there is no transportation at all in Anternesh because vehicles run a high risk of becoming stuck. Villagers must walk 12 kilometres to access any motorized transport.

If someone falls ill during the monsoon, several men take turns in carrying him or her on a mattress through the flooded areas out of the village to find transportation. Because it is difficult to travel in and out of Anternesh during the monsoon and people find it difficult to obtain food, SEWA has made arrangements to store enough food in the village to last through the monsoon months. Ranbai keeps the supply in her home and the villagers go to her whenever they need any foodstuffs.

Anternesh constantly faces an acute water shortage, though ironically the village is isolated by flooding during the monsoon.

bus service is inconvenient or simply unavailable. While transport facilities such as *chhakdas*, jeeps, trucks, and so on, may be more readily available, they are both more expensive and unregulated by any government agency or other formal entity.

In the case of the privately owned jeep and *chhakda*, the most readily available means of motorized transport, the departure and arrival times, number of trips per day, and price are at the sole discretion of the owner. The average number of trips one of these vehicles makes is about three per day. There is no fixed schedule. The jeep or *chhakda* leaves when enough passengers have assembled. Villagers cannot always rely on this same vehicle to return to the village and are at the mercy of whatever means of travel are available.

In most villages the price of a trip in a *chhakda* or jeep is fixed any-where between Rs 5 and 10 (as compared to Rs 2.5–4 for the bus). In villages far from the *taluka* centre, the fare may be a high as Rs 20. The owner of the vehicle is free to change whatever he pleases. In Babra, the women explained that a trip in the *chhakda* might be Rs 5 one day, Rs 8 the next and Rs 10 on the third day. If a villager has to hire a vehicle in extraordinary circumstances such as a medical emergency, he or she may have to pay anywhere from Rs 50 to 150 for the service. In one instance, when Jamuben of Patanka fell ill during a pregnancy, she paid Rs 215 to travel from her village to see a doctor in Radhanpur.

The cost of private transport does not deter villagers from using the services. In one village in Banaskantha, the owner of a *chhakda* makes a net profit of Rs 100 per day on short trips between villages. It is not economically viable for the GSRTC to run buses on short routes, though it could perhaps use smaller vehicles to provide such services at a lower cost and with greater reliability than the privately owned vehicles. For longer distances, it might try running smaller vehicles at greater frequency. The demand for these services is currently being met primarily by private and informal transport facilities.

Villagers also opt to use private transport facilities because of their greater accessibility. Often, a villager may have to walk several kilometres to a main road in order to catch a bus. Even then, he or she may miss the bus or it may not come when it is supposed to. Privately owned vehicles generally depart directly from the village, saving the villagers' time and energy. However, one woman described how, even though a *chhakda* leaves from her village, she walks 6 kilometres to the next village to board the vehicle because it saves her Rs 10. Many villagers are also forced to use privately owned vehicles even if an appropriate bus service is available because, if not used on a regular basis, the owner may refuse to provide a service in time of need.

When walking seems to be the only option, some villagers, including women, get a lift in a truck carrying goods. Because transporting pas-sengers is a secondary function for these goods carriers, it is only by chance that a woman villager may get a ride on one. Women will only ride in the trucks if they know the driver, and the driver will only carry women he knows. The women have to pay the driver whatever he asks for, though it rarely costs more than riding in a jeep or *chhakda*.

Although the women of Banaskantha only ride with truck drivers with whom they are acquainted, there is still a question of safety. Often the truck drivers are reckless or under the influence of alcohol and riding in the truck can be a frightening experience. Dharmistaben, a SEWA organizer, narrated an experience of travelling from their village to Santalpur, the *taluka* centre. She and two other women were sitting in the cabin with the driver and some other men:

> It was clear that he had been drinking and he kept taking his hands off the wheel and clapping. We were scared but we couldn't say so. He would just cause more mischief if he knew we were frightened.
>
> I asked him a question about how long he had been driving a truck and he stopped playing around long enough to answer me. I knew I had to keep him from being mischievous without letting him know I was scared. I started asking him more questions about his family, where he lived, if he was married, etc. I managed to keep him occupied enough to keep his hands on the steering wheel until we reached our destination. We were all very scared the whole way.

Private transport is also risky because, in order to make their business commercially viable and profitable, transporters overload their vehicles with goods and people. On average a jeep will take around 30 to 35 passengers and a *chhakda* around 15 to 18, compared to the official capacity of 10 passengers for a jeep and 6 for a *chhakda*. Young girls are also perceived to be at risk from harassment and are often prevented from travelling alone in private vehicles, adversely affecting their education and exposure to outside experiences and ideas.

Walking

While GSRTC buses, jeeps, *chhakdas*, bicycles and animal-drawn carts are all available and visible on the roads of Banaskantha, villagers rely, to an overwhelmingly degree, on walking from one point to another. This includes walking within and between villages, from the village to a workplace or to a district centre. Children often walk several kilometres to and from school each day. Women may have to walk up to 7 kilometres just to fetch drinking water for their families.

Walking is the most common way of travelling short distances (up to around 5 kilometres). Even though for longer travel walking is the last resort, inadequate transport facilities often make it the only alternative. Villagers walk long distances in extreme heat, with adverse effects on their time, health, income-earning ability, productivity and overall quality of life.

Impact of floods on routes, roads and buses

Banaskantha experiences floods every few years, causing widespread damage to the roads. During every monsoon around 40 per cent of the GSRTC-operated bus routes are temporarily terminated and private operators also cut down their trips. This severely affects the workers and women. Travel to work becomes difficult. Women are forced to walk to the nearby *taluka* town to procure the daily rations and head-load it back or to buy from local private traders at exorbitant prices.

WOMEN AND TRANSPORT PLANNING

Currently, women are denied direct access to any transport planning activity. Privately owned vehicles are controlled by their owners, and few women, if any at all, have the means to purchase their own vehicles. In the case of the GSRTC, any access to transport planning is restricted to the village *sarpanch*. S/he may or may not choose to take the villagers' concerns to the Corporation. In the few instances where women have approached the GSRTC to demand better service, the results have been negligible. Though the officers are outwardly receptive to the women's requests, they are slow to respond. Sometimes they ask the women to come back with their requests in writing, knowing most of them are illiterate.

The recognition of SEWA's intervention within water resource planning and management activities has enabled women to gain access and agency. Similar involvement in transport planning might bring about changes benefiting not only these women, but the entire village.

WOMEN'S TRANSPORT NEEDS

Even though women's access to transport planning is very limited, many of their tasks require access to transportation.

Transporting water

One of women's most crucial and laborious responsibilities is fetching water for drinking, cooking and other household uses. Women head-load water from a local source to their homes. The distance that women have to travel for water, the number of trips they have to make and the number of hours they spend collecting water each day all illustrate the burden of this task.

Though half a kilometre is the distance most frequently travelled to the water source, women often walk anywhere from 1 to 4 kilometres to collect 1 beda (10–15 litres) of water. In one village where the pipeline has failed to provide water, the villagers are entirely dependent on a government tanker. If the tanker fails to arrive, the women must walk 11 kilometres to another village to fetch water. Depending on the number of family members and how many of those are responsible for collecting water, women make from two to seven trips to the water source per day. On average, four to six hours per day are devoted solely to fetching water.

Effects of head-loading water

The cost and consequences of head-loading are significant. Head-loading limits the amount of water that one woman can carry to 10–15 litres a time and necessitates several trips a day just to meet the bare minimum water requirements of the household. The extraordinary amounts of time and energy women spend collecting water detracts from their ability to tend to other household and income-generating activities. Often, children are left hungry waiting for their mothers to return from collecting water.

Head-loading, especially in the severe heat, affects the health of the women villagers, causing chronic backache, foot pains and fatigue. It is also injurious to the head. One woman commented that if she didn't have to head-load water, she might be able to think as clearly and effectively as the SEWA organizers!

Young girls often accompany their mothers to help carry water. The pressure of head-loading not only affects their health, but also stunts and distorts their growth. The energy that these girls (and their mothers) expend generally exceeds their nutritional intake, leading to chronic nutritional deficits and long-term detrimental effects on their health. The time girls spend on water collection is one factor that keeps them from going to school.

Finally, head-loading places limits on the amount of water available and restricts it to only the most essential uses. The primary uses for water are drinking and cooking. These needs must be met. Because of the scarcity of water in Banaskantha, the women have learned to reuse water as efficiently as possible. They use water from washing dishes and bathing to water plants and to give to the animals. Bathing is something of a luxury for these villagers and they may go several days without a bath.

In some cases, the bulk of the time spent collecting water is not in actually transporting water from the source to the home but either in pulling water out of the well when the levels are low, or on waiting in line. In villages that are dependent on a government tanker for their water requirements, the women wait for the tanker to arrive before they attend to any other tasks, for fear of missing the tanker and thus their daily supply of water. In one instance, the women were left waiting until 5 p.m. before a tanker arrived, thus sacrificing a whole day's work and income.

Jamuben Ratnabhai Aahir lives in Patanka village with her husband and four children. She has two sons, aged 15 years and 8 months. Her two daughters are 12 and 8 years old. She has been a member of SEWA for over eight years and is a leader of several groups, including an embroidery and a savings group.

Jamuben's eldest son attends school every day. They used to pay Rs 20 each day for him to ride in a *chhakda* from Patanka to the school in Santalpur. They recently bought a used bicycle, which he now uses to ride to Babra. From there he rides in a *chhakda* and only has to pay Rs 10. He has to leave early in order to catch the *chhakda* and then has to pass two hours in Santalpur before school begins. He returns home between 4 and 4:40 p.m.

Jamuben earns for the family by both collecting gum and doing embroidery work for SEWA. When she first started collecting gum she could earn between Rs 12 and 18 a day, but the price of gum dropped from Rs 12 to to Rs 8, and at one point Rs 4, per kilo. However, with the aid of SEWA's intervention, the gum collectors were able to secure a rate of Rs 10 per kilo. Thus Jamuben is able to earn between Rs 400 and 450 per month by collecting gum.

On a typical day, Jamuben will wake up at 5 a.m. to collect water for her family. At 6 a.m. she begins walking to the jungle, where she spends six hours in the heat collecting about 1 kilo of gum. She returns home around 1 p.m., again to collect water and feed her family. Then she does embroidery work until dark. She again collects water and cooks for the family around 7 p.m. She resumes her embroidery work at 8 or 9 p.m. and works late into the night. Sometimes she stays up until 2:30 a.m. doing embroidery.

Jamuben faces many hardships with regard to transportation. First, she must walk 6 kilometres to and from the jungle every day in addition to the walking she does to collect the gum off the trees. She must spend Rs 200–300 of the Rs 800–1,000 that she earns each month for her son's transportation to and from school. If she needs to go to Santalpur to buy food or for her household necessities, she must walk 4 kilometres to Babra and then take a *chhakda* and lose a whole day's income from collecting gum and doing embroidery.

If Jamuben needs to go to Radhanpur, she must either walk 7 kilometres or take a *chhakda* to Sidhara village, and then take a bus from there. On one occasion, when she went to Radhanpur to fetch materials for her embroidery, she left the office later than usual and only found transportation as far as Sidhara. She then had to walk 7 kilometres in the dark, holding her baby and carrying the embroidery materials on her head.

Once when Jamuben was pregnant, she fell ill with chest pains, difficulty in breathing and diarrhoea. She had to pay Rs 215 to hire a *chhakda* to take her to Radhanpur to see a doctor. She then paid Rs 5 to get to SEWA's office in Radhanpur, where she rested a while. On her way home, she took a bus to Charanka for Rs 8. From there, because it was late and she was ill, a passing jeep took mercy on her and gave her a free ride home. Though in the end all was fine, the day cost nearly one-quarter of Jamuben's monthly income.

The people of Patanka have only had access to a *chhakda* for twelve months. A second vehicle arrived in their village only three months ago. Before that they walked 4 kilometres to Babra village or 6 kilometres to Sidhara to find any form of motorized transport.

Because Jamuben is the sole income earner in her family, the burdens she carries are overwhelming. She must feed her family and send her son to school with the money she earns. Transportation is a major expense, both in terms of monetary cost and in terms of income lost due to time spent travelling.

Possible alternatives to head-loading water

The women proposed several alternatives to head-loading. One was to have a pipeline to carry water directly to the home, but this would require resources that simply do not exist. Another was more effective harvesting of rainwater. This is a technique that has been used for years in other parts of Gujarat. SEWA has begun to construct underground tanks to store roof rainwater in four districts of Gujarat. In Banaskantha they have planned to construct tanks in 27 different homes in two villages. The government will provide 70 per cent of the cost, while the remaining 30 per cent will be provided by the household. If the rains are good and water is used conservatively (only for drinking), the supply should last about six months. This will provide relief both from water shortages and from having to head-load drinking water.

A third alternative was the use of animal carts (generally camel or bullock carts) to carry water from the source to the home, but there are several problems that need to be overcome before this becomes a viable solution. First is the availability of animal carts. There would undoubtedly be a charge for using these carts, which many women may not be willing or able to pay. Second is the problem of carrying the water. There are no smooth roads within villages and the movement of the carts causes water to spill out from the containers. However, with some group planning and creativity, this might be a viable alternative to head-loading. The women also suggested that the effects of head-loading water must be brought to light to all who use this water and to all who have a hand in water resource planning and management. The most effective solutions will be an integrated approach not only to building water resources but also to distributing water to users.

Transport and women's other responsibilities

Women are responsible for bringing household necessities such as food-stuffs and kerosene from a centre outside the village. Such items are not always regularly in stock and the women must go to get them as soon as they hear that they are available, using whatever transport facilities are available, at whatever cost. In one instance, the women of a village heard that rations had arrived so they immediately hired a *chhakda* at Rs 30 to go to Santalpur. When they arrived, they found out that the shopkeeper had already sold off the food rations to one of his relatives. The women had spent their valuable time and money only to return empty-handed.

In cases where food rations and other necessities are regularly available, the women must still invest time and money to collect them. If they travel by bus, they may spend a full day on the task. If they travel by a jeep or *chhakda*, they might save time, but they will spend more money. Often women must sacrifice one day each week to collect food and other household necessities. The amount of goods they can bring is limited by how much money they can spend and how much they can carry. In this case, the major costs of transport deprivation are measured in terms of time, money and sometimes the nourishment and nutrition of the family.

Transport deprivation also limits women's participation in social and economic development activities. Although SEWA members make concerted efforts to attend meetings, workshops and training sessions, they do so at great cost. Again, they must leave their villages early in the morning and usually cannot return until late in the evening. For women who don't have a child or a husband who might assume their responsibilities for a day, participating in activities that might better the living conditions for them and their families becomes very difficult.

In India, the rural economy is still very much interwoven and interlinked. Within such a social fabric, travel between villages is crucial.

Transport, water and earning a living: women salt workers and gum collectors

Salt workers and gum collectors suffer from such transport deprivation. These women work in unimaginably difficult conditions and are among the poorest of villagers living in Banaskantha.

The salt farming season in Gujarat runs from September through April, during which nearly 4,000,000 metric tonnes of salt, nearly 60 per cent of the country's total salt requirements, are produced. Salt farming in Gujarat takes place in the Little Rann of Kutch near the Santalpur *taluka* of Banaskantha. It is a major source of employment for both men and women during the agricultural off-season.

Women salt workers wake up early to attend to household chores before walking between 5 and 10 kilometres to the salt farm. They leave

> There is a sanctuary for wild asses in the Kutch desert where they are assured food and even drinking water, but we are not even that lucky – **Maganbhai, a salt worker**. (Nanavaty and Buch, 1990)

their homes around 8 a.m. to reach the farm by 9 a.m., and leave after work ends around 5 or 6 p.m. to return to their homes around 8 p.m. Most salt workers cannot afford gumboots to protect their skin against the corrosive clay. Their feet suffer from both fungus and numerous cuts, making the walk to and from the salt farm slow and painful.

Many salt workers relocate themselves and their families to the vicinity of the salt farm because there is no daily transport to and from the farm or because they come from far-off villages. This disrupts their lives for six months. They live in makeshift temporary shelters and face the most extreme heat and cold of the desert climate. Children's education is interrupted and they usually end up working on the salt farms with their parents. There are no childcare facilities so mothers are forced to bring young children to the worksite, exposing them to the harsh desert climate all day. These salt workers suffer from inadequate nutrition and cannot access medical care in case of serious illness. There is no medical facility near the salt farms and the workers cannot afford to travel to a large village or town.

Availability of water is the most severe problem facing the relocated salt workers. Water is always scarce in the desert. The salt workers spend Rs 150–300 per month on water and still they cannot meet all their needs. Salt workers should bathe thoroughly each day to wash off accumulated salt particles but only very few of them do this. Most bathe only once a week.

CONCLUSIONS AND RECOMMENDATIONS

Water resources and appropriate transport facilities are both grossly insufficient in Banaskantha district. The most obvious effect of water and transport deprivation is on women's time allocations. Because most of the women are generally poor, self-employed workers who rely on their labour and productivity to survive, time is a valuable resource. Time lost is often income lost, if and when work is available.

Transport deprivation and lack of adequate water resources and of efficient means of distributing water force women to spend a great deal of energy and time in travelling and in collecting water. Visiting the *taluka* centre to buy food and other necessities takes long hours and constrains women's participation in activities, such as those organized by SEWA, that might improve their social and economic conditions and that would have positive effects on the entire family and the village. Head-loading and walking long distances to collect water or to access employment, together with the lack of water for drinking and sanitation, has detrimental effects on women's health. The heavy time and energy allocation that inadequate water resources and transport deprivation impose on women restricts their ability to look after the home, care for the children and earn income. The welfare of the entire home suffers as a consequence.

While much work has been done to improve the availability of water in Banaskantha district, equal attention must be paid to the transport situation. Women's needs must be taken into account during transport planning activities. Women are major economic players who are not given proper attention by the Gujarat State Road Transport Corporation. Transportation plays an important role in women's lives, affecting food security, empowerment through employment, timely access to medical care and the availability of essential goods and services for rural populations. Women feel the impact of the lack of transport more intensely because they are responsible for the wellbeing and welfare of the family.

15

A FOREST ECONOMY AND WOMEN'S TRANSPORTATION

DUMKA DISTRICT, BIHAR, INDIA

Nitya Rao

The Santhal Parganas, lying in the southeastern part of the state of Bihar, India, gets its name from the Santhal tribals, who constitute a large proportion of the local population. The area includes hilly portions running from north to south covered in many parts by jungles, and by valleys with small villages with clearings for cultivation. About half of the land area to the west and southwest is rolling country containing long ridges with intervening depressions, rocky in places and covered with scrub jungles in others. The rest is plains, lying between the Ganga and the hills, largely cultivated with rice.

The division has a fairly good system of roadways, though the divisional headquarters at Dumka has no railway connection. The major towns are well connected by buses, but the bullock cart remains the major source of local conveyance. Most people walk. Bicycles are gradually increasing in number, but are currently used only by men.

The mostly rural Santhal population is spread over several districts of South Bihar, Northern Orissa and Madhya Pradesh and the western part of West Bengal. Despite severe deforestation in this area, wherever forests remain the Santhals still depend on them for a supplementary source of livelihood and survival. They collect fuelwood, food items, such as roots, berries, greens, mangoes, and so on, medicinal herbs and forest produce, such as mahua, sal seeds, tamarind, kendu leaves, and so on, for further processing and sale. They also farm a single rain-fed crop.

Society considers the Santhals as labourers in agriculture and construction, and for generations they have been employed to clear the land and work in the tea plantations of the northeast, as well as in agriculture and construction in eastern India. Even though there have been special tribal schools established in the district, and there was a campaign for adult literacy during 1993–4, the lack of adequate post-literacy and continuing education programmes has meant that literacy rates and educational levels among the Santhals and Paharias are low. Despite the establishment of primary health centres (PHCs) and health sub-centres, and the setting up of a malaria control unit, diseases such as malaria, Kala-azar and diarrhoea continue to be major causes of mortality in the area. The PHC at the block headquarters is ill equipped for diagnosis and treatment. Because of the lack of any transport from the villages to the PHC, sick people are usually brought in when it is too late to save their lives. Many of the traditional medicinal plants used by local people until recent times to cure disease have disappeared with the clearing of the forests. Faith in medicinal herbs has also declined due to the exploitative rituals that are often associated with the practice of traditional medicine.

The Santhals consider all lands and forests the common property of the village in which they settle. They have a leader, a *manjhi*, to administer the rights, rules and ceremonies of the community. The institution of *manjhi* has now become more or less hereditary, and is officially recognized for collecting rents and reporting crimes. Most village issues are discussed and decided locally by the panchayat or council of village elders, headed by the *manjhi*. Punishment under Santhal law is usually not very severe, except in the case of intimacy between a Santhal girl and a *dikku*[1] (non-Santhal) boy, when the offenders are excommunicated from the society. This tradition was the way the Santhals attempted to maintain their social purity and solidarity, and prevent the transfer of Santhal lands to non-Santhals. The post-independence formation of community development blocks to which people had to go for their basic needs resulted in a decline in community spirit.

THE SITUATION OF SANTHALI WOMEN

According to Santhal law and tradition, women are perceived as 'objects' or 'property', to be transferred from the father to the husband. The father or husband is held responsible for any offence that a woman may commit. Women do not have any claim over the property of either the father or the husband, whether movable or immovable. Santhal law does, however, provide maintenance for widowed women, unmarried girls, divorced daughters and wives. This custom, codified during British rule, has been misinterpreted by the Santhal Pargana Tenancy Act, formulated after Independence in 1949, which does not provide any opportunity for the woman to inherit land on the excuse that 'Santhal tribal law is quite definite in not allowing women to inherit' (Rana and Rao, 1996).

Traditionally, in the absence of a male heir, a man could get one of his daughters married with a *ghar jamai* – a son-in-law who is formally adopted at the time of marriage as a son by the girl's father. He is supposed to stay in the girl's village and sever all links with his own family. The land can then be transferred to the daughter. In practice, however, even if a *ghar jamai* is taken, the male agnates most often harass him and drive him out of the village. If a *ghar jamai* is not taken, then the man's property will go to his other male agnates, rather than his daughters. Even the widow gets no share and, unless she has a son, is virtually homeless on her husband's death. The practice amongst Santhals of marrying more than one woman, named as *badki, majhli* and *chutki* according to the order of their marriage, worsens the situation of women. If the first wife allows it, other wives are given some gifts as an insurance against friction; otherwise they do not receive anything. A large number of Santhali women, deprived from inheriting land and quite frequently victims of polygamy, are thrown out of their homes without any maintenance and are forced to lead un-imaginably hard lives with hardly any resources.

As in other patriarchal societies, the gender division of labour makes ploughing, hunting, sacrificing animals and other ritual ceremonies exclusive male preserves. However, in addition to all the household maintenance functions, it is the woman who collects paddy, borrows seed-grain, negotiates loans, goes to the market and in general manages the household. There are no restrictions on her mobility.

SURVIVAL AND LIVELIHOOD STRATEGIES

Agriculture, along with the collection and sale of forest produce, used to be the mainstay of the Santhal economy. With the decline in forest cover and lack of substantial improvement in agriculture, the Santhals have been forced into wage employment, both local and migrant, to sustain their livelihoods. Livelihoods today are finely balanced between the availability of forest produce, ownership of land and the ability to cultivate it, and wage employment, each of which sometimes supports, but more often hampers, the development of the others as viable livelihood options.

Table 15.1, derived from a study of 21 villages in Dumka district by the researcher in 1997, shows the high degree of dependence on wage labour

TABLE 15.1   Primary occupation of households

Block	Agriculture	Labour	Service	Artisan/ trader	Others (NTFP)	Total
Gopikandar	210	101	8	43	30	392
Jarmundi	75	257	4	1	–	337
Dumka	291	273	21	4	11	600
Total	576	631	33	48	41	1,329

Source: Rao, 1997.

for survival in the district. Gopikandar block, which still has considerable forests and forest produce, is less dependent on wage labour than the other two. Jarmundi lacks forests or any artisanal or trade activity based on forest produce, and is the most dependent on wage labour.

Since the major focus of this study was on women's transportation needs in a forest economy, villages in Gopikandar and the adjacent Ramgarh blocks of the district were selected for study. In these areas more than 33 per cent of women and 22 per cent of men are dependent on the forests for their survival.

TRANSPORT, LIVELIHOODS AND GENDER RELATIONS

The forest economy is primarily a female one, with women responsible for collection, processing and sale of forest produce. As forests dwindle, women walk longer distances to collect their produce. They head-load firewood, leaf plates, puffed rice, vegetables or liquor from the forests to the village, and to the market. Though roads have now been constructed to the markets, transport planners have ignored women's journeys to the jungle and to the fields. There are no regular means of transport available, not even to the markets. A few lucky villages have a single bus service during the day that can take the women one way to the market, but the majority of villages in the interior and hilly areas are inaccessible to buses. Even bullock carts find it difficult to traverse the slopes. Motorbikes are rare. A few bicycles are now found in these villages, but these are entirely under the control of and used by men.

The marketing of firewood and of fruits such as mangoes and jackfruits is gradually being taken over by the men, who take them to the markets on their bicycles. For women, this has meant a reduction in their transport burden and in time and labour. The negative consequence has been that while they collect the firewood and fruits from the jungle, they have lost control over the income from their sale. An attempt has been made in this study to analyse this development more closely and assess its impact on women's income and status.

The state's intervention in the area of transport provisioning seems to be restricted to road construction and focuses on connecting villages to towns. Roads are important for facilitating development of public transport in the area, such as buses, trucks and other heavy vehicles. However, if not maintained regularly, they become unusable by all except heavy vehicles. In several parts of Dumka district, the metalled roads are in a pathetic condition – perhaps because they have not had any maintenance since their construction in the 1940s or 1950s.

Three villages in Dumka district were selected in 1998 for detailed study: Jadopani, an interior forest village with no proper road and means of transportation; Pandhini Duma, connected once a day by a jeep to Dumka; and a roadside village, Mohalo. In all three villages the collection and sale of forest produce was a major source of livelihood. While Jadopani and Mohalo are in Gopikandar block, Pandhini Duma is in Ramgarh block, adjoining the Gopikandar villages. The villages were studied in detail using a population listing, detailed interviews of selected households and participant observation.

The study examined the consequences of changes in the socio-economic and environmental context on the transport components of the roles and responsibilities of women and men in the area. It looked at the extent of women's transport burden, and at the existing transport provision and how it is used and whose needs it meets. It examined recent changes and their effects on gender relations and transport tasks and considered the scope of non-transport interventions (drinking-water supply, fuelwood plantations) to reduce women's transport burden.

WOMEN AND TRANSPORT IN THE THREE VILLAGES

Jadopani village

Jadopani is an interior, tribal village comprising two major hamlets – with 19 and 24 households respectively. The hamlet at the lower level is inhabited entirely by Santhals. The upper hamlet has a mix of a few Santhal and

Paharia households. Some Paharias live in smaller groups of two to three households, scattered on the hilltops near the jungle. While almost all the households own some land, only a few villagers, living in the lower hamlet of the village, have land beside the stream, which they irrigate and which takes a summer paddy crop, in addition to the major rain-fed one. They are more prosperous than those living in the upper hamlet. Members of about a quarter of the households engage in wage-labour seasonally, but migration for survival is negligible. Not many in this village own bicycles, bullock carts or other means of transport, as the path to the village is rocky, steep and difficult to negotiate with a vehicle.

The village headman or *manjhi* is one among the more prosperous Santhals; the Paharias felt that he did nothing for them, but only for the lower Santhal settlement. The Paharias have only one well for their water, located at a distance of almost a kilometre. Though only a 10-minute walk, collecting water involves making at least three trips in the morning and two to three in the evening. During the summer months of April and May, this well dries up, and then the Paharia women have to go to the stream flowing beside the lower settlement to collect water. Carrying the water uphill to their settlement is a difficult task. There is a hand-pump just near the headman's house but not in their hamlet.

The headman said that they had tried boring a well in the upper settlement, but met with a rock crust and no water. He had, however, got loans sanctioned from the government for construction of houses for 23 Paharia households, but explained that service provisioning was difficult because they lived in scattered groups in the jungle, rather than together in a settlement.

The Santhals in the upper hamlet are also poor and mainly depend on the collection and sale of forest produce for their livelihood. Each family has about 30–40 mahua[2] trees allotted to them in the *jamabandi* (land settlement), and this is a major source of support, both for the food and income it provides. A household can earn Rs 500–1,000 from the sale of mahua in the lean summer months of April and May. The Paharias in this village are poorer than even the poor Santhals. They do not have land but depend for their livelihood upon shifting cultivation in the forests and firewood selling.

The better-off households have access to the services of the health worker as well as the PHC doctor, while the poorer households find it more difficult, and often end up paying high amounts to private doctors.

As Jadopani is a village high up in the hills and surrounded by forests, there is a year-round availability of forest produce such as tendu leaves, mahua, fruits (jackfruit, mango, tamarind, etc.) and their products, such as

Seasonal calendar of forest produce

January	Firewood, sal leaves
February	Firewood, sal leaves
March	Kendu, taro, mahua flowers, firewood, sal leaves
April	Mahua, raw mango, tamarind, bel, tiril (kendu fruit), firewood, sal leaves
May	Kendu leaves, mango fruit, firewood, sal leaves
June	Mahua fruits, mushroom, firewood, sal leaves
July	Mahua fruits, mushroom, firewood, sal leaves
August	Vegetables, sal leaves
September	Vegetables, sal leaves
October	Roots, firewood, sal leaves
November	Roots, firewood, sal leaves
December	Roots, firewood, sal leaves

sal leaf plates (see box). This provides villagers with supplementary income to meet daily needs throughout the year and reduces the need for migration in search of employment. Despite this, most of the Paharias and poorer Santhals have taken food loans from the local moneylender at Gopikandar, which they have to repay with 50 per cent interest within a year.

In Jadopani village women spend between six and ten hours daily collecting water, fuelwood and other forest produce as well as working in the fields. There is a clear gender division of tasks. All household maintenance tasks, including earning money to purchase food supplements such as oil and spices, fall into women's domain. The men in Jadopani are responsible for household agriculture, for the supply of grains for the family, wage labour tasks and the sale of certain kinds of higher value forest produce. The remote location of the village on a hilltop, the poor state of the track connecting it to the main road, and the lack of formal or informal transport services mean that both women and men walk. Women carry head-loads of fuelwood to the market, men carry poles on their shoulders. Men may walk longer distances to the market, carrying heavier loads, but not daily. The women make many more trips to the forest, to collect produce not only for sale but also for home consumption. The men are mainly concerned with collection of produce for sale.

Lukhi Murmu is a widow with three daughters and a son. Her husband had cleared 2 bighas (about 0.8 acres) of land in the jungle, but after his death, with small children to take care of, she was unable to cultivate this. She goes to the forest twice a week and collects sal leaves, and with her daughter makes these into leaf plates and sells them in the local markets twice a week. They save one person's earnings for the purchase of accessories such as clothes, footwear, and so on, while spending the rest on daily food needs. The markets are 10–15 kilometres away, and on market days the entire day is spent on the trip.

At the wedding of her eldest daughter, Lukhi Murmu made the arrangement of *ghardi jamai*, and her son-in-law came to stay in the village for a certain number of years. With his assistance, they resumed cultivation and the condition of their household improved, but he died suddenly and once again the family is in a precarious condition, back to selling leaf plates for their survival. Even though women here are well acquainted with agricultural practices, the difficult terrain makes it hard for them to manage the cultivation without the support of men.

One of the Paharia women from the upper hamlet, Durghi Maharani, took us to the well, the fields and the forests where she travels daily. The well was a little more than ten minutes away along a narrow path. Durghi makes two trips in the morning and two in the evening, carrying two pots of water on each trip. From the well, we walked with Durghi across the fields belonging to the Santhals, and into the forest up a steep climb. On the other side, in the middle of the forest, by a small stream, Durghi and her husband had cleared a small plot of land on which they grow pulses. A crop had just been harvested (February) and was being carried home by women on their heads and by the men on their shoulders. Although it was only 2 kilometres from their house, it took almost half an hour to get to their plot of land.

The Paharias practise shifting cultivation in a systematic, well-planned and non-destructive way. Another plot of land was being cleared for the next year. The plot would be cultivated for a year and then left to rejuvenate. Durghi collected some wood for fuel, *dantvan* or tooth-twigs for cleaning teeth, and sal leaves for making plates for use at home. These she bundled up to carry home. Durghi makes four to five trips to the forest every day. From December to about June the work in the forest peaks, and Durghi stores a stock of fuelwood and plates for use at home during the rainy months, when it is difficult to go to the forest, and also for sale. During the monsoons, they are also busy with their own cultivation and agricultural wage labour.

While Durghi takes fuelwood to the market at Gopikandar, her husband goes to Amrapara, about 15 kilometres away, with poles of wood needed for construction work. He can carry about four poles, each of which is sold for about Rs 10. This *haat* (local market) is held on Saturdays, but as it is far away he leaves the previous evening and stops overnight on the way. After selling the poles, he returns home the next night. Though the poles are sold only once a week, Durghi's husband goes to the forest at least three or four times a week and collects poles to be stored for sale in the monsoon months.

Sundari Marandi, after finishing household chores in the morning, goes about 3 kilometres into the forest and spends about two hours collecting sal leaves. After bathing at the stream and eating she settles down to making leaf plates. She goes to the forest again in the evening to collect firewood. Once a week, she goes to the local market to sell her leaf plates. She earns about Rs 40 a week, and this takes care of her family's need for oil, pulses and spices. Her husband, Chunka Hansdak, takes the cattle out to graze in the morning and works at ploughing, sowing and guarding the fields. They have three sons and a daughter. While the daughter helps Sundari Marandi with making leaf plates, cooking and other household chores, the sons often engage in both agricultural and non-agricultural wage labour tasks.

Esther Murmu is the only woman in her household, and so bears the entire burden of household tasks, including the collection of water and fuel for the house, and the responsibility for house repairs and maintenance, such as coating with a layer of mud, to be done in the summer every year. She has no time to engage in any forest-related activity. Her husband and sons look after the fields and the animals. The produce from the fields is enough to meet their grain requirements, and for other needs they sell their goats and pigs. Occasionally, Esther Mirmu sells firewood.

Mohalo village

Mohalo is a roadside village, well connected to both Dumka and Pakur[3] by buses. There are four or five buses that operate each way every day, but they don't take people with loads, as they are already crowded with passengers. Almost 50 per cent of the households in Mohalo own a bicycle. The PHC is located at Gopikandar, and this is one place to which people either cycle or go by bus. Cycles are used for many purposes, such as travelling to government offices in the block headquarters of Gopikandar, going to the market, and also carrying loads of wood for sale. As mentioned at the start of the chapter, however, the cycle is an entirely male asset.

Preliminary information about the village was collected from 34 out of the 60-odd households. Of these households 29 were Santhals, 4 Paharias and 1 from a higher caste. Most of the households had some land, but were unable to cultivate it properly; 12 households had leased out a part of their lands, many forced to do so as collateral for loans taken from the moneylenders. Of the 34 households, 21 were indebted to the moneylenders, mostly for loans to buy seed or for consumption. Wage labour and migration are not high in this village.

In Mohalo, both men and women go to the forest for collection of fuelwood. Women are also responsible for collection of water, food preparation and household maintenance. There are four hand-pumps on the road but they are often in disrepair, so the women collect water from the stream. There are also two wells located near the stream. The men graze the cattle in the fields near the village, and chop and bundle the wood for sale in the markets. Depending on the size and composition of the household, men also assist their wives in a few household tasks, such as cooking and childcare. If they have a bicycle, they play a more active role in marketing; otherwise they go to the market once a week with the women.

Men and women carry two bundles of fuelwood each to the local market at Kharoni, 10 kilometres away, every Friday. Some men take cycle-loads of wood to the slightly more distant Pakuria, 19 kilometres away, every day. While they can get Rs 10–12 for a load at Pakuria, the price at Kharoni is about Rs 8. However, men often get harassed by the Forest Department officials and, if caught, end up paying a fine of as much as Rs 150.

We accompanied one couple, Barsa Kisku and Lukhi Marandi, on their daily trip to collect firewood. The forest is about 6 kilometres from the village, and it took almost an hour to get to the top of the hill, from where the wood was being collected. Though there is a forest adjacent to the village, the villagers themselves are protecting it for the future and no one is allowed to collect fuelwood from it. The couple spent several hours cutting the wood, arranging and bundling the long pieces. Lukhi then took the larger bundle on her head, and Barsa the lighter one on his shoulder. Maintaining one's balance with a load on one shoulder on a steep slope is difficult but men are unable to carry the wood on their heads.

The couple slowly found their way down, holding on to roots and stems for balance; where there was thick vegetation Barsa moved the bushes and branches so his wife could pass. At one point there were steep rocks. The couple put their loads down. Lukhi went down first, and then her husband slowly passed down the bundle. She pulled it down, balanced it against a tree, then raised it onto her head again. It was a most treacherous journey, yet the couple moved down the hill slowly and carefully. They decided to rest only once they had reached the plain land outside the forest. At this stage, Barsa untied his sandals from the bundle of wood and put them on. Lukhi didn't have any footwear.

The trip to the forest started at 11 a.m.; by the time the researchers and the couple returned, it was 4 p.m. The trip had taken a good part of the day. The couple's two young children were at home. They are used to their parents' absence, as going to the forest is a daily routine. Once home, Lukhi started on her household chores, while her husband cut the logs, and prepared the bundles to be carried to the market the following day. Both Barsa and Lukhi do the selling. Lukhi goes only to Kharoni market once a week. Her husband uses his cycle to sell wood three times a week at Pakuria, taking two bundles on each trip. At the rate of Rs 10 per bundle, he earns Rs 60 per week from the sale of fuelwood.

Where there are more members in a family collecting wood, men with bicycles go to sell wood every day, leaving the task of collection to the others. A young boy, Simon Hansdak, who left school when his father died several years ago, now cultivates their small plot of land and also takes loads of wood collected by his mother by bicycle to Pakuria every day.

Several non-tribal traders buy firewood from the Santhals and Paharias at the local markets and take it to the district headquarters of Dumka, where it is sold at almost double the price. The tribals will not travel that far because they are afraid of the harassment of the police and forest guards. The sale of fuelwood is illegal, despite it being the mainstay of the livelihoods of the tribal people. The non-tribals are more confident of handling such situations. Access to markets, then, is not only related to access to transport, but also a result of complex social relations based on gender, caste and class, and the number of working women and men in the household.

In Mohalo we tried to understand whether cycle-loading fuelwood by men had affected intra-household relationships in any way. Traditionally the collection and sale of forest produce have been the woman's responsibility and the resultant income has been hers. Did expenditure priorities and decision-making roles change with men doing the selling?

Barsa Kisku usually buys rice, vegetables, pulses, oil and spices for the house after selling the wood at Pakuria. He realizes the importance of proper care and food for his two young children, and helps Lukhi with childcare and cooking. This seemed to be the rule rather than the exception amongst the families of this village. Budhan Hembrum actually makes two trips to the Kharoni *haat* on market day so that he can reduce the trips to Pakuria and go to the forest for collection of firewood on more days. While by and large the money earned through the sale of firewood is spent by the men on the household, the women no longer have access to cash for any of their personal expenses. If there is a surplus, the men spend it on their own needs.

Bitia Soren goes to the jungle with a group of women to collect fuelwood, while her husband Manuel Murmu works as an agricultural labourer. On days when he does not get work, he helps with cutting the logs, bundling them and taking them to the market at Pakuria to sell. Though he buys the food and essentials for the household, he spends the remaining money on liquor.

As it is a recent phenomenon, it is difficult to comment on the long-term impact of the shift of marketing functions to men, and on women's mobility and status within Santhal society. Though they have lost direct control over income, at the moment at least, the overworked women find the reduction in workloads and transport burdens a relief. Their ability to negotiate intra-household gender relations in the future to maintain this position will be worth observing.

Pandhini Duma village

Pandhini Duma is a small village of 23 Santhal households in Baliyakhoda panchayat. Though there is a road leading up to the village, it is poorly maintained. There is one jeep that connects the village to Dumka every day. There is plenty of land in the village, but much of it is unproductive uplands. The amount of paddy-growing lowlands is limited, yet the primary occupation of the majority of households is agriculture.

The headman of the village has a large family and only about 3 bighas (1.2 acres) of paddy land. He described how land in the village was alienated, with most of the lowlands being transferred to non-resident, non-tribals about a hundred years ago. He blamed the Paharia tribe for destroying the forests. Now the women have to go more than 5 kilometres away to the jungle for collection of fuelwood.

Of the 13 households available in the village at the time of the study, a third were very poor, and perpetually indebted to the moneylender. Four households had taken loans for seed, household expenses and medical expenses at an interest rate of 50 per cent for six months. In the absence of a primary school in the village, very few children study. Only 2 out of 33 children were going to school.

Women from six of the households and three men migrate seasonally to West Bengal[4] for agricultural labour. Migration takes place in mixed groups because of the increased incidence of physical harassment of and violence against women when they travel alone. Migrants need to take the bus from Dumka to Bengal. To go to Dumka, they use the jeep that operates to the village. They use the jeep only when they are migrating because then they have luggage, including a few pots and pans. At other times when they need to get to Dumka they walk to the next village 3 kilometres away and then take a bus. The regular users of the jeep are the non-tribal traders and other professionals such as schoolteachers or nurses with jobs in the area.

When we went to the village in the morning, it was deserted. Several couples were working on the common threshing floor on the outskirts of the village, and many of the women had gone to the forests. Around noon, groups of women and girls started returning from the forests. Firewood collection takes five to six hours. If they leave home around 6 a.m., they return by noon. The women go to the forests almost every day in order to store up fuelwood for use during the rains. While in the forests, the women also collect sal leaves to use as plates at home. Owing to the distance to the forest and the effort required to collect fuelwood, it is no longer common for women from this village to engage in the sale of fuelwood or any other forest produce. They collect it mainly for consumption at home. One man who had gone to the forest with his wife was bringing the fuelwood back on a bicycle, but with an uneven path this was not an easy task.

There are some open-cast coalfields a few kilometres away. Several of the men go there regularly, cut the coal and bring it back for use at home as well as to sell. In the local market, they can sell a bag of coal for Rs 50, in Dumka for Rs 150. But they rarely go to Dumka as the effort is too great. Most men who go to the coalfields own bicycles and use them for transporting bags of coal. Out of 13 households studied, 9 had bicycles. One of them had two, and one three. The number of bicycles is directly related to the number of adult males in the household. Women have no access to bicycles.

Both women and men in Pandhini Duma wake up at 4 a.m. Men take the cattle out to graze around the village, while women clean the house, fetch water and cook the morning meal. The well is close by, yet they have to collect six to eight pots of water, which takes them more than half an hour.

The grain had just been harvested (January–February). By the time the men returned, the women had finished their household chores. After having a light meal, both the men and women went to the threshing floor, built about a kilometre outside the village. For almost the entire day they engaged in threshing, collecting the grain, bundling the chaff and transporting it home. This is seasonal work and would be completed in a few days. The exclusively gendered tasks are going to the jungle for women and to the coalfields for men. While the distances are more or less the same for both, and the loads as heavy, men use bicycles, while the women walk.

Maino Hembrum is a widow who lives with her two children, a daughter aged 20 and a son aged 17 at the time of the study. During the study, Maino's daughter was in Bengal, where she had gone for the harvest work. In the Santhal Parganas, life changes greatly from season to season with the availability of forest produce, employment, and so on, and Maino Hembrum's day varies accordingly. Maino gets up in the morning and quickly finishes cooking and cleaning the house. She then goes three times to the well, fetching two pots of water each time. During the summer months this well dries up, and then she has to go 3 kilometres away to fetch water. When her daughter is at home, she helps her with this work. By 7 a.m. she is ready to go to the threshing floor. The straw has to be bundled up and brought home. If she does four or five trips every day, then this task will be completed within a week.

Maino regularly looks for wage labour, both agricultural and non-agricultural, in a large village, Dando, located 2 kilometres away. Though the family has fields, she does not spend too much time on their own cultivation. The output is always low as the lands are not of very good quality. In labour work, she can earn up to Rs 20 per day, during which she will have one snack of puffed rice.

The forest is almost an 8-kilometre walk away so Maino doesn't go every day, but only once or twice a week. The trip takes a whole day. From the forest she collects both fuelwood, mostly for domestic consumption, and sal leaves for making leaf plates. If she doesn't go out to labour, she makes leaf plates at home. When a sufficient number of leaf plates are made, she sells them from her home to any trader. She doesn't go to the market for this purpose.

Maino's son has a bicycle and uses it for getting coal. At the time of the study he had to help his mother with agricultural work, so he was not going to the coalfield. He usually goes once or twice a week, and then the earnings from coal are sufficient for their weekly provisions of oil, spices, pulses and vegetables. He sells a sack of coal for Rs 50 locally. If he could take it to Dumka, he would earn three times as much, but the distance is too far and the road is bad.

Jhumri Hansdak and Sarkar Soren have four children. Sarkar goes every day, carrying a packed lunch, to the coalfields at Bargo village, 10 kilometres away. After taking a permit for Rs 15, he starts work cutting the coal. It takes the whole day to get a full sack of coal. He loads it on his cycle and brings it home. The road is uphill, so the journey is difficult and tiresome. He sells it to a big coal depot in Kidva village for Rs 60. It is with this money that they run the household. Jhumri takes care of all the household tasks, with some support from her daughter. With one small baby, she is unable to go out to work, but spends much of her time cooking, fetching water and taking care of their own agriculture. At the time of the study, she too was engaged with work on the threshing floor. During the rainy season, her daughter goes out for labour, but she usually finds jobs within the village, though the wage, Rs 15 per day, is much lower than she could earn outside. But this means she can look after their own fields, even though they don't yield much.

The composition and size of the family make a lot of difference to the women's workloads. Miroo Hansdak and her daughter-in-law Arsoo Marandi share the tasks of cooking, cleaning and fetching water. Arsoo has a small baby. Once she has fed it, she fetches water from the well, then leaves her child with Miroo and goes to the fields along with her husband. Her husband takes the cattle out for grazing early in the morning, then for the rest of the day is engaged in the fields. They both come home for the afternoon meal and then rest for a while.

ISSUES AND LESSONS

Employment and transport

In Jadopani and Mohalo, for six months of the year, people depend on the collection and sale of forest produce, and for the remaining time on their own cultivation and some wage-work. During this time their transport needs are more local in nature, including trips from the village to the forests, fields and markets. In Pandhini Duma, however, there is a greater dependence on wage-work and seasonal migration. Trips to the forest are necessary, but forest produce is no longer a source of earnings, though it does still provide livelihood support. Travel tends to be over longer distances for trips in search of wage-work and outside sources for earning income: to surrounding villages, the coalfields or still further for migration, particularly in the winter months from November to January.

Women make daily and more regular journeys to the forests, fields and markets, and to the sources of water – the well, stream or hand-pump.

Women mainly carry the loads on their heads. Fodder collection is not one of their tasks, as the cattle are largely left to graze in the fields and forests. Some women may travel for wage-work to neighbouring villages and towns or migrate to more distant destinations.

Some men have access to bicycles, which they use to go to the coalfields, the market or sometimes even the fields. Women have no access to bicycles, even though many travel long distances to the forests, to markets and to neighbouring villages for wage-work.

Household composition and transport

There is a strong relationship between household size and composition and the transport needs and burdens of different members of the household. The transport needs are a corollary of the gender division of tasks and responsibilities, with men responsible for providing the basic grains and women for all other household maintenance functions, including finding food supplements. There is, however, a provision for sharing tasks amongst members of the same sex.

In the case of a nuclear family, the man often helps and supports the woman in the collection of forest produce, and takes responsibility for its sale. In larger households with more than one adult woman, the women take care of the forest-related activities while the men are more likely to engage in agriculture or waged work, only providing assistance in marketing if required.

Transport provision

Transport interventions have been few. The state has constructed roads and set up bus routes, interventions that address the demands of the market rather than the transport needs of village women in performing their daily tasks. Even where transport services do exist, as in Mohalo, neither women nor men with loads are allowed. In Pandhini Duma, the major users of the daily jeep service to Dumka were non-tribal traders and professionals such as schoolteachers who needed to commute to the villages. The local tribals rarely used the service.

The Regional Transport Authority (RTA), located in Dumka, enjoys full powers with regard to the issue of route permits and other control measures. Routes are decided mainly according to public need and demand. The bus owners' views on the profitability of the route are also taken into account. The RTA invites applications from bus owners for different routes, who are also free to suggest new routes. As the Bihar State Road

Transport Corporation does not make applications, the RTA deals mainly with private owners and has to give in to many of their demands. The routes are developed in response to the needs of the market rather than those of local people. The RTA, however, does fix the fares for the region, which it claims are lower than in other parts of the state.

The RTA has given about 100 permits for operation on 57 main routes in the region. It estimates that there are about 150 buses plying these routes. Local people estimate the number of buses to be greater than 300, but very few connect the interiors to the towns. Many bus owners take on the interior routes for the sake of obtaining a permit, and then only serve the main road, a fact unofficially confirmed by the District Transport Officer. Bus owners maintain that it is difficult to ply the interior routes because of the poor road conditions. They argue that women head-loaders prefer to walk to the markets even if there is a bus on the route, so they can save money, but at Mohalo we learned the contrary.

The introduction and use of bicycles has not directly benefited women. As the area is very poor, and the society strongly patriarchal, the acquisition of any asset goes first to the men. While this has meant that the task of taking the loads to the market is gradually shifting to the male owners of bicycles, the impact of this is as yet not very clear. Most of the men interviewed spend the money earned from the sale of the forest produce in the markets on household necessities. Women, who have lost direct control over the cash income, are unable to save or utilize it for their personal expenses. However, they continue with the task of collection from the forest.

Non-transport interventions

The scope for non-transport interventions to reduce women's transport burden can be clearly seen when one compares the task of collecting drinking water in the lower and upper hamlets of Jadopani village. In the lower hamlet, this is a relatively easy task due to the presence of a handpump near the houses, and when this doesn't work the stream is close by. For the women in the upper hamlet, the closest well is about 1 kilometre away; when this dries up, they have to walk down to the stream and then undertake the hard climb up to their settlement, carrying loads of water.

Protecting and regenerating village forests, as is being done in Mohalo, could help in reducing transport burdens relating to the collection of forest produce.

AREAS FOR POLICY INTERVENTION

Improving agricultural transport

Agricultural transport could be improved by upgrading the paths to the fields and by providing small carts or wheelbarrows for carrying loads, mainly seeds and harvested crops, to and from the fields. The use of inputs is low since agriculture is rain-fed and manured by grazing cattle. Promoting changes in agricultural practices that could make farming the mainstay of the Santhals' livelihoods could create a demand for the transportation of other inputs.

Transport for market needs

Markets are distant and the issue of market linkage needs to be seriously addressed. Bicycles are of course one option, but access to bicycles does not necessarily mean access to the best markets or access irrespective of gender, caste and class relations. Non-tribal traders are able to carry wood and coal to the district headquarters of Dumka but the Santhals are constrained by their poverty, lack of capital and resources, and unequal social relations. Even amongst the Santhals, the men, with access to bicycles, greater freedom to stay away from the house for longer periods of time, and fewer household maintenance responsibilities, can access better markets than can the women. Having to return home as soon as possible, with no option to stay out and no access to transport, Santhal women get the lowest prices for their produce. From this broader development, poverty-sensitive and social relations-sensitive perspective, there are several options with which to address this issue:

- *Special buses for women carrying loads on market days* In the southern state of Kerala, such a service is provided to women fish vendors bringing the fish from the harbour into town because they are not allowed on the regular buses with their loads.
- *Collectivization of marketing* Though not possible in the case of fuelwood due to its bulk, traders often collect and sell the produce of several people. They go from house to house in a village and collect the leaf plates, fruits, mushrooms, and so on, from the women and take them to the market for sale on their bicycles or in vans. The women receive a lower price when they sell the produce to such traders. Santhal women have experience of interacting with the market. If they could collect their produce and arrange for transport to the village or to the nearest point from where it could be taken to market, they

could probably get a higher price for their products and increase their bargaining power vis-à-vis other market forces.

* *Attention to improvement of paths*   Road construction policy has mainly related to linking towns and market villages with each other. Though some roadside villages, such as Mohalo, have benefited, this is more accidental than intentional. There has to be greater attention paid to improving the paths connecting interior villages such as Jadopani with the main road-head, since it will create an opportunity for hiring transport if it is not possible to provide state-run buses to all villages.

CONCLUSION

The case study has highlighted several interesting features regarding transport needs and provisioning in the forest-dependent villages of Dumka district in the Santhal Parganas. First, despite a clear gender division of tasks and roles particularly in activities related to household maintenance functions, with collection of drinking water, cleaning, cooking and collection of fuel for home consumption being primarily women's tasks, in terms of the collection of forest produce for sale both men and women appear equally engaged.

Second, the rigidity of the above gender division of tasks is mediated to a large extent by the size and composition of the family. In a nuclear family, the men do take on several of the above roles, particularly cooking and childcare. It is interesting to note, however, that the men usually do not take on the tasks involving distance and transport burdens, such as the collection of water.

Third, existing transport provision mainly caters to the requirements of the market, primarily the transport needs of professionals commuting to work and trade between markets. Apart from the long-distance transport needs of Santhal women and of men for local or migrant wage employment, provision does not cover their other market needs, as forest produce in most cases is not carried on to the buses. Bicycles are slowly emerging in the region, but, in the absence of well-maintained paths and infrastructure, their use is limited. They are also essentially a male asset, at least at present.

Given this situation, what is required is a combination of non-transport interventions for provisioning basic services such as water, education and health facilities in the village itself, and innovative transport and organizational interventions to ease the transport burden on the local tribal population, without adversely affecting gender relations.

NOTES

1. *Dikku*, or one who gives trouble, is the local word for non-tribals.
2. Mahua is a large tree whose flowers are collected and used for the production of liquor. The fruit is ground and used as food, and oil is extracted from the kernel.
3. Dumka and Pakur are both district headquarters.
4. A neighbouring state of India with irrigated paddy land; it is dependent to a large extent on migrant labour from the Santhal Parganas for cultivation of the land.

16

MY DAILY ODYSSEY:
TRANSPORTATION IN THE LIVES
OF SEWA BANK CLIENTS

AHMEDABAD, INDIA

Sangita Shresthova, Rekha Barve
and Paulomi Chokshi

'What do you mean by transportation?' Surajben, a SEWA Bank member asked. During the course of our research, we heard this question often.

Few of the women clients of SEWA Bank consider transportation to be a separate aspect of their lives. Yet women's professional lives often revolve around transportation. A woman employed as a head-loader, a porter who carries goods from one place to another on her head, spends most of her twelve-hour day moving around in the streets. A farmer in rural areas on the outskirts of Ahmedabad spends two hours every day commuting to her field. A vegetable vendor pushes her pushcart – a four-wheeled trolley made using bicycle wheels and wooden planks – around the city for nine hours every day. Transportation plays a central role in many self-employed women's lives and is a meaningful issue for the Self-Employed Women's Association based in Ahmedabad, India.

Established in 1972 by Ela Bhatt, the Self-Employed Women's Association (SEWA) is a trade union registered under the Trade Labour Association. SEWA functions as an umbrella organization which encompasses a large number of sub-organizations.[1]

The Shri Mahila SEWA Sahkari Bank Ltd is a major SEWA organization, registered as an urban cooperative bank under the Banking Regulations ACT 1949. SEWA Bank was founded in 1974 as a direct response to a need felt by SEWA's members and provides a way for SEWA members to save safely, reduce their dependence on moneylenders, and increase their technical professional proficiency through training and

Used clothes/utensils peddler

Surajben Himanlal Jagaria was one of forty founding members of the Self-Employed Women's Association (SEWA), in 1972. Surajben commands respect from all those around her and she is conscious of this position. She has taken out between ten and twelve loans from SEWA Bank for many different purposes. Surajben explained her trade as a used clothes/kitchen utensil peddler in Ahmedabad. 'I walk around the residential societies shouting a slogan offering my goods. The wives hear me and come downstairs. In high-rise buildings, I even ring the door bell to ask if the housewives have any clothes to exchange.'

Three times a week, Surajben walks to Manechowk, a market where kitchen utensils are sold. The walk takes one hour. After making all her purchases, Surajben takes an auto rickshaw home. This trip costs Rs 10. She usually returns home by 1 p.m. and prepares lunch for everyone. Lasan (a garlic paste), buttermilk, kichadii and chutney are a standard meal for the family. In the afternoon, Surajben stays at home and washes clothes to sell at the flea market. Surajben also employs a *dhobi* (washer-person) to help clean the used clothes, which decreases her net income significantly.

During the rest of the week, Surajben walks to residential areas in Ahmedabad with the utensils in a basket on her head. Once she reaches these areas she exchanges utensils for used clothing. The areas she frequents are 10–15 kilometres away from her house and she spends up to two hours in transit. She reaches them around 1 or 2 p.m. and spends the next five or six hours wandering around the neighbourhood shouting a slogan offering her wares. Surajben carries the entire load on her head. She never sits down to rest. She has many residences to visit before the day is over.

After 7 p.m. she returns home. Usually, she walks carrying the load of clothes and utensils (weighing anywhere between 20 and 40 kilograms) on her head. On rare occasions, if the load is physically unmanageable, Surajben takes an auto rickshaw home, but this is an extra cost to avoid if possible. After she reaches her house, she prepares a simple dinner and goes to bed.

On Sundays, Surajben's family sell the repaired clothes at the Ellisbridge weekly flea market in Ahmedabad. Currently, this is the only opportunity the family has to sell their goods. If they try to sell clothes on the roadside, the police and other officials harass them. Occasionally, there are state-sponsored *melas* (fairs) where Surajben can sell used clothes.

Twice a year, Surajben makes a four-day trip to purchase second-hand clothes in Mumbai. She travels in unreserved seating on the train. The ticket costs Rs 120 for a round trip. She walks to the train station. In Mumbai she sleeps at the train station and spends days collecting used clothing from Bombay neighbourhoods and merchants. Collected clothing is stored at the Mumbai train station but Surajben worries that her clothes could get stolen. She uses the city's transportation facilities. By the end of her stay in Mumbai, Surajben usually collects 100 kilograms of clothing. She takes the train back to Ahmedabad and hires a pullcart (Rs 60–70) or auto rickshaw (Rs 50) to get the clothes to her house, where they are washed and repaired.

Surajben uses the bus only on very special occasions. However, she feels that a pushcart would make it easier for her to transport used clothing and kitchen utensils around Ahmedabad. Though Surajben would still walk everywhere, carrying loads would be more efficient. Surajben estimates that she spent Rs 500–700 on transport during the last month. Most of this money was spent on rickshaw and pullcart/pushcart fees. Given Surajben's estimated income of Rs 1,000, transportation constitutes a considerable cost.

consultation. SEWA Bank also provides credit facilities. It recognizes that women's economic productivity relates directly to their social, economic and political empowerment.

THE TRANSPORT STUDY DEFINED

Though transport is an important component of self-employed women's lives, its role has been little researched. This study, conducted by SEWA Bank's newly established Research Department, represents a pioneer effort to investigate transport in SEWA Bank's clients' professional and personal lives. The study describes the forms of transport women are using for income-generating, leisure and social purposes, and examines to what extent women's transport decisions are affected by economic, cultural and gender-based considerations. This is linked to the larger picture of the provision of transport in Ahmedabad city and neighbouring areas. The final section includes tentative recommendations for future transport-related action to be undertaken by SEWA and SEWA Bank on behalf of SEWA women. This research is a pilot study to be used as a guide for future investigations in this area. It is in no way a transportation policy proposal for SEWA or any other organization.

The study is based on three types of information: secondary information from SEWA and from the Ahmedabad Municipal Corporation, Ahmedabad Municipal Transport Service, Commissioner of Transport and State Transport Office; six case studies of women engaged in different trades – used clothes/utensils peddler, pullcart labourer, bidiroller, sweeper, ragpicker and farmer; and a survey of women coming to deposit money at the SEWA Bank collection centres and women along the SEWA Mobile Bank and rural routes.

Characterization of a typical transport survey respondent

'I am 35 years old and married for the first time. I live in a household with six other family members. I earn Rs 1,500 per month. My husband earns Rs 3,000. I joined SEWA in 1995 and SEWA Bank in 1996. I have taken out no loans from SEWA Bank.'

DESCRIPTION OF SURVEY RESPONDENTS

SEWA Bank is predominantly an urban institution. Of the respondents to the survey, a majority were town-dwellers. The respondents' ages ranged from 20 to 60. Ninety per cent of the respondents were married (first marriage); 7 per cent were widows. The household size in which the women lived ranged from 2 to 21. The average household consisted of six members and had two main breadwinners. Women's monthly income ranged from zero to Rs 5,000. The average monthly income was Rs 1,300.

The respondents belonged to six occupational categories: head-loaders; hawkers and vendors; recycling wallahs; primary producers; home-based workers; and labourers and commuters (see Table 16.1).

Head-loaders are porters who earn money by carrying goods on their heads from one location to another. Hawkers and vendors sell goods on the streets of Ahmedabad, often moving through the streets pushing or pulling a cart with their wares. Recycling wallahs make their living by

TABLE 16.1 Breakdown of occupations included in the survey

Transportation labour type	No. of respondents	% of respondents
Head-loader	6	7.9
Hawkers and vendors	16	21.0
Recycling wallah	4	5.3
Primary producer	18	23.7
Home-based workers	17	22.4
Labourers/commuters	15	19.7
Total	76	100.0

exchanging used clothes for new items in residential areas. They walk through the streets either carrying their goods on their heads or pushing them on a cart. Primary producers are self-employed women who produce the goods themselves. They include farmers who grow their own vegetables, wheat or rice. Home-based workers work in their residence. They pick up raw materials and deliver the finished goods to a contractor. Finally, labourers and commuters include those who 'travel' or 'commute' to set locations for employment.

GEOGRAPHICAL AND DEMOGRAPHIC BACKGROUND

SEWA Bank is based in Ahmedabad, an urban centre in Gujarat State in the western region of India. Formerly the state capital, Ahmedabad is still the productive and economic 'power-house' of the state. Administrative institutions of both state and central government have been moved to the new capital, Gandhinagar, 32 kilometres away. The Sabarmati River runs through Ahmedabad city dividing it into two distinct parts: new and old. The western region of the city boasts new, 'modern' architecture. High-rise apartment buildings, housing the 'up-and-coming' middle-class population, are flanked by educational, business, shopping and research centres including Gujarat University, the National Institute of Design, Darpana Center of the Performing Arts, the British Library and the Calico Museum.

To the east, across the river, lies the old walled city of Ahmedabad.

> Streets are narrow and crowded with all manner of vehicles – bicycles, three-wheeler rickshaws, cycle rickshaws, hand-carts, scooters, cars and buses.... There are big wholesale markets of grain, fruit and vegetables, cloth, timber, sugar, spices, etc. where goods arrive by the truck- and train-load and are sold to retailers. There are many retail shops which sell everything a person could possibly want. And then there are the street vendors – men and women – who walk around the streets shouting their wares. (Jhabvala, 1990, p. 274)

Owing to recent rapid urbanization, more than thirty villages located on the periphery of Ahmedabad city have been enveloped within its borders.

There are three main intra-urban roads connecting different areas of the city. Tilak road runs through the heart of the two sections of the city and connects it from west to east. Gandhi Road runs parallel to Tilak road and passes through the crowded sections of the 'Walled City'. Lastly, Ashram road 'connects the north–south areas on the western side of the river and serves shops, offices, cinema houses etc. which have come up

---

The pullcart labourer

Maniben Chandubhai Thakora, a 45-year-old widow, is a pullcart labourer. She pulls a pullcart loaded with customers' goods and bundles for a charge based on distance covered. Maniben joined SEWA Bank in 1982 and has taken out one loan for Rs 10,000. She also has a savings account at the Bank. The other members of Maniben's household are also employed as pullcart labourers. As no one in the family owns his/her own pullcart, they rent carts at a weekly rate of Rs 30. The load on the pullcart often exceeds 100 kilograms. Maniben estimates that her income is Rs 25–30 a day (or Rs 150–180 a week). She pulls a cart for six hours a day.

Maniben complained about several health problems related to her strenuous employment. She suffers from a heart problem which is difficult to control given the physical strain of pulling a cart. Maniben also complained about other physical problems. 'Sometimes my legs hurt so much that I cannot work. On those days, I can't walk at all.'

Pulling a pullcart in the monsoon rains is unpleasant and the goods have to be covered and kept dry. Congested streets and traffic pollution in Ahmedabad also make manoeuvring a cart a daily struggle and Maniben often spends time waiting in traffic jams. She complained repeatedly about the pollution 'Sometimes it is difficult to breathe.' The police sometimes harasses pullcart labourers. 'Once the police released the air in our tyres to slow us down.'

Maniben would need approximately Rs 6,000 to purchase her own pullcart. This would eliminate the weekly cart rental fees. If she owned her pullcart, Maniben wouldn't have to haggle with the dealer in the market about renting his pullcart. The new cart, however, would be registered in her son's name. It would be left chained at the market at the end of the day, and Maniben would not use it for any other purpose.

---

along both sides' (Central Institute of Road Transport, 1996, p. 9). These roads carry a heavy weight of traffic; the lack of sufficient parking, loading and unloading facilities results in frequent traffic jams during peak hours.

Ahmedabad has a multimodal transport system. There are pedestrians and cyclists. Women walk carrying loads exceeding 40 kilograms on their heads. Fewer men carry loads on their heads; more often they use push- or pullcarts. Pullcarts are simple two-wheeled carts constructed to allow one or two people to stand behind the handlebars in the front. They then literally pull the cart forward. Though usually person-operated, animals, mainly donkeys, can also be used to pull the carts. Pushcarts range from simple wooden boards set up on four bicycle wheels to elaborate box-like constructions designed to serve a specific trade.

Camel carts, donkey carts, bullock carts and occasionally elephants are also used to transport goods within and without Ahmedabad city. Scooters, *lunas* (simple mopeds) and other two-wheelers are used by the middle classes and are popular because of their relatively low cost and convenience. Auto rickshaws are also widespread and are used as taxis, 'school buses', private and official vehicles. SEWA Bank staff use auto rickshaws to reach the outlying areas in the city. Larger 'shuttle rickshaws' operate along set routes picking up and dropping off passengers along the way. Slightly more expensive than the public buses of the Ahmedabad Municipal Transport Service (AMTS), shuttle rickshaws complement Ahmedabad's public transportation network. Urban public transportation is provided by AMTS, which operates 187 routes in Ahmedabad. The fully nationalized Gujarat State Road Transport Corporation serves the outlying rural areas and claims to provide bus services to 95 per cent of the towns and 99 per cent of the villages (Gujarat State Transportation Corporation, 1998).

Areas outside Ahmedabad and other states are also accessible by train. Private cars, jeeps and minibuses are also heavy users of Gujarat's urban and rural motorways.

Ahmedabad is the seventh largest city in India, with a population of 4,684,700 in 1997, growing at 2.8 per cent per year and expected to reach 6.2 million in 2011. A Central Institute of Road Transport study indicates that if the population growth continues as projected, the 'subsequent travel demand in the city will be 7.7 lakhs[2] per day by 2011' (Central Institute of Road Transport, 1996, p. 5). This means that the already highly congested urban motorways will have to serve greater volumes of commuters (Central Institute of Road Transport, 1996, p. 11). This investigation of SEWA Bank's clients' use of transportation is relevant not only to the immediate needs of SEWA women and the long-term goals of SEWA Bank but also to Ahmedabad city's infrastructure and future development.

THE FINDINGS

In this section, the focus is on issues relating to SEWA women's personal and professional mobility, the use of public and other transportation facilities, the cost of available transport options.

Personal and professional mobility

The degree of professional mobility of the respondents varied greatly. Home-based workers' work required only minimal mobility. Usually this amounted to picking up raw materials from the contractor and delivering

The ragpicker

Manjulaben Atmaram Senma earns her income through ragpicking. She joined SEWA Bank in 1994 and has taken out four loans for house repairs. Manjulaben's eldest daughter, Pushpa, works in a factory but the largest portion of the household's income comes from Manjulaben's ragpicking. Ragpickers wander through the streets of Ahmedabad collecting discarded materials such as glass, metal, plastic, paper, wood, iron, and so on, which they sell to a middleman and which eventually gets recycled.

After completing all her household chores, Manjulaben sets out for Kalupur, a wholesale market in Ahmedabad. She estimated that the market is a 30- to 45-minute walk away. There she collects 'rags' until around 7:30 or 8:00 p.m., when she begins her journey home. She carries the collected material in a sack on her head. Usually the load weighs around 30 kilograms. If the load is too heavy to carry, Majulaben makes two trips from Kalupur to her house. This happens two to four times every week. Manjulaben never takes a rickshaw or other form of motorized transportation, as this would cut too much into her net profit. At home she sorts the 'rags' according to the type of material. Her income from ragpicking is Rs 3,000 a month.

On Sundays the Kalupur market is closed. Manjulaben and her daughters use this time to sell the week's 'rags' to the merchant. The merchant is not far away from their house and the women walk to drop off the collected goods.

Two or three times a year, Manjulaben travels to see her relatives outside Ahmedabad. She takes the bus, which costs her Rs 10 each way. She also takes the bus if she is too ill to walk to visit a doctor.

Walking takes up more than ten hours of Manjulaben's day. She complained about occasional sharp pains in her legs: 'Sometimes I have to sit down while I am ragpicking, because my legs hurt too much.' Bending constantly to pick up articles off the ground also gives Manjulaben backache. Despite these problems, she hardly takes a day off. 'If I do not go, there is no money', she explained simply.

---

the finished goods after they had been processed. Head-loaders, ragpickers and labourers require a high level of mobility.

Table 16.2 shows the total hours the women spend travelling every day. All the home-based workers spent 2 hours or less every day on travel. Around 50 per cent of the labourers and commuters spend 6–12 hours travelling. All the head-loaders estimated that they are on the move between 4 and 10 hours every day; two of the four recycling wallahs said they were on the move 6–8 hours every day. The estimated time spent moving while working was very erratic for hawkers/vendors and primary

TABLE 16.2   Total time spent on the move according to occupation

Hours	Head-loaders	Hawkers/ vendors	Recycling wallahs	Primary producers	Home-based workers	Labourers/ commuters
0–2	0	2	1	2	17	4
2–4	0	3	1	7	0	2
4–6	3	2	0	7	0	2
6–8	2	6	2	2	0	3
8–10	1	2	0	1	0	2
10–12	0	1	0	0	0	2
Total	6	16	4	19	17	15

producers (both ranged from no time to 10 hours). Hawkers and vendors walk along the streets carrying goods on their heads or pushing a rickshaw. The distance they cover depends on the number of 'transactions' they are able to execute in one location. Primary producers in our survey were predominantly farmers. Their mobility patterns depend on seasons and on crops planted and vary from season to season and from location to location. In addition, some of the primary producers surveyed had an additional source of income. For example, several of the women kept buffaloes and sold milk to the local dairy. The buffaloes needed to be fed and cared for. This affected their mobility.

Overall, 53 per cent of all the respondents estimated that they travelled between 2 and 8 hours for their professional needs. Table 16.3 summarizes the mobility of urban (within Ahmedabad city) and rural (in villages outside Ahmedabad) respondents. Only 27 (34 per cent) of the respondents were able to offer any estimate of the distance they covered. Time was a much more accurate measurement of distance for the respondents. For them the time spent in commuting and the time spent working was more important than the number of kilometres walked on any particular day. For example, head-loaders carry goods from one location to another for 8 or 9 hours every day. Within those 8 or 9 hours they do not keep track of the distance they cover. Rather they keep track of the time, because they know that they must return home, begin their second form of employment, and so on. Overall, estimation of distance proved to be ineffective in measuring women's professional and personal mobility.

TABLE 16.3 Time spent on the move per day: urban versus rural workers

Hours	Urban	Rural	Total
0–2	23	1	24
2–4	8	7	15
4–6	8	6	14
6–8	13	2	15
8–10	6	1	7
10–12	2	0	2
Total	60	17	77

The total time respondents spent on the move included time spent commuting to work. The self-employed members of SEWA are largely employed in the informal sector of the economy and do not have a set location where they work. Out of 79 respondents, 65 (82 per cent) considered the streets of the city as the location of their work. Only one respondent stated she worked in an office. Five respondents (6 per cent) worked exclusively at home. The rest commuted to different locations in search of work (i.e. head-loaders) or customers (i.e. vendors). As a result, the estimated distance women covered to get to work varied. Often women did not 'commute' to work in the conventional sense of the word. For example, a kitchen utensil/used clothes merchant begins her work the minute she steps out of her home. If she finds customers within five minutes of her house, she is happy to sell to them. Alternatively, she has to cover large distances to reach the middle-class residential groups located in more affluent parts of the city. The majority of the women who estimated distance travelled said that they travelled 1–3 kilometres to reach their work every day.

Use of public and other transportation services

To come to the SEWA Bank or a SEWA Kendra (Centre) most women took an Ahmedabad Municipal Transportation Service bus. If bus routes were inconvenient or infrequent, the women used a metered or shuttle rickshaw. Of the women surveyed, 55 (70 per cent) used rickshaws and

Farmer

Amrutben Umedsingh Zaler is a farmer by profession and lives in Kaniyal village, 60 kilometres outside Ahmedabad city. She farms land she co-owns with her husband's family, her husband having died several years ago. Amrutben receives 200 kilograms of crop per season (once a year) as payment for her work. 'Usually this breaks down into 100 kilograms of rice and 100 kilograms of wheat.' To supplement her income, Amrutben sells milk to the dairy from the five buffaloes she owns. At any time only one buffalo is able to produce milk that Amrutben can sell. She retains a litre for family consumption and sells the rest, for which she gets Rs 50 a day on average. To increase the fat percentage of the milk, Amrutben pays the dairy Rs 25 a day for *khan* (buffalo diet supplement) to feed her buffaloes. This decreases her net income substantially.

Amrutben's daily routine depends on the season. When there are crops to attend to and harvest, she gets up at 5 a.m. After washing her buffaloes and collecting their *chat* (buffalo dung), which she dries and uses as cooking fuel, and selling milk to the dairy and going to the nearby market for vegetables, Amrutben sets out for the fields.

The walk takes her 15–20 minutes. 'The field is about one kilometre from my house', Amrutben estimated. Upon reaching her field, Amrutben harvests the crops using a sickle. At 1 p.m. she walks home, carrying the harvested crop on her head. If there is time, she also cuts grass to feed to her buffaloes.

Out of season, when there are no crops to harvest, Amrutben still walks to the field every morning. There she cuts grass to feed to her buffaloes. In or out of season, Amrutben estimated she carries a 60 kilogram load on her head when she walks back home from the field. In the afternoon she cuts a second load of grass for the buffaloes. This trip takes two hours.

Between 4 and 5 p.m., Amrutben collects a second batch of milk from her buffaloes and sells it to the dairy collector. The dairy closes at 5:30 p.m. and Amrutben has to deliver the milk on time. After 7:30, children from the neighbourhood gather at Amrutben's house and she leads them in evening prayers and devotional singing. The gathering lasts until around 10 or 11 p.m., when everyone goes to bed.

Amrutben walks almost everywhere. There is no scheduled bus connection to Kaniyal. The nearest bus stand is 7 kilometres away. An auto rickshaw is available for this journey and costs Rs 5. 'Usually, I walk to the bus, because the rickshaw is too expensive', Amrutben explained. For example, to go to SEWA Bank in Ahmedabad, Amrutben walks the 7 kilometres to the bus stand and catches the bus from there. A bus ticket costs Rs 3 one way.

Currently, both of Amrutben's daughters attend school. Bharti is 18 and attends grade 11 at a public school. Bhawana is 16 and in grade 9. Commuting to school costs Amrutben and her family Rs 20 a day.

Though Amrutben has joint ownership of a tractor (shared with her in-laws) she doesn't use it. 'Women don't drive tractors', she explained. A bicycle was also out of the question.

buses and 17 (22 per cent) used state transportation services. Those within a reasonable distance from the bank, understood to be less than 6 kilometres, walked.

Modes of transportation used for professional (business) purposes were not as uniform. Most commonly, women walked to carry out their work (52 per cent). Seventeen respondents used a pushcart (22 per cent) to transport goods. The pushcart also served as a mobile shop for a wide range of merchandise. Bus was used by 17 (22 per cent) respondents. Seven (9 per cent) took an auto rickshaw. The rest of the respondents used a combination of these modes of transportation.

SEWA Bank's clients use a range of transport modes for personal travel; 80 per cent of the respondents walked to do their shopping; 15 per cent, many of whom were from the rural areas, used a combination of state transportation and walking. The rest of the respondents (5 per cent) used a combination of bus, walking and *tempo* to do their shopping.

For social visits to friends and relatives within Ahmedabad city (or in their respective villages) women sometimes walked or used a combination of public transportation and walking; 65 per cent took a bus, metered/shuttle rickshaw or walked to visit people; state transportation, *tempo* and walking accounted for 13 per cent of the respondents and 28 per cent of the women walked without using any other form of transport.

Most of the women surveyed rarely visited family (usually the women's parents) or friends outside Ahmedabad (or respective villages). Often these trips were not even an annual occurrence and many of the respondents had not left Ahmedabad for several consecutive years. Yet, when travelling outside Ahmedabad, an overwhelming majority took state transportation buses and trains.

Frequent use of public transportation facilities also applied to the choices made by the respondents for health purposes. The responses regarding women's choice of transportation for health purposes for themselves and their family (household) members are shown in Table 16.4.

Around 75 per cent of transportation needs for health reasons in both categories were solved by taking the public bus or (if the illness was not too serious) by walking. In emergencies, 14 per cent of the respondents used a rickshaw for illnesses of family members. Only 8 per cent used a rickshaw for themselves in the same situation, showing that the women were more willing to bear a higher transportation cost for their family members than for themselves.

The survey also aimed to find out how women travelled for leisure or for a second income-generating activity. Only three of the respondents were engaged in a second income-generating activity (and they all walked).

TABLE 16.4 Mode of transportation used for own health reasons according to occupation

	Walking	Rickshaw	Bus and walking	State transportation
For self	2	6	59	12
(as % of total)	(3)	(8)	(75)	(15)
For family members	4	11	59	5
(as % of total)	(5)	(14)	(75)	(6)

None of the women engaged in any leisure activities on a regular, or even irregular, basis. Most of the women worked six to seven days a week. During the week they had no free time to spare for leisure activities. Some of the women did not engage in an income-generating activity on Sundays. Their Sundays, however, were far from free. They were used to catch up on all the household chores and to prepare for the next week.

In summary, respondents walked to any place within a reasonable distance, but the importance of public transportation facilities (AMTS buses, state transportation, train and, less frequently, rickshaws) cannot be underestimated. To run personal and professional errands in Ahmedabad city, women took a public bus. If the bus routes were too inconvenient, they opted for a shuttle or metered rickshaw. Metered rickshaws were usually seen as a luxury to be used on festive occasions or in emergencies. For visits outside Ahmedabad, state transportation facilities were the most popular choice. The train was also an option. State transportation was used more frequently in the rural areas. In areas not served by the state transportation network, women resorted to walking or taking shuttle rickshaws to the nearest ST depot.

Financial costs of transportation

To reduce transportation costs, all of the surveyed women walked anywhere even remotely accessible. Since 89 per cent of the respondents earned less than Rs 2,000 per month, finances were very tight. Yet most did incur at least minimal transport expenses on a regular basis.

Sweeper

Lilaben Dipakbhai Galiyar works as a sweeper at Kundan and Bhagirath residential societies in Vasna, Ahmedabad. She sweeps the common grounds and porches of the bungalows, and also cleans the bathrooms and toilets. Lilaben joined SEWA Bank in 1994 and opened a savings account. She has taken out two loans from SEWA Bank and has used the money to rebuild her house, which is registered in her name (not her husband's).

Lilaben gets up at 4 a.m. every day. She makes two trips to fetch water from a neighbour's house, which takes about 30–40 minutes. The family pays a Rs 15 monthly fee for this facility. Rekha, the eldest of Lilaben's six children, has taken over a substantial portion of the household chores, while Munni, her second child, helps her with her job and with the ragpicking which Lilaben engages in to supplement her income.

At 6 a.m. Lilaben and Munni leave the house to begin their 45-minute commute to the residential colonies. Lilaben always walks to work, because the Rs 2 bus fare is too expensive. Lilaben and Munniben sweep the outside pavements and driveways of all the bungalows. Lilaben uses a short thistle broom, which she buys at a cost of Rs 10. Each broom lasts a month. She works without stopping (no tea breaks) until approximately 1 p.m. and then walks home. Lilaben earns Rs 900 a month for sweeping.

Around 4 p.m., Lilaben leaves the house to do her second job: ragpicking. She carries a large sack (with a capacity of about 200 litres) and walks around the streets of Ahmedabad collecting discarded objects (glass, metal, plastic, paper, wood, iron, etc.) off the streets. Ragpicking requires that Lilaben moves around constantly, bending over to pick each object off the ground. Lilaben ragpicks until around 7 p.m., earning approximately Rs 25 for three days' work.

Lilaben returns home to drop off her ragpicking sack, and once again makes the 45-minute trek to the residential societies to collect leftover food from the societies' families to supplement her family's meal. She carries a large steel bowl on her head, covered with a cloth to protect the food from flies.

On Sundays, when the residential colonies do not have to be swept, Lilaben sorts the week's ragpicking and with her daughters carries the sacks to a middle-man, who buys their merchandise. The merchant is a 30-minute walk from Lilaben's house, and they usually have to make several trips to deliver all the sacks. They do not take a rickshaw or bus because that would decrease the limited profits they are able to earn through this business.

Though Lilaben never takes an auto rickshaw or bus even in emergencies, her husband takes a bus to work every day. He is a sweeper in a corporation approximately 30 kilometres away, and the commuting costs him Rs 8 a day.

The physical strain of working both as a ragpicker and as a sweeper have given Lilaben health problems. She complained about severe pain in her neck, back and legs and knees. 'But I have no time to rest,' she explained. Lilaben learned how to ride a bicycle when she was young, and would like to purchase a bicycle to ride to the residential colonies. A new bicycle costs Rs 1,500.

Respondents were asked to distinguish between professional transportation costs and total transportation costs per month. Professional transportation costs included all payments made for transportation related to the women's form of employment. Total transportation costs were a sum of business costs and included all additional transportation costs.

Professional transportation costs ranged from zero to Rs 1,500 per month. The mean professional costs were Rs 169.75 per month. Using the mean monthly income (Rs 1,300) as a base, the respondents spend approximately 13.06 per cent of their income on transportation costs directly related to their business.

Similarly, the total transportation costs (which included business cost) ranged from zero to Rs 3,000. The mean total cost of transportation was Rs 375.46 per month. This accounted for 28.89 per cent of women's monthly income. In other words, the respondents were spending almost one-third of their income on transportation required by their business and personal needs.

The women surveyed spend a very high percentage of their incomes on transport. As the analysis of the modes of transportation used for personal and professional purposes showed, most women cannot cut these expenses further. Almost all walked anywhere even remotely within walking distance and used public transportation for longer journeys. Public transportation (AMTS and state transportation) is currently the cheapest form of transportation available in Ahmedabad and surrounding areas. Transportation costs were, however, a real concern for the respondents and many expressed a need for alternative solutions to their transportation problems.

WOMEN'S COMPLAINTS AND RECOMMENDATIONS

Difficulties

The cost of public transportation facilities was the most frequent complaint, expressed by more than 80 per cent of the surveyed women. Relatively few respondents in comparison voiced other complaints such as the lack of a vehicle, the long wait for public transportation or physical strain.

More than half (58 per cent) of the respondents felt that their transportation difficulties would best be addressed through the purchase of a vehicle. One urban respondent was interested in starting up her own transportation business and in taking out a SEWA Bank loan for this purpose. Only 5 per cent openly stated that an increase in the frequency

Bidi roller

Nagmaniben Naranbhai Padmushali, 35 years old, works primarily as a bidi roller.[3] She also assists her husband, Naranbhai, in producing idlis, a popular South Indian snack, which they prepare at home. Naranbhai walks around Ahmedabad streets and neighbourhoods selling the idlis from a specially adapted four-wheeled pushcart.

Nagmaniben explained that it would be culturally unacceptable for her to push the idli cart around the city. 'What kind of woman would stand on the street selling idlis?' 'All kinds of people roam the streets', she elaborated, 'and I never know if I am going to be safe with those drunkards and gamblers around.'

Nagmaniben picks up the materials for bidi rolling from a contractor situated only a 10-minute walk away from her house. Bidi rolling is a popular occupation in the area. Sometimes, Nagmaniben has to stand 45–60 minutes in a queue to pick up the tobacco, thread and leaves needed for rolling bidis. She carries the materials home and begins rolling.

Work is interrupted to run errands like shopping and visiting neighbours. Nagmaniben usually walks to all destinations. The market for purchasing vegetables and other food for the family is only a five-minute walk from Nagmaniben's house. To cover larger distances, Nagmaniben takes a bus, train or, in an emergency, a rickshaw. These trips, however, are rare and on a daily basis Nagmaniben does not travel beyond a 20-minute radius of her home.

Social and gender-based restrictions play an extremely important role in Nagmaniben's transportation decisions. The couple could significantly increase their income from the idli business if they purchased an additional idli cart. Doubling the number of idlis produced is not a difficult task. Nagmaniben, however, does not feel she could push a cart on her own. She even claimed she would rather hire another labourer than do this work herself, but that would make purchasing an extra idli cart a less lucrative venture.

of public transportation would help them. One respondent expressed a need for financial assistance to help her bear her transportation costs.

Some 65 per cent of the women said that a vehicle would help them carry out their business more efficiently, 27 per cent answered negatively, and one respondent was undecided. Primary producers were by far the most interested in purchasing a new vehicle, followed by the vendors and hawkers. Head-loaders were the most hesitant about purchasing a vehicle.

The primary producers' eagerness for the new vehicle can be explained by the fact that most were farmers who conducted their farming (including ploughing and harvesting) manually. They said that a bullock cart or a tractor would increase the efficiency of their work. For vendors and hawkers a pushcart, for example, would allow them to carry more goods around the city and help bring in more income. A pushcart also eases the physical strain of carrying goods on one's head. Some of the vendors surveyed also proposed to purchase a rickshaw, which could be used to pick up vegetables in the morning and distribute them to individual merchants. For these vendors, purchasing a rickshaw was a way of moving from small-scale enterprise into wholesale market entrepreneurship.

A large number of the urban women said that they would operate the vehicle themselves, but a majority of the primary producers were hesitant. The social constraints and gender-based limitations women face in villages may play a large role in their transportation decisions. Unfortunately, no conclusions can be drawn from our study on this issue and we recommend that this be further investigated.

Though none of the women surveyed was restricted to her household, there was a definite gender bias in the use of modes of transportation within the families. Many of the respondents stated they would not use a bicycle, scooter or rickshaw because it isn't culturally permissible. Others argued that they would give preference to another family member who 'needed' the vehicle. Six women said that their husbands would not give them permission to use a vehicle, and 37 felt they did not have the skills. Most of the women were, however, willing to take out a loan from SEWA Bank for the purchase of this vehicle. They explained they would let their son, husband or other male members of the household drive it.

The wider context

SEWA Bank's clients' transportation needs are set in the context of the traffic and transportation situation in Ahmedabad. Connecting the broader transportation issues with the findings of this study is the first step towards addressing women's transportation difficulties. A Central Institute of Road Transport study conducted on behalf of the Ahmedabad Municipal Transport Service identified typical passengers on the AMTS public buses as being 25–44 years old and earning Rs 1,250–4,000 per month. (One-third earned Rs 1,250–2,500 per month.) They take the bus on a daily basis, commuting to and from work, and spend Rs 100 or more on bus tickets every month. (One-third owned no vehicle at all.) If the bus network breaks down they resort to one of several alternative means of transportation. They walk (4 per cent), ride a bicycle (21 per cent), ride a scooter (22 per cent), or take a rickshaw (34 per cent) (Central Institute of Road Transport, 1996). Up to this point it appears that the findings of the

AMTS research team correspond with the investigation involving SEWA Bank's clients. The two studies might be describing the same passengers. There is, however, one major distinction. According to the AMTS study, only 29 per cent of the passengers on public buses are female! Our study on SEWA Bank's clients' use of transportation suggests several possible reasons for this. Women tend to be relatively less mobile than their male counterparts. They cover a relatively smaller distance on any given day. This gives taking a bus a high opportunity cost. Possibly, the expense of using a bus (a major concern for our respondents) makes many women decide to walk. In comparison, 'physical strain' and 'time' are more expendable commodities.

There are long-term implications associated with these priorities. Women save money at the expense of time and health. They use extra energy to walk large distances. This can lead to chronic health problems.

Our study suggests that the biggest deterrent for the respondents in taking advantage of the AMTS public transport network is cost. Initially, this appears to be an insurmountable hurdle and the only solution could be for these women to turn to alternative modes of transportation (i.e. cycling, walking).

The study conducted on behalf of AMTS warns that 'Traffic engineering measures have failed to keep pace with the increased demand for transportation facilities and the condition of traffic is fast deteriorating' (Central Institute of Transport, 1996, p. 8). In a direct response to these worsening traffic conditions in Ahmedabad city, the AMTS study calls for a 'reorganization' of public transportation facilities to ensure that this network appeals and provides service to different strata of society.

CONCLUSIONS

Our study raises a number of specific and general policy issues. It highlights several transportation issues affecting SEWA Bank's clients and shows that, though transportation is not often considered as a separate issue, it plays a vital part in women's professional and personal lives.

Given the anticipated shift in focus of the AMTS as it tries to attract more passengers, it may be possible for SEWA Union to negotiate a concession for SEWA members on public buses. Therefore it is imperative that SEWA carry out a detailed study of SEWA members' use of public transportation. Special attention must be paid to the financial burden borne by the women. If conclusive, this study could be used as the basis for a fare concession proposal to be negotiated with AMTS.

Likewise, other issues highlighted in this study should be carefully analysed. Conclusions can be used as guidelines for SEWA transportation policy.

First, a detailed study of urban mobility habits needs to be undertaken to determine the viability of an AMTS fare reduction for SEWA members. The study must investigate to what extent women's lives depend on transportation. In addition, it should also address the positive impact of a fare reduction in terms of increase in net income, increase in efficiency and reduction of physical strain.

Second, the physical feasibility and financial viability of communal transportation services (especially in the rural areas) must be investigated. The study should determine whether there is a real interest among the women themselves in operating such a service communally. Possibly, in areas where public transportation facilities are unavailable, communal transportation services may be financially lucrative.

SEWA Bank should investigate the positive impact that the purchase of a vehicle would have on SEWA Bank's clients' net income. Initially, this study should identify the exact transportation needs expressed by SEWA Bank's clients that cannot be addressed through public transportation facilities. These needs will vary according to profession and location. The economic viability of owning a vehicle (including subsequent maintenance and operational costs) needs to be carefully evaluated. Based on this investigation, SEWA Bank should consider providing low-interest loans for professional transportation purposes.

NOTES

1. For more information about and SEWA, see Biswas, 1997; Jhabvala, 1990; SEWA, 1996.
2. One lakh is 100,000.
3. *Bidis* are locally produced cigarettes. *Bidis* are rolled using dry leaves, tobacco and thread. Individual bidis are then tied into sets of 20 and packaged to be sold on the market. In Ahmedabad *bidi* rollers are predominantly home-based workers. The vast majority of these workers are women.

17

FROM DAWN TO DUSK: TRANSPORTATION OF RURAL WOMEN TO AND FROM THE METROPOLIS

CALCUTTA, INDIA

Mahua Mukherjee

The rate of urbanization is increasing in India, though 70 per cent of the population continue to live in rural areas. Urban growth is concentrated in major metropolitan cities and a few other industrial and coastal towns. The lack of basic facilities in rural areas and the economic disparity between rural and urban areas has led to urban migration.

Some rural people migrate to the cities to live, and start off by living in the slums. Others commute during the day for work and return to their houses in rural or suburban areas. Daily commuters belong to all economic classes – low-, middle- and high-income groups. A large number of women also commute daily.

Indian society has always imposed direct or indirect restrictions on the movement of women. Mobility of women was initially related to either household work, such as collection of firewood, fetching drinking water and collecting crops, or to visits to the parental home and relatives. Over time, however, women began to travel for income-generating activities.

The modes and problems of urban transportation vary considerably from those in rural areas. Urban women are more vocal than their rural counterparts and their transport problems have therefore been more clearly articulated. The problems of transportation for rural women, and particularly for rural women commuting to the city, have yet to be identified and recognized. They are the victims of both the almost non-existent rural transport system and the badly managed and overcrowded urban system. The number of women in this category is steadily increasing. They suffer

---

Long hours away from home

Bijoli Mashi starts her journey at 3.00 a.m. She is a vendor. She walks through the darkness on a *kutcha* road (so slippery during rainy seasons). She collects her vegetables for sale and reaches the station after a 45-minute journey by tricyle van. She looks at the sky and worries about the weather and security. The first train in the morning is overcrowded as usual, but she can't wait. The heavy load of vegetables is sometimes unmanageable but somehow she manages the 10-minute walk to the market. Bjoli Mashi is in her late thirties. She is the only daughter-in-law in a family of nine and she has hardly saved anything. She sometimes worries about her future. It's a relief that the return journey is not so hard. She comes back home around 5.30 p.m. after six hours of travel and eight and a half hours of work. Then it is time to attend to her household chores. She never gets time to think about herself.

---

from mental and physical strain because of the enormous time they spend travelling.

Calcutta metropolis is surrounded by Howrah, Hoogly, Nadia, North 24 Parganas and South 24 Parganas districts, among which South 24 Parganas' boundary with Calcutta city is the longest. Owing to close proximity and connection by rail and roads, large areas of this particular district are extended suburbs of Calcutta and the city plays an important role in the district's economy. The district supplies labour, vegetables, fish, flowers and other produce to the metropolis. The city links the district to the state as a whole (West Bengal) and to the rest of the country. Both men and women from the South 24 Parganas commute to the city in large numbers, and for this reason the district was chosen as the location for this case study.

South 24 Parganas is one of the largest districts in West Bengal. It has an area of 9,962 square kilometres and a population of almost six million. The district has different modes of transportation such as train, bus, auto, rickshaw, van, motorized and non-motorized boats, cycles and carts (for goods transport mainly). Approximately 0.7 million people commute daily, of whom approximately 2 per cent are women, most of them poor.

The women travel to the city primarily to earn an income, but also to pay a visit to a hospital or to meet relatives. Women earn incomes in the city as maidservants, as vendors of flowers, vegetables and fish, as workers in industries like leather, plastic, glass and building, and as assistants in hospitals/nursing homes and in offices. The jobs are not necessarily permanent.

Spending money, earning money

Janaki Patra prepares food for her family and also supplies one office canteen in Calcutta. She wakes up early in the morning and does her daily chores. After preparing the cooked food she gets on a rickshaw to the railway station. She uses the same rickshaw for her return journey. She pays the rickshaw Rs 200 per month. The railway journey costs her Rs 90 per month. The office for which she caters is near the railway station. She walks there. Her profit from catering is about Rs 1,200. Meals for her family of four come out of what she cooks for the canteen. Janaki Patra is satisfied with her profits.

The first objective of the study was to document the present situation. Based on this information the study also aimed to detail action plans and to make suggestions for meeting women's transport needs.

There has been little work on the subject so the study had to rely on collecting primary data from rural women who commute to the Calcutta metropolitan area. The number of women commuting daily is estimated at between 10,000 and 25,000 and they make the journey by rail and bus to a number of locations. Because of time, money and manpower constraints, the study selected a purposive sample of women from locations such as Jadavput and Ballygunge railway stations and the Sakherbazar (bazaar) and Ramgarh (Garia) Market.

Recognizing that the women are always busy and only available to be interviewed while waiting for their train or bus, the main tool for the study of women at their destination was a questionnaire that was simple, short and direct. It aimed to find out who the commuters are and why

Hopes for better days

Sonali, like her name, is full of golden smiles. She is not much bothered by the hard journey. Everyday she has to fight while boarding the crowded trains. But this does not deter her from laughing and sharing jokes with her friends. It takes more than one hour to reach school but since she had started her early education in the same school, both she and per parents thought she ought to continue there. When you ask her about the hazards of the journey, she simply giggles. But slowly she gives details about journey hazards. There is some sexual harassment and pick-pocketing and the late running of the trains is a problem. She is optimistic that these issues will be solved and she will see better days.

and how they are commuting; what problems they face and how far these problems are gendered; how their choice and use of transport are affected by their roles and responsibilities in their homes and communities; and what ideas they have about improving their transport facilities. The questionnaire was pre-tested and modified accordingly.

The survey at the commuters' destination was complemented by interviews in three villages of South 24 Parganas with family members of the working women and with some women who had not gone to work on the days the interviews were carried out.

FINDINGS

Table 17.1 shows that most of the commuters interviewed belong to the age group 20–40, with over a third being between 30 and 40. Girls under 20 mainly commute for educational purposes. Women who belong to the 20–30 age group are engaged as maidservants, while vendors are older, mostly from the 30–40 age group, possibly because being a vendor requires investment of money as well as labour (see Figure 17.1). Older women who used to commute when they were younger are now crippled by ill health and living in bad economic conditions. They constitute a relatively small proportion of the commuters.

Most of the respondents earn a very small income (see Table 17.2). A majority are also the sole income earners in the family either because they are single or because their male partners are too ill to work. The women who are vendors earn more than the others but face the problem of fluctuating incomes.

TABLE 17.1   Distribution of sample respondents by age

Age in years	% of respondents
Below 20	12
20–30	28
30–40	38
above 40	22
Total	100

TABLE 17.2 Distribution of respondents by income and occupation

Monthly income (Rs)	Maid-servant	Veg./fish vendor	Service	Other	Total
<250	15	0	0	0	15
250–500	28	2	0	0	30
500–750	11	0	0	2	13
750–1000	7	3	0	2	12
1000–3000	0	10	1	0	11
>3000	0	0	4	0	4
Total	61	15	5	4	85

Most of the respondents are engaged as maidservants. Depending on their health and stamina these women offer their services to more than one household. A total of 46 per cent of the maidservants earn between Rs 300 and 500 per month (i.e. an average of US$10 per month). Another 25 per cent earn even less than this.

A few women (less than 6 per cent of the respondents) work in the formal sector. These women feel that they can afford an increased trans-portation cost but they would like a comfortable journey, which is next to impossible in the current circumstances.

Some 47 per cent of the sample live in nuclear or extended families in which there are one or two adult females. The women of these house-holds shoulder all household responsibilities. Even though there is a greater number of households with more than one adult woman, not all the women will commute for work or share economic responsibilities.

Time

Some 54 per cent of the women are away from home for more than 12 hours and only 5 per cent stay for less than 8 hours. The women who start their journey before dawn, despite the rain or the cold, have to face the problems of travelling in the dark. They walk through areas infested with insects and snakes and are also in danger of being robbed or sexually harassed. Many respondents spend at least three hours or more in a train or bus and waste about an hour daily simply waiting for transport.

Hard work for the family's happiness

Kanchandidi is in her late thirties. She is too busy to chat with her friends today. Her mother-in-law has been seriously ill for a week. She now has the sole responsibility for the family. The family is a large one. It consists of her parents-in-law, her own family of five, two brothers-in-law, one of whom is married with two children, and one widowed sister-in-law with two children. She is proud that the family has stayed together – but it takes its toll on her. Her husband is too ill to work. She has been working as a maidservant for two years. She spends 11 hours or so out of her home so that she can earn enough income for her joint family.

In most cases the respondents use more than one mode of transport. In every case they walk – on average for about 90 minutes, in some cases for 150 to 180 minutes. Two-thirds of the respondents commuting by train never buy tickets. Non-ticket travel is one reason why the government is trying to close this section of the railway.

The respondents spent very little money on transport (see Table 17.3). The entire railway system in the South 24 Parganas district is running on the basis of a subsidy by the government.

TABLE 17.3 Distribution of sample respondents by daily expenditure and mode of transport

Mode of transport	Daily expenditure (Rs)					
	0	5	5–10	10–15	15–20	Total
Train	64	14	3	6	2	89
Bus	0	12	0	0	0	12
Auto	0	2	5	0	0	7
Van	0	3	6	0	0	9
Rickshaw	0	5	0	0	0	5
Total	64	36	14	6	2	122

Watching the trains to forget

Padmadida is an old lady – she is frail and wrinkled and looks older than her actual age of around 67. Padmadida starts her day at 6 a.m. She walks for an hour to reach Jadavput Railway Station. By train she reaches Sealdah Station, a stone's throw away from Koley wholesale market. Here she buys vegetables, which she carries back to Jadavpur Station to sell. But the process takes time. She settles with her vegetables on the platform of Jadavpur Station at around 11.00 a.m. But she extends her stay on the platform. She tries to avoid her family. Her only son died ten years ago along with her grandchildren. Her daughter-in-law is now in an abnormal state of mind. So Padmadida tries to forget the agonies of her family by watching the trains pass by. She prefers to return home as late as possible – around midnight.

VILLAGE SURVEY

Nabhashan village under Pratapnagar Anchal *panchayat*, Tana Sonarpur, has about 685 people who are lower middle class and poor. The infrastructural facilities are minimal, though better than in many of the surrounding villages. The primary road through the village is a metalled one. The village has brick-laid collector roads 2.4 metres wide but all the accessory roads are *kutcha*, earth roads. The bus stop is at the junction 'Prasadpur More', which is 15 minutes' walk from the village main road. Vans, autos and a few express buses from Sonarpur are available there. The nearest railway station is Kalikapur, about 40 minutes by cycle or rickshaw.

The village has no piped water supply or waste disposal system. Tubewells and ponds are the main sources of water. The main market is 10 minutes' walk away.

There is one primary school in the village but for secondary education children have to go to school in Prasadpur. The school is situated by the bus stop and is a 10- to 15-minute walk from Nabhashan village. Students continuing their studies to higher secondary and undergraduate level commute to Kalikapur, which takes about an hour by bicycle.

The nearest post office is in Kustia (25 minutes' walking distance). Allahad Bank in Kalikapur provides the nearest banking facilities. The closest medical centre is also situated in Kalikapur. Kalikapur also has a youth club for boys, and a temple. The women from Nabhashan participate in the festivals at the temple.

Interviews were conducted with families where at least one female member commuted to the city daily. The researcher met Sabina Bibi, Upali Dasi, Lalita Did, Madhumasi, Amaladevi and a few others. Sabina Bibi is working as a maidservant. She has four children. Her relatives take care of her children while she is away. On the day of the interview, Sabina was sick and had not gone to work. She was uneasy that her employers would reprimand her harshly for this. She did not go to work for several days in the previous month because her children were ill. She was afraid she would lose her job. Because the sector is unorganized, maidservants have no formal leave, income protection or pay scales. Sabina was more vocal about the discrepancies in her working conditions than about the journey to work.

Upali Dasi gave a completely different story. Though old and no longer working herself, she was so impressed with her employers that now her daughters and daughter-in-law were working as maidservants in those households. But the journey to and from work was becoming hazardous for them. The women who commute complained to Upali Dasi about safety, overcrowding and the lateness of the trains. Upali Dasi felt that if women were educated and trained to carry out home-based work such as food preservation, weaving, printing on cloths or embroidery work on saris, they could have a better life. It would be better for both the younger women and their children. She felt that the literacy rate would increase automatically if the children could get guidance and supervision from their mothers.

In the nearby village of Taldi, most of the women are engaged in prawn processing. Because of the opportunity to set up a local industry, commuting from the village is reduced. The women earn their livelihood at home and are more involved in local development and in the development of their household. Their energy is used only for work – there is no energy wasted on travel.

The attitudes reflected by the women in the villages complement the ideas obtained by talking to women at their commuting destinations.

CONCLUSIONS

The surveys showed that economic reasons are the driving force behind women commuting to work. The women commuters are vegetable/fish/fruit vendors, maidservants, needleworkers, and so on. They all play an important role in their households. Their main responsibility is to generate income, and in several cases they also have to carry out domestic responsibilities.

The women commuters stay away from home on average about 12 hours per day. Their journeys take about four and a half hours and they waste about 50 to 60 minutes between journeys. They start their journey early in the morning (sometimes around 3 a.m.) and reach their homes late in the evenings (around 7 p.m. or so). They also have to perform some household tasks.

The problems the women face are varied: it is too cold at dawn during winter, too hot during summer; there are no street lights; they are unable to pay for travel by van, auto or train. In the crowded buses and trains passengers do not welcome the vendors' loads. During the rainy season the *kutcha* roads are muddy. There are no toilets at the roadside and the women's train compartments are inadequate. Trains are cancelled without warning or run late. Women lose money to pickpockets and from bribery to the railway police.

Rural women who commute daily are in most cases extremely poor. They explore different ways to earn money – they are ready to work hard, to travel a lot. The family members who live on the earnings of these working women are not always in favour of this. They resent the women going out on such a difficult journey and carrying out such hard work. In most cases, however, the families are too big to be supported even by two people's meagre earnings.

Lack of time for interaction with other members of the household and the strenuousness of commuting and housekeeping often lead to neglect of the family. In most cases the women's husbands are either too ill to support the family or have deserted their wives without any formal divorce or compensation. Malnutrition and unhygienic living conditions have led to asthma and tuberculosis, which are common among both children and adults in these families. Family members feel that it is impossible to expect proper housekeeping from a woman who travels daily to the city. This leads to family feuds and children are badly affected. Often nobody takes care of them. They are undernourished, uncared for, uneducated and in poor health.

As maidservants the women get old clothes, saris and other household items, which they accept gladly. They even accept leftover and stale food.

For modes of transport like bus, boat or auto, women pay the fare, but they can rarely afford railway tickets. To pay regular train fares they would need to raise their income or seek an alternative way to commute.

The women do not have any alternative source of work, so poverty forces them to stay away from their homes for a large part of the day and this affects their families' education, health and housing.

Though the women made recommendations for the solution of their problems, they don't think they can play any role, however minor, in the improvement of the present situation. They lack the confidence.

RECOMMENDATIONS

The women commuters had several suggestions to improve the situation. They proposed an increase in the number of buses and trains and a double-decker train to increase passenger capacity. They also recommended dual tracks for both outward and return journeys, to minimize delays.

They recommended better lighting on the streets, a cemented walkway, toilets by the roadside, a direct bus route, and new roads to shorten their journey. They also suggested that the number of women's compartments on the trains should be increased and called for an end to corruption among railway staff and police. They also recommended that income-generating activities be established near their villages.

The present overcrowding of the transport system could be lessened by reducing the number of commuters and/or improving the service. The number of commuters can be reduced by controlling the population in the area or by introducing local income-generating activities. More attention from the government and the *panchayat*, with involvement by NGOs and community-based organizations, is needed for family planning, for provision of health facilities and for providing incentives for small families. Government and private investment in small- or large-scale local industry should be introduced.

The improvement of transport facilities requires human and financial resources and needs to take into account the existing infrastructure. Since economic viability is essential for the sustainability of any system, the commuters will also have to take some responsibility. Buying tickets should be made compulsory and corruption should be eradicated. The women commuters' employers will have to bear the additional travel cost.

18

GENDER AND RURAL TRANSPORT DEVELOPMENT

CHATTRA DEURALI, NEPAL

David Seddon and Ava Shrestha

In a predominantly hilly and mountainous country like Nepal it is hard to overestimate the critical importance of modes of transport and transport facilities as an issue in rural development. For decades, road construction has been assumed to be a prerequisite for development. Yet there has been no systematic attempt to investigate in detail the economic and social significance of rural transport development in Nepal or to consider the relationship between transport development and the status of women or gender relations. Reference to the role of women in transport development, or to the impact of transport development on women, is rare in any of the existing documentation on Nepal. Even rarer is reference to the implications of transport development for gender relations in the rural areas.

But in the hill areas in particular (and also in the plains or Terai), women bear much of the burden of transporting heavy goods. Nepali women also travel widely within the country and outside for social as well as economic reasons, and a significant minority are involved in a variety of commercial activities along trails and along the roadside. Women are fetchers of water, fuelwood and fodder, and work as porters, labourers and construction workers in rural transport systems.

This study attempts to explore gender and rural transport in Nepal and to consider in particular the effect of transport development on gender relations and on the lives of women.

INTRODUCTION TO CHATTRA DEURALI

Chattra Deurali is a Village Development Committee 10 kilometres and some two hours' drive from Kathmandu along the Bhimdhunga–Lamidanda road which now connects Dhading district to Kathmandu. Dhading district is situated in the Central Development Region of Nepal and includes both hill and mountain areas. Chattra Deurali was connected to Kathmandu by road in 1988.

There were 1,270 households in Chattra Deurali at the time of the survey (Ministry of Local Development, 1994). Several caste and ethnic groups were represented: Tamang, Brahmins, Chhetris, Thakalis, Newars, Rais, Magars and Thakuris. Strikingly, no 'artisan' ('untouchable') castes were present. The sex ratio indicates that 51 per cent of the population were male and 49 per cent female. Unusually for the hill regions of Nepal, the sex ratio in favour of men was greatest (1.09:1) in the age range 15 to 44, while women outnumbered men (0.94:1) in the age range 45 to 59. Some 10 per cent of households were female-headed.

Few men were employed permanently outside the Village Development Committee; the majority were employed as wage labourers, with a significant minority involved in construction work. About 10 per cent of the workforce were employed as porters (some of whom were women). A minority were active in trade or employed in 'service'. Seasonal labour migration to Kathmandu was undertaken on a regular basis.

The Dhading Development Plan was initiated in 1983. Since then two 'green roads' have been built. 'Green roads' are environment- and community-friendly roads whose construction involves the local communities in some way (Impact Monitoring Unit, 1994). The concept emerged from the experience gained first in the construction of rural roads in Palpa district and subsequently in Gorkha and Lamjung districts in the western hill areas. The environmental element is directed towards minimal degradation of existing natural resources by careful planning and construction. The concept emphasises not only appropriate technology but also quality in design and construction methods. Methods are essentially labour-intensive, using blasting only where manual alternatives are unavailable, and then under strict supervision. The built road is subject to revegetation and bioengineering measures for exposed surfaces; mass waste is prohibited during construction.

Existing trails are not disturbed, but are integrated where possible with the new road. Existing features, such as resting places (*chautaras*), temples, water sources, and the like, located adjacent to the road are respected and not affected. People are educated about the possibility of dust pollution generated by road traffic, and the construction of new houses within 50 metres of the middle of the road is discouraged. Children under 16 are not employed in road construction, but women are encouraged to work and are paid the same wages as men.

The roads built under this programme are single-lane, earthen, fair-weather roads open only for eight or nine months of the year, and are closed during the monsoon months. These roads are considered suitable for light vehicles only (tractors, pickups, minibuses and private cars) and for a low traffic volume of up to 75 vehicles a day (Impact Monitoring Unit, 1994).

Local people are supposed to be involved in all decision making, and local collective responsibility for construction and maintenance of roads is encouraged. Project implementation (or users') committees are formed at two levels: the Dairy Development Corporation (DDC) and project level. Local people and organizations undertake overall responsibility, mobilize labourers and do the construction work. The aim is to make use of local, unemployed labour and road construction is timed to coincide with the agricultural slack period from October to May.

The first green road connects Bhimdhunga on the western edge of the Kathmandu Valley to the hilly agricultural hinterland of Lamidanda, while the second links the agricultural plateau of Salyantar to the district headquarters in Dhading Besi. Kathmandu itself is connected to Bhimdhunga by a road running through paddy fields from the Chakra Path (ring road).

The roadworks undertaken between Bhimdhunga and Chattra Deurali are reported to be 'technically successful' (Meyer and Acharya, 1995), but it is certain that the women of Chattra Deurali were not involved in community decision making. The construction of the road involved male and female labourers, and although it generated employment opportunities it is not clear to what extent *all* of the members of the local community contributed their labour. Wages were paid according to the nature of the work involved and, as there was a distinction made between tasks assigned to men and to women, there was effective wage discrimination, with women being paid lower wages.

However, the concept of utilizing only locally available labour and resources for road maintenance has permitted the creation of work during the agricultural off-season for local people.

CHANGING TRANSPORT PATTERNS

Reduction in transport costs and time

One of the immediate consequences of the building of roads is the development of a transport sector, as vehicles begin running along the roads; another is the restructuring, dislocation or demise of previous methods of transport – portering or mule trains. Whatever the particular outcome, there is a clear 'revolution' in rural transport methods.

The major consequence of the revolution in modes of transport is a reduction in transport costs and in the time taken to travel or transport goods. In Dhading district, when goods were carried by back- or head-load, transport costs amounted to 60 per cent of the value of the total product cost, while after road construction it amounted to only 13 per cent (Impact Monitoring Unit, 1994).

The development of the rural transport infrastructure not only reduced direct costs; it also decreased time taken (thereby also affecting a saving) and the effort involved. In Chattra Deurali, a drive that today takes less than two hours previously took some four hours' walk. This reduction in time and effort significantly affects the willingness of individuals to make journeys as well as the cost-effectiveness of transporting goods. People also use the road to walk along as it is easier, faster and safer than the old trail. Traditional foot trails of the area are no longer in use.

Growth of personal travel

Another consequence is a dramatic increase in the demand for passenger transport. The number of persons travelling between Chattra Deurali and Kathmandu has increased significantly as individuals travel by bus, mini-bus, truck or taxi both to transport goods and for personal reasons. Increase in personal mobility is considered in Chattra Deurali to be a major benefit of road construction. An average of 144 persons were travelling daily on vehicles – although nearly twice as many were still walking.

Bus travel overwhelmingly dominates passenger movement in Nepal. Women travel by bus, both in urban areas and long-distance. They may sit in groups, or next to men – there is no formal and little apparent segregation. At bus stops in towns, there are generally food stalls, washing/toilet facilities, and so on, though these are rarely 'separate'. Even twenty years ago it was becoming more common for women to travel as passengers on buses running on the few motorable roads in Nepal. In Chattra Deurali, many women who used to walk are now using various forms of passenger transport, including the more expensive private taxis.

Some 37 per cent of the travellers from Chattra Deurali were transporting agricultural products to market; 25 per cent were going to school
or college in Kathmandu; 18 per cent were travelling to visit relatives,
attend weddings or visit holy places; and 13 per cent were shopping in
Kathmandu. Surprisingly few people were travelling to access government
services or for health reasons (2 per cent each). Studies conducted in the
mid-1970s also show that 'visiting family and friends' accounted for between 26 and 27 per cent of 'on-road' trips. Social visits (the use of
transport facilities as a consumption good) increased very considerably
after the provision of roads (Blaikie et al., 1977). Such trips involved
women as well as men. The importance of being able to shop in
Kathmandu for the people of Chattra Deurali is worth noting as it has
been significant elsewhere also.

Among those travelling by vehicle between Chattra Deurali and
Kathmandu, there appeared to be no discrimination by gender: women
accounted for about 34 per cent of those travelling by vehicle and for 27
per cent of those walking. Women travelled alone to Kathmandu when
necessary; mobility was not restricted and travelling alone was not considered against social norms. Other studies suggest that 'greater social
mobility, resulting from institutional and infrastructural interventions which
have subsequently affected gender roles and gender specific potentials, is
visible' (Shtrii Shakti, 1995, p. 104).

The overall significance of travel should not be overemphasized, however. According to the World Bank's study on poverty alleviation (World
Bank, 1990, p. 17), in the mid-1980s only 1 per cent of the monthly
consumption/expenditure of poor rural households in the Terai went on
transport.

Roadside benefits (and costs)

The beneficiaries of the Bhimdhunga–Lamidanda road are those living
along the roadside, those in the immediate hinterland of the road and
those in market centres downstream from the road all the way to
Kathmandu (Apedaile, 1996). The first to benefit economically are the
landowners immediately adjacent to the road. They benefited from major
appreciation of their land value even before the road was constructed.
These households have replaced their traditional thatched roofs with metal
or tile roofs. There has been an increase in the availability and ownership
of a variety of consumer goods bought with the savings that families
generate from lower costs overall. Households along the roadside have
televisions, radios and other such goods.

Next are the traders and vehicle owners. Fourteen shops have opened alongside the road in Chattra Deurali. The most dramatic growth has been in the number of teashops, restaurants and small lodges catering to the new clientele travelling along the roads. Although the shops are run by both men and women, it was generally women who were responsible for them. The women who run these businesses were knowledgeable and were taking decisions independently.

Benefits have also accrued from investment in vehicles. In Chattra Deurali, light trucks (being cheaper) are generally owned by local farmers, whereas larger trucks mostly belong to the rich merchants of Kathmandu. None of those who own or drive these vehicles is a woman, although elsewhere in Nepal there are examples of women drivers of trucks, buses and other vehicles. A few of the drivers of 'clean' electric *tempos* (small three-wheeled taxis) in Kathmandu are women and in several areas of the Terai women, even women from Muslim communities, ride bicycles. In Narayanghat (the major town in Chitwan) the use of bicycles is regarded as 'modern', and women who cycle are viewed as desirable wives.

Citizens are also beneficiaries as consumers, travellers and socially mobile people. Large and medium-sized landowners benefit from new investment opportunities, cheaper inputs and new markets. Farm households and service providers with limited or no land are the last to benefit.

In parts of Nepal the growth of the informal sector and of new employment opportunities along the roadside and in urban centres has encouraged young women from the poorer and more remote areas to migrate in search of employment. While trafficking in girls and young women exists, for many women commercial sex is a means of maintaining an adequate livelihood for themselves and their families. Average earnings from commercial sex were three times that of wage labour. Improvements in transport infrastructure have facilitated this trend, though such development is less significant along the smaller feeder roads and fair-weather roads like the Bhimdhunga–Lamidanda road than along the major highways.

The restructuring of non-road transport systems

One of the major consequences of road construction in Chattra Deurali is that vehicles have almost completely replaced porters. In 1993 roughly 10 per cent (41 out of 416) of those employed in Chattra Deurali worked as porters and included a small number of women. While the wealthy families have benefited because now they pay less when using minibuses to transport their products to Kathmandu, the poorer (low-caste families) find no loads to carry. Before the road was built, men and women from poor families were hired to transport food grains, vegetables and fruit. Now porters, especially women, find it difficult to obtain work.

Both male and female porters operate during the monsoon months, when the road is closed. The rest of the year the men from these poor (low-caste) families work as hired labourers – work which is not all that easy to find; women from the low-caste families are even worse off because they find it even more difficult to obtain work as wage labourers. Other studies elsewhere in Nepal reveal the importance of porterage (mainly involving men but also sometimes women) in hill and mountain areas away from roads. In two hill districts in Rasuwa Nuwakot IRDP (Integrated Rural Development Project) portering accounted for 9 per cent of incomes among low-income households (World Bank, 1990).

Several other studies also reveal the tendency for roads to dislocate 'off-road transport systems' (porterage and mule trains), sometimes reducing demand for these systems and throwing porters and muleteers out of work, but sometimes simply resulting in a relocation of off-road routes, and on occasion actually increasing the overall demand for off-road transport. Road construction in West Central Nepal in the late 1960s and early 1970s, for example, resulted in a massive increase in the flow of goods and an increase in opportunities for various kinds of traders, merchants and middlemen in new roadside locations, especially in the hills. It also resulted in more opportunities for shorter-haul porterage from these new roadheads to off-road locations. (Blaikie et al., 1980). Even so, the 'space' for porters and muleteers would appear to be progressively reduced as roads are extended further into the hill areas. Those households dependent on these branches of the transport business for their livelihood will find themselves squeezed – as have the households in Chattra Deurali who were dependent on porterage.

Effects on the farming economy

Many studies have examined the relationship between road construction and agricultural change. Despite significant doubts, the idea that roads help promote agricultural development remains central to Nepal's current strategy for agricultural development. Nepal's Agriculture Perspective Plan is committed to a major programme of 'agricultural roads' with a heavy emphasis on such roads in the Terai, where it is argued the greatest potential for agricultural development exists. The draft Transport Master Plan contradicts this view and stresses that in the Terai most areas are now accessible to wheeled vehicles, whether animal-drawn or motorized.

In Chattra Deurali, however, there is evidence of significant changes in agricultural production consequent on the construction of roads. Land in the Village Development Council comprises lowland irrigated land (5,547 ha), upland dry land (14,037 ha) and pasture (2,280 ha). Land ownership was high, with only 10 per cent owning less than 4 ropani and 2.4 per cent landless. Just over half the households were food self-sufficient for the whole year, 32.6 per cent for more than six months, 3.3 per cent for four months and 13.4 per cent for less than four months. This is, therefore, a relatively well-off rural community. Paddy rice, wheat, maize, millet and potatoes are the principal crops, using improved seeds and chemical fertilizer fairly intensively. Food sufficiency had improved slightly in the area opened up by the Bhimdhunga–Lamidanda road (Impact Monitoring Unit, 1994). There had also been a change from the consumption of maize and millet to rice. This increase in rice consumption was linked not only to a rise in incomes but also to higher rice yields through increased fertilizer use, and an increased availability of rice in the local shops. Farmers in Chattra Deurali now cultivate a finer variety of rice for sale to consumers in Kathmandu, where it is in high demand; the coarser variety consumed locally is no longer cultivated, but instead purchased in Kathmandu.

Vegetable cultivation has been increasing since the road construction. As there is a growing and dependable market in Kathmandu for vegetables and fruit, men and women are growing more vegetables and fruit than before. As a result, more land is cultivated with vegetables The Small Farmers' Development Programme provided low-interest credit to farmers and stimulated the initial increase in production. After the construction of the road, however, production increased further because of the improved opportunities for transportation to markets in Kathmandu and the existence of a reliable demand.

Land is now being leased on contract to grow vegetables, and even *khet* land previously used for rice and wheat is being used for vegetable production. Fruit production is also important. Both vegetables and fruit are largely exported from the Chattra Deurali to Kathmandu.

Before the road was built, men and women carried their produce on their backs in bamboo baskets (*dokos*); now motor transport is available (particularly minibuses) to take local produce to market. It is still the men who travel with products to sell in Kathmandu; but the increase in cash crop cultivation has not excluded women from marketing activities because women now travel more frequently to Kathmandu. Also, during the three months of the monsoon when the road is closed to traffic, men and women carry their vegetables and fruit to Kathmandu.

Livestock production is important in Chattra Deurali: chickens are produced in large numbers, as are cattle and buffalo. Chickens are looked after mainly by women and children, and sold in Kathmandu. Livestock are stall-fed all year round with straw and fodder gathered from fast-growing fodder trees grown in the fields. Milk production is popular, and milk is sold to the Dairy Development Corporation . It is collected by the Small Farmers' Development Project (now a cooperative) and transported to the DDC in Kathmandu. This arrangement is particularly convenient as the farmers themselves do not have to travel to sell the milk.

It is suggested that the increases in agricultural output have also resulted in an increased demand for agricultural labour. Previously, men used to travel to Kathmandu for seasonal work, to return home during the planting and harvesting period, leaving a good number of *de facto* female-headed households in which women managed the farm, the family and the home. Local people stated that they would have liked to pursue other income-generating activities during the off-farm season, but opportunities did not exist within the Village Development Council. Men spent their spare time playing cards (which the women were unable to stop, despite protesting and, on occasion, tearing up their cards). Now nearly everybody is active in farming activities.

It is not clear, however, whether the increased level of agricultural activity and output has affected the division of labour within agriculture, and within the overall farming economy more generally. One implication is that those put out of work as porters may be able to find work in a local economy with an increased demand for agricultural and other forms of labour. But the changes in gender relations that accompany the transformation of the local economy are not entirely clear.

In general, however, it seems that the gender division of labour in farming and other tasks has persisted, with the women undertaking those activities falling within the 'private' sphere and the men undertaking activities within the 'public' sphere. Women continued to be responsible for household and farm tasks, while men were undertaking farm and market activities. The construction of the road has not changed the gender division of labour but has increased the workload for both women and children. More women are being left to look after the home, farm and children. The progressive shift from the extended family to the nuclear family has increased pressure on women, who can no longer share the burden with other members of the family (this shift is largely attributed to the construction of the road).

Social benefits of the roads

Increased travel for personal reasons – to visit relatives, attend weddings and other ceremonies and to visit holy places – has been remarkable in the case of Chattra Deurali, as elsewhere in Nepal when connected by road to the outside world. One-fifth of all those travelling by road from Chattra Deurali gave personal travel as the reason for their journey. Increase in mobility has resulted in more exposure to and interactions with 'outsiders'.

The literacy rate is higher along the road corridor. Since the road was constructed, the number of students attending school increased more along the road corridor than in off-road areas, probably as a result of the construction of additional primary schools along the road. In all areas the proportion of boys and girls was about equal in primary school (40–50 per cent girls); in secondary schools, the proportion of girls was around 44 per cent along the road corrridor, while in the off-road areas it was still 30 per cent (Impact Monitoring Unit, 1994).

Female literacy in Chattra Deurali remains low, however, relative to that of men (720 females literate, compared to 1,350 males). So, too, does female school attendance: of a total of 995 enrolled students in the nine primary schools, 58.8 per cent were boys and 41.2 per cent were girls; while in the high school, out of a total of 330 students, 60.6 per cent were boys and only 39.4 per cent were girls. Both figures are higher than the national average – and higher than the figures cited by the Impact Monitoring Unit for off-road areas in this region.

To pursue college education, young people have to go to Kathmandu; both men and women in Chattra Deurali debated the advantages and disadvantages of pursuing higher studies. It was clear that there was a lack of employment opportunities in the village and no guarantee of finding suitable jobs elsewhere – students who had completed college education were accepting lower-level jobs. Students from wealthy families were continuing higher studies while students from less well off families were dropping out of school and working as labourers on the construction of a link road from the Village Development Council to the Bhimdhunga–Lamidonda road.

There is a health post in Chattra Deurali, but the traditional practice continues of calling on a local faith healer first. Before the road was constructed, those who were too ill to be treated locally were carried to Kathmandu, often by hired porters. For everyone, the availability of motorized transport was the most important benefit of road construction. At the same time, as mentioned above, only 2 per cent of road travellers interviewed were travelling for health treatment. Nevertheless, the health situation is reported to have improved, as a result perhaps of increased consumption of vegetables, better diffusion of primary health care by NGOs, improved information on sanitation and hygiene and increased water availability.

Chattra Deurali has 26 water taps, which provide drinking water to 840 households. Fetching water is normally a woman's task. The improved availability of drinking water has reduced the walking distance and the time women spend daily collecting water. Before the taps were installed, water had to be fetched from the river, an hour's walk away. Women consider themselves very fortunate in this respect. However, the availability of water has little to do with the construction of roads; it is rather the result of bringing water closer to the users. Women still have to travel to the forest, alone or more usually in groups, to collect firewood and fodder.

Seventeen drinking-water user groups exist, initiated in the early days of the Small Farmers' Development Project (it started in 1985, three years before the road). Fourteen irrigation user groups were also formed, as were nine mothers' groups (one for each ward) and a handful of forest and pasture users' groups. The most numerous – 111 – were the credit groups (for which the Small Farmers' Development Project was designed); these groups included men's groups, women's groups and mixed groups.

These and many other developments that have taken place in the village over the last decade or so cannot be attributed to the road in any direct way; it can only be concluded that the road may have contributed indirectly to some of the economic and social changes that can be observed. We hope that we have been able to demonstrate that an explicit focus on the relationship between rural transport and gender relations can help to reveal aspects of change in rural areas that might otherwise remain unseen.

19

TRANSPORT IN THE MOUNTAINS AND THE TERAI

KUSHIYA DAMRANG AND SHIVPUR, NEPAL

Ganesh Ghimire

This study addresses how men and women in rural Nepal share travel and transport tasks. It comprises a review of selected documents, interaction with relevant authorities and individuals, and participatory rural appraisal in two rural sites: one in Kushiya Damrang, in the mountain district of Dolakha, and the other in Shivpur, in the Terai district of Rupandehi.

The scope of the research was limited to three basic questions only. What is the existing rural travel and transport task structure? Is this structure taken into account by policies and plans? How have travel and transport interventions impacted on this task structure?

RURAL TRANSPORT

The overwhelming majority of Nepal's population live in rural areas. The country is divided into 3,912 Village Development Committees (VDCs), 54 municipalities, 1 metropolitan and 3 sub-metropolitan areas. All the VDCs are rural by definition. Some municipalities have included the peripheral rural population into their boundaries to make up the minimum population for the area to qualify legally for the status of a municipality. At the same time, there are market centres that have urban features but have not yet received the legal status of municipalities. Thus, the distinction of rural and urban population on the basis of municipalities is rather unrealistic, but it is generally accepted that only 20 per cent of Nepal's population is urban.

TABLE 19.1   Nepal: terrain type and related details

Topography	Elevation (m)	Population (% of total)	Area (% of total)	No. of districts	Remarks
Mountain	4,877–8,848	7.3	35	16	Includes trans-Himalayan areas
Hills	610–4,877	46	42	39	Includes highly populated valleys like Kathmandu, Pokhara and Surkhet
Terai	up to 610	47	23	20	Includes inner Terai
Total		100	100	75	

Source: *Statistical Yearbook of Nepal*, 1997.

Topographically Nepal has three major strips running east–west parallel to each other: the Himalayas, the mid-hills and the Terai (see Table 19.1). The Himalayan belt is the northernmost strip, comprising the high mountains and fringes of the Tibetan plateau. The mid-hills is a mountain belt with a few remarkably fertile valleys at the south of the Himalayas which extends down to the southern plains. The southernmost strip at the foothills, called the Terai, is the main portion of the plainland in the country. Part of the Terai is trapped between the Mahabharat mountain range and the Churiya hill range and is called inner Terai. Total plain terrain of the country, comprising the valleys, inner Terai and the Terai, amounts to some 23 per cent of the country's 147,181 square kilometres and is crisscrossed by rivers and streams.

The topography, the rivers and the jungles pose difficulties in moving goods and people in Nepal, whether in mountains, in hills or in the Terai.

The settlement pattern in the hills and mountains is generally scattered and sparse except where there is thriving commercial activity or where there are better natural resources. Rural communities with sparsely distributed houses inhabit the cultivable slopes. Houses are connected to each other and to the farms by local trails. The communities are connected with each other by major trails. In many cases the households are located along the major trail.

The prevailing system of travel in the rural hills and mountains is predominantly walking, and transportation is by human load-carrying. In these rural communities localized movement of goods and people involves a lot of climbing up and down and significant physical effort. Access to the outside world from these communities is difficult, especially where a motorable road does not connect them. Where a motorable road or an airport exists, the influence of such access may be limited to the closer vicinity of the roadhead/airport.

Clusters with some scattered housing dominate the settlement pattern in the Nepalese plains. Set amidst agricultural lands, these settlements are normally connected among themselves as well as to outside areas by a network of tracks or wide trails, which local people upgrade or repair, so that walking, plying animal-drawn carts, handcarts and pack-animals is possible. Bicycles are becoming popular, but their use is constrained by the bad condition of the non-engineered village roads. These capillary roads comprise the basic transport infrastructure of Nepal. It is estimated that the total length of these village tracks is anything between 15,000 and 20,000 kilometres, but as they are officially unrecorded there is confusion over whose responsibility it is to build and maintain them. The condition of these roads is not good and a large proportion are in an almost abandoned state. The overall efficiency of the mobility of people and goods in the rural Terai and of the transportation system as a whole depends on the serviceability of these roads.

Historically, a prominent feature of Nepalese society has been isolation as a result of the difficulties and drudgery associated with travel and transport. Topography was the barrier to movement and the cause of isolation in the mountains and hills. In the Terai the malarial infection and seasonal swelling of the north–south rivers constrained movement. This situation in travel and transport over a long period has had a definitive role in shaping Nepalese society and has made some contribution to sustaining the cycle of low-production, low-consumption, no-surplus, subsistence economy and to the perpetuation of scarcity and widespread poverty. The difficulties, inefficiency and drudgery associated with transport have often been considered the main hurdle to achieving quicker economic and social development.

The network of trails in the hills and localized earth tracks in the Terai have evolved over time. The communities themselves built and maintained the trails, earth tracks and other related infrastructure like *chautaras*. (*Chautaras* are stone resting places built along the trails in the hills and mountains. Usually a banyan and a pipal tree are planted for shade. The *chautaras* have social and religious value as well.) The major trails in the hills and mountains and long-distance tracks in the Terai were developed by successive rulers to consolidate their empires and were complementary to the localized trails and earth tracks. Suspended bridges, *ghats* (ferry boats) and other infrastructures like *pati* (a kind of permanent shade or a little building alongside major trails for travellers staying overnight, free of cost) were also developed. This is the transport infrastructure that still serves the rural areas of Nepal.

Improvement of rural transport in hills/mountains and in plains may involve different approaches. A motorable road may be less viable in a mountainous rural area owing to its limited utility and high cost, and improving earth tracks and building stream crossings could substantially improve the transport situation in the plains. Similarly, a new mode of transport like rope-ways could be of significant advantage for some hill/mountain areas.

RURAL TRANSPORT PLANNING

A systematic planning-in-development process began in Nepal in 1956 with the first Five Year Plan (1956–61). During the first three decades of planned development there was no exclusive policy statement on rural transport. Rural transport was part of overall transport planning, and policies and plans relating to rural transport and related interventions were embedded in the transport and communication sections or in the rural development sections. More recent plans have included rural roads, but now (as then) the overall assumption is that the physical infrastructure will automatically generate economic growth in the area, and that everybody irrespective of gender, economic class and culture will benefit from these developments.

Several projects and programmes relating to rural transport have been implemented with support from several donors. These include: the Seti Development Project (ADB, 1997); the Karnali Bheri Integrated Rural Development Programme (CIDA, 1980s); the Trail and Bridge Building Programme (SNV, 1987–92); the Palpa Development Programme (GTZ, SDC, Helvetas, 1986); the Dhading Development Project (GTZ, 1997); Bridge Building at the Local Level (SDC, Helvetas, ongoing); the Lamosangu–Jiri Road Project (SDC, 1976–85); the Rehabilitation of Flood-Damaged Rural Infrastructure Project (WFP, IFAD and UNDP, 1994–96); the Main Trail Study (UNDP, 1980s); the Pilot Labour-Based Road Rehabilitation Project (World Bank, 1993 to date); the Rapti Integrated Development Project and the Remote Area Access Study (World Bank, UNDP); Bhattedanda–Jhankridanda in the Context of the Bagmati Watershed Project (European Union, 1997).

None of these projects was found to have considered gender interrelationships in an explicit way in planning or in the implementation of

A Day in the life of Phul Maya Thingsha, a 17-year-old Tamang girl

6:00 a.m.	Woke up and left for the mill to grind corn
7:15 a.m.	Returned from the mill
7:20 a.m.	Morning wash, cleaned and prepared buffalo shed
7:45 a.m.	Rested and watched the morning dairy crowd
8:20 a.m.	Cut corn stalks for the buffalo
8:45 a.m.	Rested beside fire and ate left-over rice
9:15 a.m.	Left for private *pako*
10:30 a.m.	Began collecting fodder
12:30 p.m.	Brought fodder home
12:40 p.m.	Went into hut and cut corn stalks for buffalo
1:15 p.m.	Fed fodder to buffalo
2:00 p.m.	Sat down to eat lunch of rice and curry
2:15 p.m.	Washed plate and other dishes
2:20 p.m.	Mixed pre-packaged buffalo feed in luke warm water and fed buffalo; put out fodder for goats
2:50 p.m.	Left for Paribas [government] forest
3:50 p.m.	Arrived and started looking for fuelwood
5:15 p.m.	Arranged fuelwood sticks into a bundle and began walking home
6:00 p.m.	Arrived home and milked buffalo
6:30 p.m.	Prepared dinner
7:15 p.m.	Ate dinner
7:30 p.m.	Washed utensils
8:00 p.m.	Started shelling corn
9:30 p.m.	Finished shelling corn, left it to dry for next day; began cutting corn stalks for next day's buffalo feed
10:15 p.m.	Rested; had cigarette
10:30 p.m.	Went to sleep

rural transport improvement components. In some cases, however, for example the Lamosangu–Jiri Road Project and the Pilot Labour-Based Road Rehabilitation Project, there has been some consideration given to women's participation as construction labour.

TABLE 19.2 Travel and transport task structure in the rural mountains

Context	Travel- and transport-related tasks	% share of responsibilities		Remarks
		Women	Men	
Farming, growing food staples	Travelling to field and transporting tools, manure, seeds	25	75	Over half the families have farmlands more than an hour's walk from home
	Transporting snacks	75	25	
	Transporting harvest back	25	75	
Preparation of food	Transporting grains to and from milling	75	25	
	Fetching water and fuelwood	75	25	
Raising cattle	Taking cattle for grazing and watering	50	50	
	Collecting fodder and mulch	75	25	
Travel to market	Taking milk, yoghurt and ghee to market to sell	25	75	
	Going to market to buy manure, seed, etc.	25	75	
	Taking farm output to market to sell	25	75	
	Going to market for kitchen supplies, educational materials, medicines, clothes, etc.	50	50	
Taking care of children and old people		100	0	
Others	Travelling to take part in social activities	25	75	
	Administrative, legal and political needs	25	75	
	Travelling for health care to the local health posts or distantly located hospitals	50	50	
	Travelling for entertainment fairs, religious gatherings	25	75	
	Visiting relatives and friends	50	50	

Market travel	Taking milk, yoghurt and ghee to sell at market	50	50	In about half the cases dairy produce collectors come to individual households
	Going to market to buy manure, seed, etc.	25	75	
	Taking farm output to market to sell	50	50	
	Going to market for kitchen supplies, educational materials, medicines, clothes etc.	50	50	Women usually take kitchen garden products
Others	Taking part in social activities	25	75	
	Administrative, legal and political needs	25	75	
	Travelling for health care to local health posts or distantly located hospitals	50	50	
	Travelling for entertainment: fairs, religious gatherings	25	75	
	Visiting relatives and friends	50	50	

TABLE 19.3 Travel and transport task structure in the rural Terai

Context	Travel- and transport-related tasks	% share of responsibilities Women	Men	Remarks
Farming, growing food staples	Travel to fields; transporting tools, manure, seeds	0	100	Farmlands are usually not far from the house; also usual to have small plot of land around the house
	Transporting snacks	100	0	
	Transporting harvest back	25	75	Harvest usually brought home on a bullock cart
Preparation of food	Milling the grains	50	50	Grain is partly milled at home and partly taken outside for milling, usually in bulk
	Fetching water and fuelwood	50	50	Fetching water does not involve traveling; fuelwood is transported in bulk by bullock cart or in head-loadings if quantity is small
Raising cattle	Taking cattle for grazing and watering	50	50	Very little grazing space
	Collecting fodder and mulch	75	25	Collecting mulch is less usual
Taking care of children and old people		100	0	

HOUSEHOLD AND TRANSPORT TASKS

In meeting the needs of the rural households, men and women take up different tasks. The division of responsibilities depends on various socio-economic and cultural factors and on social values. In the context of rural Nepal, women in general are found to play a greater role in running the household, from taking care of children to producing and processing food. Transport and travel tasks are also divided with respect to gender, arising from the differentiated nature of household responsibilities.

In the mountains

The act of travelling and transporting in the hills and mountains involves a lot of physical effort due to the amount of uphill and downhill climbing involved. The majority of travel and transport takes place at the local level on trails and suspension bridges. Motorable roads and mechanized vehicles are used only for long-distance travels. Female members of the households take responsibility for fodder and fuelwood collection. A typical daily routine of a young rural woman in the mountains illustrates women's role in a rural household (see box).

Table 19.2 shows the structure of major rural transport needs and tasks by gender in Kushiya Damrang, Dolakha district.

In the Terai

In the Terai, as the terrain is flat and there are many earth tracks and motorable roads, travelling and transporting tasks are relatively easier. Use of vehicles like bullock carts, bicycles and motorized vehicles is also common practice. Table 19.3 shows a travel and transport task structure with respect to gender in Shivpur, Rupandehi district.

These tasks are not exhaustive. In the mountains, for example, women are usually involved in the planting of rice and other food staples; going to the field involves a significant amount of walking. Similarly, in large parts of the Terai dairy produce collectors do not come to households; instead, mostly, it is the women who have to transport the dairy produce to the market.

IMPACT OF RURAL TRANSPORT INTERVENTIONS

Rural transport interventions like road-building are found to have particular impacts on travel and transport tasks. First, the total range of households' travel and transport tasks changes due to such interventions. Second, a change occurs in the share of responsibility for travel and transport tasks that men and women take.

In the mountains

Kushiya Damrang, Dolakha district, is located in the vicinity of the Lamosangu–Jiri road. This road passes through Charikot, the district headquarters. From Charikot a branch road was extended in 1987 to Dolakha bazaar. This brought motorable transport about one hour's walk closer to Kushiya Damrang.

Long-distance travel has become much easier. Men and women have to walk either to Dolakha or to Charikot and then catch the bus from there. As all the travelling involves some goods transportation this has also helped associated transport.

As a result of the increased market, perhaps due to the road, the demand for dairy products, particularly milk, has increased. The people of Kushiya Damrang have consequently raised more cattle. This has generally added a burden to the households, and because women undertake a larger share of responsibilities for raising cattle (see Table 19.2), including the tasks of collecting fodder and mulch, the volume of women's work and their travel and transport have increased. Men do not volunteer to share this added burden. Thus, one of the impacts of the building of the road is that women's share of travel and transport tasks has increased significantly.

In the Terai

Shivpur is located right at a junction of an earth track upgraded recently to motorable standards and a perpendicularly crossing earth track built by the local people. This seems to have had a tremendous impact on the travel and transport condition of the locality.

The improved road condition has facilitated the introduction of motorized vehicles like motorcycles, light jeeps and minibuses in the area. Now there is a regular bus service from Shivpur to Manigram Chauk via the Butwal–Bhairahawa road. Some minibuses operate between Shivpur and Bhairahawa and between Shivpur and Butwal. Shivpur serves as a junction for all the peripheral rural areas. Motorcycle ownership has increased.

There has also been a greater use of bicycles and rickshaws. The bicycle seems to be the most affordable of the mechanized means of transport, and almost every household owns one, with about a third of the families owning more than one. Handcarts are also used more frequently. Though there are more women cyclists, individual ownership of bicycles or access to them is dominated by men. Male members have priority of access to a bicycle owned by a family.

The number of shops in the area has increased substantially. Repair shops, tailors and pharmacies have emerged in addition to the original teashops and general grocery. Households have widened their occupational base by incorporating more activities of a commercial nature. Cattle raising has become more commercial. As there is an absence of grazing land, fodder grass is collected from the forest or purchased. Ready-made cattle feed is used. The demand for dairy products is high and products get sold immediately. As a result, the average number of cattle per household has increased. All this change has taken place in the last few years and much of it could be attributed to the upgrading of the earth road to a motorable one.

The total stock of transport tasks for everybody has perhaps remained the same, as some original tasks have disappeared and some new ones have emerged due to the road. Generally, undertaking travel and transport tasks has become easier. For women, the major difference that the road has made has been to enable the use of mechanized means of transport. Riding bicycles has helped tremendously with women's mobility. Some change in sharing the responsibilities of travel and transport tasks has also been observed. Collection of fuelwood, particularly in small quantities, used to be women's exclusive responsibility. Now this responsibility seems to have shifted to men in many cases, who frequently use a bicycle for carrying fuelwood. Similarly, women, especially the young ones, frequently use bicycles for localized movements and for carrying small loads.

CONCLUDING REMARKS

Rural households have well-defined travel and transport tasks that are clearly divided among men and women. In general these tasks involve more physical hardships in the mountains and hills, where women take the larger share of the burden of travel and transport. In the Terai, travel and transport tend to be less troublesome physically and women seem to be less burdened.

However, a review of the policy and planning context of rural transport reveals that the gender differentiation of travel and transport tasks is not considered in the policy and planning of rural transport, nor in the formulation of rural transport-related projects and programmes. In some cases the employment of women as construction labour has been included as a project/programme policy.

The building of a motorable road does have some positive impact on rural travel and transport conditions. It reduces the hardship of travel and transport tasks of both men and women in rural areas. In some cases the improved transport condition brings new economic opportunities for households, which, consequently, require additional travel and transport tasks. Women are found to be undertaking more of the responsibility of this added travel and transport burden.

20

CASH CROPS AND TRANSPORT: CASHEW GROWING AND PROCESSING

SRI LANKA

Kusala Wettasinghe and Upali Pannila

This study focuses on shifts in the lifestyle of a rural community due to technological changes in their main source of income, and the implications of these for their transport needs. Its primary aim is to ascertain the transport implications of a non-transport intervention. It was carried out in an area where techniques of processing cashew had spread spontaneously and were later supplemented by a technology development project carried out by the Intermediate Technology Development Group, Sri Lanka.

THE ROLE OF CASHEW IN THE SRI LANKAN ECONOMY

Despite efforts to promote industrial development and due to the failure of national-level strategic planning to recognize its importance, the economy of Sri Lanka continues to be dominated by smallholder agri-culture and is highly dependent on the import–export economy. Cashew, an export crop, earns a large amount of foreign income. Cashew process-ing developed as a cottage industry in Sri Lanka. About 30,000 women and men are employed directly or indirectly in the industry. Over 70 per cent of this labour force are women micro-scale cashew processors who either are self-employed or work as casual labourers.

Cashew mainly grows under dry climatic conditions. It is an evergreen tree and highly drought-resistant. The cashew tree bears fruit approxi-mately three to four years after planting, and reaches maximum production in nine to ten years. It flowers for two to three months and the fruit matures two months after flowering. The cashew season, when the cashew nuts are attached externally to the cashew apple, continues for about three months.

The main commercial product of the cashew tree in Sri Lanka is the cashew nut. The shell of the nut has a soft leathery outer skin and a thin harder inner skin. Between these two is a phenolic material known as the cashew nut shell liquid. Inside the shell the kernel is wrapped in a thin brown skin known as the testa. Decorticating the shell and the testa in a way that does not damage the shape of the kernel is important because whole nuts fetch a higher price in the market. A skilled processor can decorticate 2,500 to 3,000 nuts a day. Casual labourers who decorticate cashew are generally paid Rs 35 for 1,000 nuts (around 8 kilograms). Cashew processors try to decorticate and stock as many raw cashew nuts as possible. The stocked cashew is decorticated during the season as well as in the off-season.

BRIEF DESCRIPTION OF THE PROJECT

Intermediate Technology Development Group, Sri Lanka (ITSL) has been working with micro-scale cashew processors since 1990. The project began working in Vanathavillu, in the Puttalam district in the northwestern part of the country, in 1994. It aimed to improve the quality of the processed kernels and value to the final product through the introduction of a drying technology, a tray drier. It also sought to empower the micro-scale cashew processors by helping them access information on markets and technologies, and by improving their status within the cashew industry.

The technology transfer was carried out through a village society formed for this purpose. The society also handled the marketing and divided the profits among the members. A Cashew-Processing Centre was set up in 1996 by the village society, and this now functions as a small private company. About twenty people in the village are involved as shareholders. Cashew is dried regularly at the Processing Centre, using the tray drier. In addition to this, shareholders, as well as other women in the village, work at the Centre as casual employees, decorticating and refining the product for marketing. The Centre also buys processed cashew from outsiders and dries cashew from villagers. The decorticated, dried and refined product is stocked at the centre and taken to an exporter in the capital, Colombo.

A paid employee manages the Cashew-Processing Centre. A management committee chosen from among the shareholders (members) supervise the work. Several other members have formed themselves into groups to deal with marketing issues, security, purchase of raw cashew, finances, and so on. The Centre continues to carry out research into and development of other technology interventions that may help increase production, lower the production cost or add value to the final product.

The object of this study is to:

- assess the impact of the technology change on people's access and mobility;
- identify changes in gender roles and responsibilities;
- assess the extent to which a non-transport intervention affects the transport requirements of a community.

The researchers had a close rapport with the community in the cluster of four villages on which the research was focused. In-depth interviews were carried out with 14 women who were involved in different ways in the cashew industry, together with their families; with the owners of 10–25 acres of cashew land; and with elders who remember the village's history. Discussions were also held with project staff and the manager of the Cashew-Processing Centre.

VANATHAVILLU

Vanathavillu is located in the dry zone of the country, about 12 miles north of Puttalam town, in the Northwestern Province. The landscape is flat with monsoon shrub jungles. Heavy rains are experienced between March and April and from October to November. The average temperature ranges between 26 and 28 degrees Celsius.

Landless families were given land in 5-, 10- and 25-acre plots in the early 1960s. The government Cashew Corporation introduced cashew as a commercial crop to the area in 1978. It helped the people to cultivate cashew in the 5-acre plots on which they had earlier grown vegetables. People grew a few cashew trees in their home gardens. It proved to be a good income earner for the villagers and a few people expanded their cultivation to cover 25 acres. At the time of the research approximately 100 families in Vanathavillu had 25-acre cashew plots, about 60 families had 5-acre plots plus the 2-acre plots on which they live, and about 40 families had only 2-acre plots.

For over ten years, the villagers of Vanathavillu sold cashew as raw nuts. Decorticating techniques were acquired by the women in Vanathavillu around 1989, when a few pioneering women, individually, tried out various methods. Vanathavillu gradually came to be known as a centre for decorticated cashew, and with more traders beginning to visit the area many families became accustomed to selling the decorticated cashew to the traders once or twice a week. A few traders began to operate 'decorticating centres' where women were employed as casual workers. But this did not continue for long. Several small shops in the local town also began to buy small quantities of cashew, which they stocked. Today for most people of Vanathavillu, the market for cashew is limited to one trader who set up a cashew-processing business in the local town and visits the village once a week, and to the operations of the Cashew-Processing Centre set up with the help of ITSL.

Occupational patterns

Most women and men have two or more sources of income. Their income pattern varies with the cashew season. Women contribute to some of men's income-generating activities while being involved in household work, in cashew processing and in their own income-generating work.

All the villagers are directly or indirectly involved in cashew-related work, and for most this is their main source of income. The work is divided into different activities like collecting cashew nuts, selling raw nuts, decorticating and processing, selling processed nuts and clearing cashew plantations. About sixty families in the area decorticate cashew, either in their homes or as casual labourers in other places. Over 98 per cent of those who decorticate cashew are women. The men in the households handle the marketing of cashew. Other cashew-related work is done by both men and women. Men have other employment in the armed forces or as village security personnel, in agriculture-related small enterprises, brick making, fisheries, carpentry, masonry and in the government sector. A small number are employed in other countries as casual labourers. Main sources of income for women outside the cashew industry are agriculture-related enterprises, food processing, dressmaking, casual labour and employment in the state sector and in garment industries, as well as work in other countries. The proportion of the labour force that is engaged in clerical and other equivalent jobs in the government and private sector is 16.4 per cent. The unemployment rate in the area is only 3.4 per cent of the total labour force.

Health

Malaria, encephalitis and diseases related to the digestive system are common in the area. Of these, malaria accounts for approximately 63 per cent of the illnesses. People are anxious to have their blood tested when high fever occurs. Such tests are carried out in Puttalam, about 19 kilometres away from Vanathavillu. Taking patients to Puttalam who are too ill to travel by bus is costly. Since transport facilities are very limited, a *canter* (open lorry) or van has to be hired for this purpose. The charge for a van is Rs 500, while for a *canter* it is Rs 350.

Owing to the shortage of doctors at the state hospital in Puttalam, each clinic treats only about twenty patients a day. People who want treatment need to travel very early to the hospital to take their place in the queue and to ensure that they are among those treated. Thus they spend a whole day on the trip.

For minor ailments, villagers visit the nearby medical centre, which has very limited facilities. The medical centre also has a maternity clinic but it handles only the birth of the second or third child. For other confinements, pregnant women go to the government hospital in Puttalam.

Water

Shortage of water is a keenly felt problem in the area. Rainfall is limited to two months of the year. The water in the area has a high mineral content, and a bad taste. People have to travel far to collect quality drinking water.

The most common supply of water is public tubewells. Various organizations and development projects have constructed a few tanks. The distance to these sources of water may be between half a kilometre and 3 kilometres. The government has also supplied water pumps and necessary pipelines to some areas. Water is pumped every two days. A bowser supplies water to the villages two days a week. It stops at certain places and people have to go to these spots to collect water. However, if people are not at home when the water is pumped or when the bowser arrives, they have to walk to a tubewell or a tank to collect water.

Collecting water is mainly done by women and children. An average of two hours a day is spent on collecting water. Where sources of water are generally over 3 kilometres away, men travel by bicycles to collect it.

Transport facilities

The road to Puttalam from Vanathavillu is paved but is dilapidated in several places. Within the village there are four main roads that are wide and motorable. These are gravel roads with a high sand content. The rest of the village has a network of footpaths and bicycle paths created from constant use. These roads and paths are difficult to use in both the rainy and the dry season, being slippery with sand in the dry weather, and eroding in the short rainy period. The railway line between the cement factory in Puttalam and the quarry also runs through the village, and this too serves as a footpath.

The main form of transport is the bicycle, with 88 per cent of the families owning and using one for their day-to-day travel. Motorcycles have the second highest ownership, with 26 per cent of the families owning and using them. Ownership of vans and tractors (which also can transport people in an attached trailer) is much lower and these are generally owned by the more affluent families in the village.

The public transport system on the main roads is satisfactory during daytime with a regular service operating to Puttalam. In the evenings, the frequency of buses is reduced and people are in the habit of hitchhiking to Puttalam. Women who travel alone don't often hitchhike and may walk a long distance until they find a suitable mode of transport.

The village interiors are not serviced by a public transport system. On weekdays, villagers who do not use any kind of vehicle have to walk to the bus route. Some villagers walk as much as 3 kilometres. On market days a private public transport service using a *canter* operates from Vanatha-villu to Puttalam. This leaves the village at a time specified by the owner, and brings the passengers back to the village by about 12.30 p.m.

During emergency situations such as accidents or serious illnesses, people hire a van or a *canter* to take patients to the hospital in Puttalam.

TECHNOLOGY

The development of the cashew industry in Vanthavillu can be broadly categorized into three stages:

1978–89   Introduction of cashew as a plantation crop to the area.
1989–94   Familiarization with the cashew decorticating technique.
1994–on   The Cashew-Processing Technology Development Project of ITSL, which introduced a tray drier to the village and familiar-ization with other decorticating/processing technologies.

Stage I: 1978–89

During this time raw cashew nuts were sold to middlemen and cashew decorticating or processing was done in Gampaha, about 100 kilometres from Vanathavillu. Most of the middlemen (*mudalalis*) came to Vanathavillu from Gampaha, but later small shops (boutiques) in Vanathavillu developed as collection centres, and people were able to sell raw cashew nuts to them on days when the Gampaha traders did not visit the village. Work related to the cashew industry during this stage was limited to tending to cashew cultivation, and collecting and selling raw nuts.

Cashew plantations need to be tended only in the first two or three years of cultivation and require regular watering only in the first year. Once the tree reaches maturity, weeding, or clearing of the shrub jungle in the area around the cashew trees, is done annually, generally in the latter half of the cashew off-season, by male or female family members, or in larger cultivations by male or female labourers. Owners needed to travel to the plots either to clear the land or to supervise the work done. Casual labourers had to go in search of work, carrying a *mammoty* (hoe) and other equipment, and their food. Most walked, but younger women and men sometimes used bicycles.

Raw cashew nuts are collected for about three months, from April to June, which is the cashew season. In the gardens around the homes and on the smaller plots, the women and children of the family did this. Owners of 25-acre plots usually hired children, who worked for about an hour to collect the nuts before going to school. Two or three children are hired for a plot, and it is customary to take them to the cultivation and drop them off at home once the work is done. They were paid on a daily basis.

In the first stage, selling raw cashew nuts hardly involved any travel because most buyers were in the habit of visiting the villages to collect the nuts. It was customary for men to do the marketing, particularly of larger quantities collected over one or two months. They usually used bicycles, and in a few cases motorcycles, to carry the sacks of cashew.

Men, women and children transported the smaller quantities when money was needed. It was usual for women to take about 5 kilos to the shop, sell it there and buy the day's provisions with that money.

Other work related to the cashew industry involved contacting the extension service of the Cashew Corporation and purchasing agricultural inputs such as pesticides and fertilizer.

Travel patterns related to Stage I

Table 20.1 is based on information given by people who were in the cashew trade between 1978 and 1989, and on responses by interviewees as they remember the cashew-related work patterns during this period. Most people remembered how their parents or other family members did these tasks.

TABLE 20.1 Tasks related to Stage 1 cashew processing

Task	Women's task	Men's task	Distance (km)	Mode of transport
Collecting raw cashew nuts from cultivation away from home	No	Yes	2	Bicycle
Collecting raw cashew nuts from home compound	Yes	Yes	–	–
Bringing collected cashew home	No	Yes	2	Bicycle/cart
Informing workers about work	No	Yes	0.5	Bicycle
Counting cashew nuts for sale (during the early stages, when cashew was sold by number instead of weight)	Yes	No	–	–
Selling to traders	No	Yes	–	–
Takeing small quantities to boutiques in the village (as the industry developed, traders began buying at boutiques in the local town)	Yes	Yes	2	Walking / bicycle

The table shows that in the period when cashew was sold as raw nuts, men were the key players in the cashew industry in Vanathavillu. Women were involved only in two tasks: counting nuts (at this stage traders bought cashew by the number of raw nuts and not by weight) and marketing small quantities. Counting raw nuts was a tedious home-based activity that was very time-consuming. Men rarely did these tasks.

Stage 2: 1989–94

The technology of decorticating cashew spread gradually in Vanathavillu. Several women claim that they introduced the technology to the area. Some say that a former resident of Gampaha, who came to live in Vanathavilu after her marriage, taught this technology to other women. Others supported the idea that the women learned it by themselves through experimenting with decortication before it became an accepted value-adding technology in the area.

It is now common for most women to decorticate cashew as an additional source of income, but young girls are reluctant to do this task, as their hands can become stained with cashew shell liquid.

Gunawathie, a pioneer in this field, went to Nedungamuwa in Gampaha to sell cashew, and learned the technology of decorticating through trial and error. Once she mastered the technique of decorticating cashew, she taught this to a few of her friends and relatives. She organized them as a group, and they pooled their stock of cashew, which they transported to Nedungamuwa in a hired van. The first few trips proved to be profitable and they were able successfully to bypass the middlemen. Once on a return trip a gang, disguised as the police, accosted them. Although they did not lose any money, the incident scared them, and their contacts in Gampaha offered to visit Vanathavillu to collect their produce.

With the spread of this technology, traders began to visit the village on specified days. This eliminated the need for people to carry their stocks of cashew to the town. Prices were paid as specified by the trader. The villagers had little knowledge of the market prices outside the area. The traders either resold these to *mudalalis* in Gampaha, who roasted the decorticated cashew and sold these to exporters, or themselves made transactions with the exporters.

Cashew being a seasonal crop, it was necessary for the people to stock as much cashew as possible to decorticate. They decorticated as much as they could, sold the stock, bought more raw nuts and continued work. If they needed money urgently, they took available stocks of decorticated cashew to the trader's establishment, about 2 kilometres from the interior of the village. Generally it was the men who transported large quantities of decorticated cashew, either by bicycle or by motorcycle. Small quantities were taken by women or children

The Rural Development Bank intervened at this stage to issue loans to cashew processors to stock cashew. This credit system required the forming of small groups and obtaining peer guarantee for loans. This increased the social interaction between women, and the time they needed to spend at meetings. They also needed to visit Puttalam once or twice to hand over the loan application and get the money. With the bank official visiting the village on specified days, the need for frequent travel to Puttalam was minimized.

Travel patterns related to Stage 2

The second stage shows that with cashew being collected for processing, women became more involved in the industry (see Table 20.2).

TABLE 20.2 Tasks related to Stage 2 cashew processing

Tasks	By whom		Distance		Mode of transport			
	Women	Men	<3 km	>3 km	Bicycle	Motorcycle	Hired van/bus	Walking
Collecting cashew								
at home	6							
from adjoining villages	2	2	4	4	1	1	2	
from other sources	2	2	4					3
Decorticating								
at home	11							
supervising labourers at home	2							
working as a paid labourer	1			1			1	
Marketing								
to traders in local town	5	6	7	4	3	1		
to traders outside the area	2			2			2	7

In 10 of the 14 families interviewed, women collected raw cashew nuts. The pattern of selling raw nuts also changed, and people began to sell small amounts of cashew within the village to the families who were decorticating it. Women usually took these for sale, but in a few cases children did so. Although the majority purchased raw cashew on their doorstep, two women travelled outside the village to purchase nuts. One used a bicycle, while the other hired a van to visit an adjoining village that had large quantities of good-quality raw cashew nuts. The men who collected cashew used a motorcycle, a cycle and a hired van.

At this stage women's interaction with outsiders and their involvement in marketing/purchase-related work of the cashew industry increased. A minority of the women in the community became more mobile.

Decorticating cashew was wholly a woman's task, done mostly at home. Women either decorticated the cashew nuts themselves or supervised one or two hired women workers. Women who decorticate cashew spend six to eight hours a day on this task, but since cashew decorticating can be done in the night too, it does not necessarily mean that women were confined to their homes because of this workload. Nevertheless, women spent as much time as possible decorticating because by selling their stock they were able to buy more raw nuts and make the maximum money during the season. With the income they earned, they stocked as much as possible for decorticating during the off-season.

Men were heavily involved in marketing the decorticated cashew and in 6 of the 13 families it was only men who did the marketing. But whereas earlier no women were involved in marketing at all, in seven families women now take part in this. Two women had travelled 150 kilometres to Nedagamuwa, Gampaha, to sell their nuts. One used the public transport system, while the other, with a group of friends and neighbours, hired a van for this purpose.

In 11 households both women and men sold decorticated cashew to traders in and around Vanathavillu. Where women carried out this task, they walked. Men used bicycles and motorcycles.

Stage 3: 1994 onwards

In 1994, ITSL introduced the tray drier to the village. During the demonstration period of this technology in Vanathavillu, the machine was located in the premises of a member of the society. Processing (drying) was done only on specified days. Members of the village society formed around the project brought in their stocks of decorticated cashew to the centre for drying. Once dried, the members took their stocks back home

TABLE 20.3 Tasks related to Stage 3 cashew processing

Tasks	By whom		Distance		Mode of transport			
	Women	Men	<3 km	>3 km	Bicycle	Motorcycle	Hired van/bus	Walking
Collecting cashew								
at home	7	1						
from adjoining villages	1	1		2				
from other sources	1		1		1		1	
Decorticating								
at home	9							
supervising labourers at home	2							
working as a paid labourer	7		5	1				7
Marketing								
to traders visiting village/home	4	1	3		2			
to traders/centres in town	3	4	6		1	1		
to Cashew-Processing Centre	1	2	2		2	1		
to markets outside the area								4

to remove the testa, and brought the stock back to the centre. When a large stock had accumulated, two male members of the society took it to the exporters in Colombo. (Initially, representatives of the society had visited potential exporters in Colombo to identify suitable markets. Exporters preferred the drying technique introduced by the ITSL project to the roasting done by the traders because it removes the moisture of the nuts without any danger of discolouring or damaging them.) This continued until the new Cashew-Processing Centre was set up in the local town, and was registered as a small company.

The Cashew-Processing Centre buys stocks of raw cashew and employs women as casual labourers to decorticate them. The centre also dries cashew brought by the villagers. The employees are paid by the number of cashew they decorticate. Owing to the availability of more decorticated cashew, the tray drier is operated more frequently and the villagers do not have to wait long, as they did initially, to have the cashew dried. The members who sell their cashew through the Centre are paid back once stocks are sold to exporters. Members expect to divide the profits of the Centre among themselves once a year.

An increased involvement of members, both women and men, in the management of the Centre is now visible. This involvement requires regular travel for meetings to discuss issues and arrive at decisions.

Travel patterns related to Stage 3

In the third stage fewer men are involved in purchasing raw cashew nuts. Most women purchase raw cashews at home while a minority travel within and outside of the village. The mode of travelling has not changed significantly. Many walk. Where men are involved, it is always away from home and involves a vehicle.

Though decorticating continues to be a woman's task, women are moving out of their homes to work as paid labourers. Most women work three days at the Cashew-Processing Centre; during the rest of the week, and in their spare time, they work at home. The Cashew-Processing Centre is close to the local town and requires a considerable amount of travelling for people who come from the interior of the village. With the increase in travelling, it is clear that the workload of women has increased. They spend on average 38 minutes a day on travel.

A few women are motivated to use vehicles as their travel needs increase, bringing a regular travel element into their lives. One woman uses a bicycle while another uses a motorcycle, which belongs to her husband, to come to the Centre. Women also use the opportunity of travelling to the Centre to buy their daily provisions.

There is an equal level of participation by men and women in the marketing of decorticated cashew. In some families women and men share the task. In others it is either the man or the woman who does the marketing. While in Stage 2 the processors or their family members went out to sell cashew, in the third stage more traders come into the village to make purchases. In the families where men do marketing, many use bicycles or motorcycles and cover distances up to 2 kilometres. Several women sell cashew to traders who come to their doorstep or are in the village. Some sell it to traders in town and to the Centre. Three women use bicycles.

Women are heavily involved in the management of the Centre. Two of the members we talked to were members of the committee on sales, which met once a month., Three others were on the committee on security, which met twice a week. Men were not very involved in the management of the Centre, but four men are involved in the purchase of cashew and in the committee on financial matters. The Manager of the Centre (a man) has 50 per cent decision-making power in the purchase of cashew.

Other travel related to the work of the Cashew-Processing Centre

Several women who are members of the Cashew-Processing Centre have visited other villages 10–25 kilometres away, to help women in those communities to start similar income-generating activities. Some of these villages closely border the areas that are conflict-prone due to the war. Travelling to, as well as interacting with women in these areas, and participating in awareness-creating activities, have helped the women of Vanathavillu to develop their self-confidence. Some mentioned that their status in the community has risen as a result of these trips. Members also participated in occasional shareholders' meetings and in small group discussions that took place once a fortnight. Some also travelled to Puttalam to access credit from the bank.

IMPACT OF CHANGED TRAVEL PATTERNS ON GENDER RELATIONSHIPS

Women's involvement in the cashew industry in Vanathavillu increased considerably with the introduction of the decorticating techniques. The nature of the technology evolved over the years, and new processing methods and machinery and new institutions have been introduced to the village. Nevertheless, decorticating cashew, whether carried out at the Centre or at home, remains a time-consuming and monotonous task that confines women to one place for six to eight hours a day. This is similar to work patterns in other sectors, where tedious, time-consuming tasks are generally handled by (assigned to) women. In the cashew industry, the technique requires a fine skill which is much admired, but which men have not been eager to learn or use, even though it generates satisfactory profits.

The adoption of decorticating techniques led to participation in small group activities, interaction with banks and government institutions in Puttalam, and more involvement in purchasing and marketing – activities which increased women's mobility and their interaction within the community and with outsiders. It has made them better informed and more confident in making decisions and dealing with financial matters. Once Vanthavillu became established as a place for good-quality cashew and traders began to visit the village, access to markets became easier but women's mobility decreased. They became more dependent on the information that was 'brought to them', and less able to compare prices and sell at a competitive rate. Unfortunately, once women are accustomed to selling the cashew without leaving the village or local town, travelling appears an insurmountable task.

The introduction by ITSL of the tray drier to process cashew was accompanied by related activities like setting up a village society to manage the technology, bringing in decorticated cashew for drying; community involvement to identify and access markets; taking the stocks to exporters in Colombo; contributing to the management of the project by sharing responsibilities; and travelling to banks, government institutions and other villages for awareness-creating programmes on the technology. These activities, especially travelling to Colombo to identify markets, participating in training and going to other villages for awareness creation, have, once more, given women the opportunity to develop their knowledge of technology, markets, bank procedures and community development issues. Although only a few women participate in these activities, other women are very much influenced by them.

The research attempted to assess any changes in gender roles as a result of the above. It was evident that women's activities have shifted into areas that were more controlled by men: marketing of cashew and making purchases of daily/weekly provisions for the family. In many families, especially those that had women on the management committee, women's status within the family had increased. Cashew processing involved handling large sums of money, often obtained as credit, and this definitely has given women more decision-making power in financial matters. But, except in a few rare cases, men had not taken over the traditional workload of women, and women remain responsible for most of the domestic work.

BIBLIOGRAPHY

Ali-Nejadfard, F. (1997) *Rural Travel and Transport Planning and Related Interventions: A Case Study in Malawi*. Proceedings of the South African Transport Conference, Vol. 3C, Johannesburg.

Amadi, B.C. (1988) 'The Impact of Rural Road Construction on Agricultural Development: An Empirical Study of Anambra State, Nigeria', *Agricultural Systems* 27 (1): 1–9.

Apedaile, L.P. (1996) *Diagnostic Review of DDP Local Roads Maintenance Issues and Related Institutional Innovations in Dhading District of Nepal*. Peer Diagnostics, Edmonton, AL, 1996.

Athreya, V.B. and S.R. Chunkath (1996), *Literacy and Empowerment*. New Delhi: Sage.

Baber, R. (1996). 'Current Livelihoods in Semi-arid Rural Areas of South Africa', in M. Lipton, F. Ellis and M. Lipton (eds), *Land, Labour and Livelihoods in Rural South Africa*. Durban: Indicator Press, University of Durban.

Bamberger, M. (1998) *Addressing Gender in the African Rural Travel and Transport Programme (RTTP)*. Gender and Development Group, World Bank, Washington DC.

Banjo, G.A. (1997) 'Rural Travel and Transport Program: A Tool for Improving Access to Rural Development'. Unpublished.

Barwell, I. (1996) *Transport and the Village: Findings from African Village-Level Travel and Transport Surveys and Related Studies*. World Bank Discussion Paper No. 344, Washington DC.

Biswas, A. (1997) *Sustainable Banking with the Poor: A Case Study on SEWA Bank, India*. AGRPW Rural Finance, World Bank, Washington DC.

Blaikie, P.M., J. Cameron and D. Seddon (1977) *Centre, Periphery and Access in West Central Nepal*. Monographs in Development Studies, University of East Anglia, School of Development Studies, Norwich.

Blaikie, P.M., J. Cameron and D. Seddon (1980) *Nepal in Crisis: Growth and Stagnation at the Periphery.* Oxford: Oxford University Press.

Booth, D., L. Hanmer and E. Lovell (2000) *Poverty and Transport.* A report prepared for the World Bank in collaboration with DFID. Final report and Poverty and Transport Toolkit, June, ODI, London.

Boserup, E. (1981) *Population and Technology.* Oxford: Basil Blackwell.

Bryceson, and J. Howe (1993) *Rural Household Transport in Africa: Reducing the Burden on Women.* World Bank, Washington DC.

Carr, M. and R. Sandher (1987) *Women, Technology and Rural Productivity: Analysis of the Impact of Time- and Energy-Saving Technologies on Women.* UNIFEM Occasional Paper No. 6, UNIFEM, New York.

Callaway, B.J. (1987) *Muslim Hausa Women in Nigeria: Tradition and Change.* New York: Syracuse University Press.

Central Institute of Road Transport (1996) Ahmedabad Municipal Transport Service (Ajhmedabad Municipal Corporation) *A Report on Structure and Strategies.* Central Institute of Road Transport, Pune.

Central Statistical Office (1992) *Zimbabwe National Census Report 1992.* Harare: Government Publishers.

Chisala, V. (1997) 'Financial and Institutional Framework for Rural Travel and Transport'. Unpublished.

Chiwanga, M.E., S. Miller and A. Wiederkehr (1992) *Makete Integrated Rural Transport Project Tripartite Terminal Evaluation. Full Evaluation Report.* United Republic of Tanzania Prime Minister's Office/Swiss Development Cooperation/ILO, Dar es Salaam.

Curtis. V. (1994) *Women and the Transport of Water.* London: Intermediate Technology Publications.

Dawson. J. (1995) *Manufacture and Diffusion of Low-cost Transport Devices in Zimbabwe.* Report of visit by Consultant Socio-Economist, 18 January–9 February. IT Zimbabwe, Harare.

Dawson, J. and I. Barwell (1993) *Roads are Not Enough: New Perspectives on Rural Transport Planning in Developing Countries.* London: Intermediate Technology Publications.

Department of Roads, Nepal (1995) *Nepal Road Statistics.*

Devies Inc. (1980) *Socio-economic and Environmental Impacts of Low-Volume Rural Roads: A Review of Literature.* AID Program Discussion Paper No. 7, USAID, Washington DC.

Doran, J. (1990) *A Moving Issue for Women: Is Low-cost Transport an Appropriate Intervention to Alleviate Women's Burden in Southern Africa?* Gender Analysis in Development Discussion Paper No. 1, University of East Anglia, School of Development Studies, Norwich.

Doran, J. (1996) *An Imbalanced Load: Gender Issues in Rural Transport Work.* Intermediate Technology Development Group, Rugby.

East Consult (P) Ltd (1985) *A Study on Low-Cost Road Construction Technology.* September.

Fernando. P. (1997) *Balancing the Load: Gender Issues in Rural Transport: Overview of Existing Information and Identification of Gaps.* IFRTD Secretariat, London.

Gandhi, G. (ed.) (1983) *Tamil Nadu District Gazetteers, Pudukkottai.* Government of Tamil Nadu, Chennai.

Gaviria, J.C. (1991) *Rural Transport and Agricultural Performance in SSA: 6 Country Case Studies.* Joint SSATP/MADIA Study, Africa Technical Department, Infrastructure Division, World Bank, Washington DC.

Gomoa District Assembly (1996) *A Development Plan for Gomoa District 1996–2000.* Apam, May.

Government of Bangladesh (1990) *Fourth Five Year Plan, 1990–1995.*

Grieco, M., N. Apt and J. Turner (1996) *At Christmas and on Rainy Days: Transport, Travel and the Female Traders of Accra.* Aldershot: Avebury.

Gujarat State Transportation Corporation (1998) *Administrative Report 1996–97.* Gujarat State Road Transport Corporation, Ahmedabad.

Hine, J.L. (1984). *Some Limitations to the Opportunities for Road Investment to Promote Rural Development.* International Conference on Roads and Development, Paris, 22–25 May.

Hine, J.L. (1993). *Transport and Marketing Priorities to Improve Food Security in Ghana and the Rest of Africa.* International Symposium: Regional Food Security and Rural Infrastructure, Giessen, May.

Howe, J. (1997) *The Impact of Rural Roads on Poverty Alleviation.* IHE Working paper TandAE-18, The Hague.

Howe, J. (1997). *Transport for the Poor or Poor Transport? A General Review of Rural Transport Policy in Developing Countries with Emphasis on Low-Income Areas.* International Labour Office, Geneva.

Impact Monitoring Unit (1994) *Impact Assessment of the Local Road Program Implemented on Dhading Besi–Salyantar–Siktar Road and Bhimdunga–Lamidanda Road, Summary Report.* Impact Monitoring Unit (IMU), Kathmandu.

International Forum for Rural Transport and Development (1999) *Balancing the Load: Proceedings of the Asia and Africa.* Regional Seminars on Gender and Rural Transport. IFRTD/ILO ASIST.

Jhabvala, R. (1990) 'Working Women: Myth and Reality. Experiences of a Group of Muslim Women Workers', in *Women Workers in India.* Delhi: Chanakya Publications.

Kaira, C., et al. (1993) *Prioritisation Study of Pilot Districts for the Rural Travel and Transport Programme.* Dar es Salaam: Government of Tanzania.

Larcher, C. and M.S. Dikito (1991) *Socio-economic Survey with Specific Considerations of Gender Issues in Gutu District Communal Lands.* Deutsche Gesellschaft fur Technische Zusammenarbeit (GTZ), Masvingo.

Latif, Z. (1999) 'The Impacts of the Use of IMT on Transport Needs and Access of These by Women in Rural Pakistan', in *Meeting Transport Needs with Intermediate Means of Transport,* Vol. II. Lanka Forum for Rural Transport Development, Colombo.

Malmberg Calvo, C. (1994a) *Case Studies on the Role of Women in Rural Transport: Access of Women to Domestic Facilities.* SSATP Working Paper 11, World Bank, Washington DC.

Malmberg Calvo, C. (1994b) *Case Study on Intermediate Means of Transport: Bicycles and Rural Women in Uganda.* Working Paper no. 12, Sub-Saharan Africa Transport Policy Programme (SSATP), World Bank, Washington DC.

Mannock Management Consultants and ILO (1997) *Rural Transport Study in Three Districts of Zimbabwe,* Vol. 1. ILO, Harare.

Marais, H.J. (1987) *Household Transportation Needs in Rural Transkei.* Council for Scientific and Industrial Research, Division of Roads and Transport Technology, Pretoria.

Mashiri, M.A.M. (1997) *Improving Mobility and Accessibility for Developing Communities.* Contract Report CR-97/041, Department of Transport, Pretoria.

Mashiri, M.A.M., D. Motha and A.K. Sarkar (1998) *Towards a Rural Accessibility Planning Framework.* Division of Roads and Transport Technology, Council for Scientific and Industrial Research, Technical report TR-98/024, Pretoria.

Meyer, W.P. and B.N. Acharya (1995) *Review of Dhading Local Roads Programme. Draft Field Report of Bhimdunga–Lamidanda Road Programme.* Dhading Development Project, DDP/GTZ, Kathmandu.

Ministry of Local Development (1994) *District/Village Profile – 1993 (A Statistical Account of Dhading District).* Dhading Integrated Rural Development Project, Ministry of Local Development, HMG, Kathmandu.

Moser, C.O.N. (1993) *Gender Planning and Development: Theory, Practice and Training.* London: Routledge.

Muthahar, S. (1998) 'On the Road to Empowerment', *The Hindu,* 19 March.

Mwaipopopo R. (1994) 'Gender Issues in Tanzanian Agriculture: An Overview', in A. Njau and T. Mruma, *Gender and Development in Tanzania: Past Present and Future.*

Mwaka, M.V. 'Women's Studies in Uganda', in *Beijing and Beyond: Towards the 21st Century of Women,* in *Women Studies Quarterly,* an educational project of the Feminist Press of the City University of New York.

Nanavaty, R. and P. Buch (1990) *Salt Farmers of Santalpur Taluka.* SEWA, Ahmedabad, September.

National Planning Commission, HMG Nepal (1985) *The Seventh Five Year Plan (1985/86–1989/90).* Kathmandu.

National Planning Commission, HMG Nepal (1992) *The Eighth Five Year Plan (1992/93–1997/98).* Kathmandu.

National Planning Commission, HMG Nepal (1998) *Approach to the Ninth Five Year Plan (1997–2002).* Kathmandu.

Nepal Transport Master Plan (1996), *Draft Final Report.* HMG Nepal, Kathmandu.

Orr, S. and P. Njenga (1995), *Manufacture and Diffusion of Low-Cost Transport Devices in Zimbabwe.* Evaluation Report, July, IT Zimbabwe.

Porter G. (1989) 'A Note on Slavery, Seclusion and Agrarian Change in Northern Nigeria', *Journal of African History* 30: 487–91.

Porter, G. (1997) 'Mobility and Inequality in Rural Nigeria: The Case of Off-road Communities', *Tijdschrift voor Economische en Sociale Geografie,* 88 (1): 65–76.

Porter, G. (1998) *Living Off-road: An Exploration of Accessibility Issues in Rural West Africa.* Paper presented at the annual conference of the Development Studies Association of Bradford, 9–11 September.

Rana, K. and N. Rao (1996) 'Gross Injustice', *Hindustan Times,* 17 October.

Rao, N. (1992) 'Cycling into the Future', *Statesman,* 15 August (New Delhi).

Rao, N. (1993) *Towards Empowerment – A Quest for Justice, A Case Study of Women Stone Quarry Workers and Gem-cutters in Pudukkottai District, Tamil Nadu,* National Institute of Adult Education, New Delhi.

Rao, N. (1997) 'Land Issues and Livelihoods of the Santhals: How Are Women Affected?' Unpublished report.

Rao, N. (ed.) (1999) *Owning their Land: Rights of Santhali Women*. New Delhi: Friedrich Ebert Stiftung.

Robson, E. (2000) 'Wife Seclusion and the Spatial Praxis of Gender Ideology in Nigerian Hausaland', *Gender, Place and Culture*, 7(2): 179–99.

Salifu, M. (1994) 'The Cycle-Trailer in Ghana: A Reasonable but Inappropriate Technology', *African Technology Forum*, 7(3): 37–40.

Samute, W.W. (1997) 'Rural Transport in Malawi'. Unpublished.

SEWA (1996) *SEWA: Self-Employed Women's Association*. Ahmedabad.

Shtrii Shakti (1995) *Women, Development, Democracy: A Study of the Socio-economic Changes in the Profile of Women in Nepal*. Kathmandu: Shtrii Shakti.

Sibanda, A. (2001) 'Rural Transport and Empowerment of Women: Policy Guidelines on Best Practices'. United Nations Economic Commission for Africa. Unpublished.

Starkey, P. (2000) *Local Transport Solutions: People, Paradoxes and Progress: Lessons Arising from the Spread of Intermediate Means of Transport*. World Bank Sub-Saharan Africa Transport Policy Program, Rural Travel and Transport Program, Washington DC.

Stephens, R.D. (1997) 'Rural Transport Infrastructure Building Technology'. Unpublished.

Tarrius, A. (1984) *Transport in Rural Areas: Scheduled and Non-scheduled Services*. European Conference of Ministers of Transport, Paris.

Wilbur Smith Associates (1998) *Road Condition Study: Final Report*. May.

World Bank (1997) *Staff Appraisal Report, Ghana Village Infrastructure Project*. Document of the International Development Association acting as the Administrator of the Interim Trust Fund Report 15942–GH.

World Bank, Nepal (1990) *Relieving Poverty in a Resource-Scarce Economy*, World Bank, Washington DC.

Zils, K.L. (1987) *The Regional Rural Development Concept*. Proceedings of the Regional Rural Development: Principles and Application in the Co-ordinated Agricultural and Rural Development Programme in Zimbabwe, 16–27 November, Great Zimbabwe, Masvingo.

ABOUT THE CONTRIBUTORS

Priyanthi Fernando is the Executive Secretary of the International Forum for Rural Transport and Development. She is a sociologist with a particular interest in gender and technology issues, networking and mass communications.

Gina Porter is a Senior Research Fellow in the Department of Anthropology, University of Durham, UK, with considerable work experience in Ghana and Nigeria.

Mac Mashiri is a transport planner for the Council for Scientific Research (CSIR) in Pretoria, South Africa. He has special responsibilities for rural transport and development and for urban transport. His areas of interest are transportation policy and strategy development, local economic development, poverty alleviation and livelihoods. **Sabina Mahapa** is attached to the University of the North, South Africa, as a lecturer in Geography. Her field of specialization is Gender and Rural Transport. She has a master's degree in Geography and is currently researching gender and rural transport in the Northern Province for her PhD.

Dorris Chingozho is an independent consultant working from Harare, Zimbabwe. At the time of doing the research she was working with the Intermediate Technology Development Group promoting appropriate technology for self-help in rural areas of Zimbabwe.

Josephine A. Mwankusye is the coordinator of the Village Travel Transport Programme under the Ministry of Regional Administration and Local Government (MRALG) of Tanzania, responsible for guiding implementation of village travel and transport activities in six pilot districts. She is a sociologist with a special interest in gender mainstreaming.

Kwamusi Paul holds an honours degree in Sociology from the Makerere University and has twelve years' experience in transport development. He has a special interest in aspects of transport safety, including the development of new approaches and policies and training and development of community communications. He is a director of Professional Driving and Defensive Systems Ltd, and the training advisor for Uganda Taxi Operators and Drivers Association

P.G. Kaumbutho is Chairman of the Animal Traction Network for Eastern and Southern Africa (ATNESA) and the Executive Coordinator of the Kenya Network for Draft Animal Technology (KENDAT), a Kenyan NGO. He is a chartered agricultural engineer with many years of experience in implementing practical solutions to everyday agricultural and rural development problems.

Suad Mustafa Elhaj Musa currently works for GOAL–Sudan, developing a model based on community participation, capacity building and sustainability for the handing over of a health clinic for internally displaced people. At the time of the research, she was working for Oxfam as a Women's Programme Officer in the Kebkabiya Smallholders' Project.

Mohammed-Bello Yunusa is a lecturer in the Department of Urban and Regional Planning at the Ahmadu Bello University in Zaria, Nigeria. He is a registered member of the Nigerian Institute of Town Planners. **E.M. Shaibu-Imodagbe** is a trained environmental scientist with interests in environmental impact assessment and gender relations and has worked as a lecturer, researcher and consultant. He is a member of many professional bodies including the Institution of Environmental Sciences of the UK and the Nigerian Environmental Society. **Y.A. Ambi** lectures on Agricultural Economics in the Department of Agricultural and Rural Sociology at the Ahmadu Bello University in Zaria, Nigeria.

Amadou Ouedraogo has been a Fulbright Scholar and the Chair of the Department of Modern Languages of the University of Ouagadougou, Burkina Faso. His non-academic experience includes working with grassroots populations on environmental issues. He is currently working towards a PhD at the University of Iowa, USA.

Nilufar Matin is an independent consultant in Bangladesh, trained in economics and in urban and regional planning, and is currently working on research in gender studies. **Mahjabeen Mukib** works for Intermediate Technology Development Group in Bangladesh in the area of social policy research. Her work has focused on food security, agrarian issues, gender and technology and community-based approaches to disaster management. **Hasina Begum** and **Delwara Khanam** are two Bangladeshi sociologists who specialize in PRA surveys.

Nitya Rao is currently working towards a Ph.D degree. She has been actively involved in the field of rural development in India. Her professional experience includes organizing women into groups and cooperatives at the grassroots, research and training support at an intermediary level, international development assistance at the national level, as well as networking, capacity-building and policy advocacy for education in the Asia–Pacific region.

Poorni Bid, **Reema Nanavaty** and **Neeta Patel** work for SEWA (the Self Employed Women's Association), a trade union of urban self-employed women in Gujarat, India. Reema Nanavaty is SEWA's elected General Secretary and is responsible for coordinating the rural development programmes of the organization.

Sangita Shresthova, **Rekha Barve** and **Paulomi Chokshi** are researchers in Shri Mahila SEWA, Shakari Bank of SEWA, in Ahmedabad, India.

Mahua Mukherjee is a practising architect working with the Centre for Built Environment in Calcutta, India. She is currently involved with Bachchau Town Planning for reconstruction after the earthquake in Gujarat, India.

David Seddon is Professor of Development Studies and a member of the Overseas Development Group at the University of East Anglia. His interest in rural access began in Nepal in the mid-1970s. Most recently he has participated in the design of a rural access programme in Nepal and the development of appropriate maintenance systems in Vietnam. **Ava Shrestha** is an independent consultant in Kathmandu, Nepal, working as a gender and social development specialist.

Ganesh Ghimire is an independent consultant based in Kathmandu, Nepal, with an interest in road planning and design, integrated rural development, rural infrastructure planning, project preparation and project evaluation. He has also been involved in environmental advocacy.

Kusala Wettasinghe is a freelance writer and illustrator. At the time of the research she was working with the Intermediate Technology Development Group, in Colombo, Sri Lanka, as the communications specialist in the rural transport and manufacturing programme and as the project manager for the gender and technology project. **Upali Pannila** is a sociologist working as the Programme Manager of the Rural Transport and Manufacturing Programme of Intermediate Technology Development Group South Asia, in Colombo, Sri Lanka.

INDEX